Anansi's Journey

Anansi's JOURNEY

A Story of Jamaican Cultural Resistance

Emily Zobel Marshall

UNIVERSITY OF THE WEST INDIES PRESS
Jamaica • Barbados • Trinidad and Tobago

University of the West Indies Press
7A Gibraltar Hall Road   Mona
Kingston 7   Jamaica
www.uwipress.com

A catalogue record of this book is available
from the National Library of Jamaica.

ISBN: 978-976-640-261-7

Book and cover design by Robert Harris.
Set in Fairfield LH Light 10.5/15 x 24
Printed in the United States of America.

For Theo

Contents

Acknowledgments

FIRST AND FOREMOST, I WOULD like to thank Tom Brown, for his love and encouragement. If I ever started to doubt the necessity of this endeavour, Tom's reassurance and practical advice gave me the strength to continue with renewed zeal.

I could not have written this book without the support of Tom Herron and Max Farrar. Tom, I would like to thank for his patience, insight and sense of humour and Max, for his extensive knowledge of the field, unending enthusiasm and keen appreciation of the Anansi spirit.

Simon Gunn and Mary Eagleton's rigorous and professional approach to academia have been a strong source of motivation. I am particularly grateful to Simon Lee, for helping to fund my trip to Jamaica. During my time in Kingston, the warmth and friendship of Jimmy and Peggy Saltou and Jean Small gave me the strength to face the challenges of my research. I am also indebted to my interviewees: Captain Smith, Isaac Bernard, Webster Sutherland, Velma Pollard, Brother Martin, George Campbell, Sylvan Sutherland, Rocky, Barry Chevannes, Laura Tanna, Jimmy Stevens, Sean Mock Yen, Olive Lewin, Kingsley Keith, Russell Keith and Lynnette Wilks. Their willingness to share their thoughts and insights have been fundamental to the creation of this book. Thanks also to all those at the University of the West Indies, in particular Barry Chevannes, who gave me access to libraries and resources.

Sections of chapters 1 and 2 have appeared in earlier forms in my articles "Liminal Anansi: Symbol of Order and Chaos: An Exploration of Anansi's Roots among the Asante of Ghana", *Caribbean Quarterly* 53, no. 3 (October–

November 2007) and "From Messenger of the Gods to Muse of the People: The Shifting Contexts of Anansi's Metamorphosis", *Jamaica Journal* 29 (2008). An earlier version of chapter 3 has been utilized in "Anansi Tactics in Plantation Jamaica: Matthew Lewis's Record of Trickery", *Wadabagei: A Journal of the Caribbean and Its Diaspora* 12, no. 3 (2009), and draft excerpts of chapter 4 in " 'The Anansi Syndrome': A Debate Concerning Anansi's Influence on Jamaican Culture", *World Literatures Written in English* 39, no. 1 (2001), http://www.tandfonline.com. I am grateful to the editors of these journals for helping me to develop my ideas and for publishing my work.

I am thankful to the staff at the University of the West Indies Press, in particular Linda Speth, Shivaun Hearne and Erin MacLeod for their editorial support and guidance. Kieran Hadley's advice and proofreading and Samuel Hodgson's expert input into the book's graphics and images have been a tremendous help. My colleagues at the School of Cultural Studies at Leeds Metropolitan University have directed me throughout my research: I truly appreciate their counsel. Pascale Gayford, Bridget Kelly, Ruth Thomas, Joanne Watkiss and Claire Chambers have sustained me with their friendship throughout the writing process. Finally, my warmest thanks to my parents, Peter and Jenny, who have been a source of constant support; I am incredibly lucky to have had such loyal and sensitive travelling companions on my intellectual journey, and to Elizabeth, Dylan, Katie, Liz and Ed, for their love, kindness and wise words.

Figure 1. Illustration of Anansi in Pamela Coleman-Smith's *Annancy Stories* (1899).

A nancy

by Andrew Salkey

Anancy is a spider;
Anancy is a man;
Anancy's West Indian
And West African.

Sometimes, he wears a waistcoat;
Sometimes, he carries a cane;
Sometimes, he sports a top hat;
Sometimes, he's just a plain,
Ordinary, black, hairy spider.

Anancy is vastly cunning,
Tremendously greedy,
Excessively charming,
Hopelessly dishonest,
Warmly loving,
Firmly confident,
Fiercely wild,
A fabulous character,
Completely out of our mind
And out of his, too.

Anancy is a master planner,
A great user
Of other people's plans;
He pockets everyone's food, shelter, land,
money and more;

He achieves mountains of things,
Like stolen flour dumplings;
He deceives millions of people,
Even the man in the moon;
And he solves all the mysteries
On earth, in air, under sea.

And always,
Anancy changes
From a spider into a man
And from a man into a spider
And back again
At the drop of a sleepy eyelid.

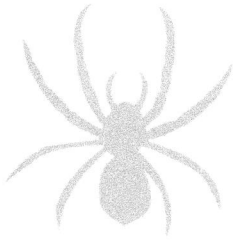

Introduction

ANANSI IS A COMPLEX and intriguing figure who has woven a fine tapestry of tales across Africa and the African diaspora. Anansi survived a cultural metamorphosis and became symbolic of the struggles of black slaves. Like Anansi, the slaves worked at overturning the structured hierarchy of their environment, developing coded strategies of survival and resistance. With its broad historical sweep, this book not only examines Anansi's role in plantation Jamaica, but it also traces Anansi's journey from his roots among the Asante of Ghana through to his contested position in contemporary Jamaican society.

The uniqueness of this book lies in its accumulation of new data on Anansi in both Ghana and Jamaica and in its theoretical analysis of Anansi's potential as a resource for resistance against oppression. No sustained analysis of the Anansi tales has been undertaken on such a scale. Moreover, there are no existing studies of the Anansi tales from a cross-cultural and historical angle. This is therefore an investigation dedicated to filling the lamentable deficit in our current knowledge of this fascinating folk phenomenon.

The book is chronologically ordered and begins by demonstrating how Anansi was used as a medium through which the power structures of the Asante were both tested and strengthened. It then turns to an examination of the changes Anansi underwent during the Middle Passage and discusses Anansi's relationship to power in a Jamaican plantation context. The text ends with an analysis of Anansi's role in postcolonial Jamaica, illustrating how he is interpreted as both a symbol of greed and individualism as well as celebrated as a modern Jamaican national hero.

It is an interdisciplinary and international study which examines cultures on both sides of the Atlantic. I argue that the Anansi story is proof that African culture survived in the Americas. Through tracing Anansi's journey, it is clear that the slave trade did not destroy African culture but rather transmitted it to the Caribbean. Moreover, the argument maintained throughout is that, while there are multiple ways of interpreting Anansi, in times of conflict and oppression Anansi has the potential to inspire a combination of psychological and practical methods of survival and resistance. I maintain that the term "resistance" correctly describes the amalgamated practices of defiance executed by both the mind and body. I demonstrate that on the plantations, slave resistance at a psychological level (exemplified in folklore) influenced practical physical tactics of resistance, which in turn contributed to outright rebellion and revolt aimed at overturning plantation power structures.

Through outlining Jamaica's long history of rebellion and resistance, the book demonstrates how slave resistance and survival methods were represented and encouraged by the Anansi folktales. Furthermore, it illustrates that Anansi not only reflected and inspired these models of behaviour, but played a multi-functional role in slaves' lives, establishing a sense of continuity with an African past and offering them the means to transform and assert their identity within the boundaries of captivity. As Lawrence Levine argues, slaves in the Americas devoted "the structure and message of their tales to the compulsions and needs of their present situation" (1977, 90).

The data for this study has been collected and analysed using a combination of three key research methods: the close reading and textual analysis of Anansi tales, the interviewing of participants in Jamaica, and both archival and library research conducted in Jamaica as well as the United Kingdom.

Key to developing an understanding of Anansi's role in Jamaica was a three-month period of fieldwork conducted on the island. I interviewed people from a diverse range of ages, ethnic and religious identities, geographical locations and occupations. These included traditional storytellers, authors, schoolchildren, actors, playwrights, taxi drivers, Maroon leaders, shopkeepers, Rastafarians and Caribbean academics who were specialists in the field.

I participated in Anansi storytelling sessions in Kingston and Moore Town and witnessed several Anansi storytelling events on stage.[1] When I mentioned my research most people would invariably launch into their favourite Anansi story, whether we were at a bar, in a taxi or in the street. One of my interviewees was so enthused by the project that he recorded and transcribed Anansi stories told by people in his neighbourhood in St Thomas and presented me with a handwritten collection of around a dozen tales. All this was testimony to the fact that the tradition is still very much alive in Jamaica.

I employ several theoretical approaches in this exploration of Anansi's journey. First, through my analyses of the impact and legacy of colonial rule, I pursue the concerns of postcolonial theory. I posit that Jamaican slaves were not passive participants in their history, but a people who played a part in shaping their own circumstances. Furthermore, through the use of interviews and in my analysis of African and Caribbean sources, I investigate the effects of colonial power and oppression on Jamaicans from their own perspectives. In doing so, I endeavour to contribute to the formation of a historiography that challenges the legitimizing strategies of colonialist discourse. As Anansi is part of an oral tradition, my exploration of Anansi's journey uses oral history, wherever possible, as a form of historical documentation. While conventional historiographical practice rejected the oral tradition as a legitimate source of material, postmodernism and postcolonialism have aided the development of new theoretical approaches. These theories give scope for the creation of alternative sources of history, informed by practices that were once rejected as too unreliable to be a foundation of knowledge.

Let us now turn to Anansi. "Ananse" is the Asante Twi word for "spider". As with all folk characters from the oral tradition, there are numerous alternative spellings of his name.[2] The most popular spelling in contemporary Jamaica is "Anansi" or "Anancy", while in West Africa "Ananse" or "Anànse" is still used (Cassidy and Le Page 2002, 10). The most popular contemporary Jamaican spelling – "Anansi" – will be employed here.

Although I focus on the Anansi tales in their Ghanaian Asante and Jamaican contexts, Anansi tales are told all across West Africa and the Caribbean. A vibrant tradition of telling Anansi tales that dates back to the beginnings of the slave trade can be found in numerous Caribbean islands as well as in parts of the United States and South America.[3]

Anansi can be found in several countries on the west coast of Africa besides Ghana, such as the Ivory Coast, Togo, Sierra Leone and Liberia. Other African spider figures rival Anansi's popularity: "Ture", the spider of ethnic groups such as Zande in north and central Africa and those in the folktales of Kakas of the Cameroon, the Ngama and Sara of southern Sudan and the Hausa of Nigeria (Craton 1982, 56; Yanka 1983, 9; De Souza 2003, 347–51). Several tricksters of West African origin, such as "Eshu" and "Legba", the Yoruba and Fon trickster deities, share similarities with Anansi. They were transported to the Caribbean by African slaves, becoming central figures in the folk religions of Orisha, Santeria and Vodun practised in Trinidad, Cuba, Haiti, Grenada and in many parts of Latin America (Chevannes 2001, 7).

Anansi also shares similarities with the trickster figure of Brer Rabbit, who originated from the folklore of the Bantu-speaking peoples of south and central Africa. Enslaved Africans brought the Brer Rabbit tales to the New World, which, like the Anansi stories, depict a physically vulnerable creature using his intelligence to prevail over larger animals. Yet while Brer Rabbit stories are told in the Caribbean, especially in the French-speaking islands (where he is named Compair Lapin"[4]), he is predominantly an African-American folk hero. His tales entered the mainstream through the work of the white American journalist Joel Chandler Harris, who wrote several collections of Uncle Remus stories between 1870 and 1906. Plantation blacks told Harris the tales, and he has been both applauded for keeping the folktales alive and heavily criticized for plagiarism, contributing to the creation of patronizing stereotypes and defending slavery. In the 1920s, American ethnomusicologist Helen Roberts stated that Brer Rabbit had become a "byword of our own nurseries". However, while Brer Rabbit was known world-wide, "there has been no Harris for Anansi" (Roberts 1926, 244). This may be a blessing, for due to appearances in several Disney films and American brands of Brer Rabbit food, the character has been distanced from his origins as an African and slave folk hero. In an angry essay, "Uncle Remus: No Friend of Mine" (1981), African-American author Alice Walker accused Harris of stealing part of her heritage and making her "feel ashamed of it" (cited in Stephenson 1998). While Brer Rabbit will be mentioned here, I do not provide a sustained analysis of him, as he does not play a significant role in Jamaican folklore.

Rather than belonging to a particular country, Anansi stories can be viewed as the folktales of West Africa and its diaspora. Indeed, the trickster figure itself, described as a universal archetype by Carl Jung[5] can be found in indigenous cultures worldwide. Ivan Van Sertima, in his essay "Trickster: The Revolutionary Hero" (2002) explains that the existence of the trickster in global cultures is not simply a reflection of the expression of a desire to thwart powerful and oppressive forces, but proof of the profound longing of the human psyche for freedom: "Freedom from fixed ways of seeing, feeling, thinking, acting: a revolt against a whole complex of 'givens' coded in society, a revolt which may affect not only an oppressed group, class or race but a whole order – the settled institutions and repetitive rituals of a whole civilization" (444).

While the trickster figure plays a role in cultures across the globe, I focus on the Anansi trickster in his Ghanaian Asante and Jamaican contexts. I concentrate on Ghana (formerly the Gold Coast) because the tales play a more central role in Asante culture than they do in other West African cultures, and on Jamaica because the majority of slaves taken from Gold Coast to the Caribbean were sold in Jamaica.

The Asante kingdom was, by the middle of the eighteenth century, the largest and most powerful on the Gold Coast (Patterson 1967, 120). The Asante were both captured as slaves as well as involved in the selling of slaves. Although there has been some dispute concerning the origins of Jamaican slaves, and a number of contemporary researchers have argued against the overemphasis of Asante or Akan (the ethno-linguistic group to which the Asante belong) prominence on the island,[6] it would seem from the evidence available that most slaves taken from the Gold Coast to the Caribbean were transported to Jamaica. Between 1641 to 1840, a total number of 587,057 slaves were taken from the Gold Coast region and sold in the Caribbean. Of that number, 225,179 were sold in Jamaica. The data shows that more slaves taken from the Gold Coast area were sold in Jamaica than in any other Caribbean island during this period (Trans-Atlantic Slave Trade Database 2009). As the Asante were a dominant force in the Gold Coast region, this would support the argument that there was a strong Asante influence on cultural forms on Jamaican slave society.[7]

Surprisingly, despite Anansi's global popularity and intriguing history, and while Anansi can be found in numerous collections of folktales, academic studies and literary texts, there have been no sustained analyses of the folktales or the folk-figure in either an African or Caribbean context. One of the few studies that examines the role of Anansi folktales among the Asante of Ghana is R.S. Rattray's *Akan-Ashanti Folk-Tales* (1930), which is referred to throughout this book. The tales were recorded directly from Asante oral storytelling sessions and published in both English and Twi, making it a valuable and unique text. The main sources for my exploration of Anansi in his Jamaican setting are five twentieth-century collections recorded and compiled by Walter Jekyll (1907), Martha Beckwith (1924), Philip Sherlock (1956, 1959, 1989), Louise Bennett (1944, 1950, 1961, 1979) and Laura Tanna (1983).

In academic and literary texts Anansi is often used as a symbol of African, Caribbean or black culture and history. Robert Pelton's *The Trickster in West Africa: A Study of Mythic Irony and Sacred Delight* (1989) and Christopher Vecsey's "The Exception Who Proves the Rules: Anansi the Akan Trickster" (1993) present Anansi as a figure who simultaneously tested and strengthened the Asante social structure. Their conceptual frameworks are examined and applied to an analysis of Anansi's role among the Asante in chapter 1, which explores Anansi's roots among the Asante of Ghana and the function of the tales in their context. The chapter provides an overview of Asante history, culture and religion, and asks whether Anansi is indeed an inverter, breaker or supporter of the rules of the their social system.

Chapter 2 focuses on the next stage of Anansi's journey, examining the changes and continuities in the transmission of the tales from Ghana to Jamaica. It shows how Anansi is symbolic of metamorphosis and cross-cultural fertilization and an emblem of opposition against the oppressive power structures of the colonial system.

Drawing from a combination of key historical sources and interviews, chapter 3 explores Anansi's role in the lives of the Jamaican Maroons and plantation rebels. It argues that the Anansi story encouraged "Anansi tactics", key to the survival of rebels and runaways. The chapter illustrates how the Maroons deployed these tactics when pursued by the British and examines why Jamaicans continue to perceive Anansi as symbolic of Maroon resistance.

Focusing on Anansi's role in contemporary Jamaica, chapter 4 draws from interviews conducted in Jamaica to explore Anansi's role in modern Jamaican communities and Jamaican oral traditions, poetry, music, pantomime and literature. It questions the legitimacy of Anansi as a Jamaican role model and folk hero and examines the sociopolitical problems that Jamaica faces, asking what are the possible uses of Anansi in a violent and struggling society.

My historical research is much indebted to the work of Michael Craton and his exploration of Caribbean slave resistance in *Testing the Chains: Resist-*

ance to Slavery in the British West Indies (1982). I also particularly endorse and make numerous references to Levine's sensitive analysis of African-American oral narratives in *Black Culture and Black Consciousness: Afro American Folk Thought from Slavery to Freedom* (1977). Craton's rigorous historical analysis demonstrates that slaves persistently resisted the Caribbean plantation system, and helps refute myths of slave compliance and submission. Levine was the first scholar to have stressed the importance of trickster narratives in the lives of black slaves, and his work has been invaluable.

Central to my exploration of Anansi's journey is the theory that while subordinate cultures are not always in open conflict with dominant cultures, they will, as E.P. Thompson explains, "negotiate the spaces and gaps in it, make inroads into it 'warrening it from within'" (1965, 311–62). As Michel de Certeau argues, opportunities for the subversion of sociopolitical systems are continually seized in the everyday lives of people operating within a system of domination (1980). I use the phrase "Anansi tactics" to explain the techniques used by slaves in their daily lives to undermine the plantation power structure and explain that Anansi tales encouraged "warrening from within", which could, in certain contexts, lead to more overt forms of rebellion. I conclude that although slaves did not bring about an end to slavery through revolution or revolt, their unrelenting resistance, both psychological and physical, weakened the structures of domination and sped up the process of emancipation.

Finally, I make clear that I aim to avoid fixing the Anansi tales within any one particular interpretive framework. Anansi tales were traditionally oral narratives, and they have continually metamorphosed, each storyteller adding their own embellishments and meanings. The tales have been told in myriad different contexts: from the villages of West Africa, to the slave quarters of the Caribbean plantations, to white children in great houses, to the hidden communities of the Maroons. The significance of the stories has been subject to continuous change, and when examining stories of this kind it is unfeasible, and undoubtedly erroneous, to attempt to assert one fixed and final overarching interpretation. The malleability of meaning in the tales facilitates their adaptation to disparate contexts and ensures both their survival and popularity.

Figure 2. Ghanaian children "ready for a story" (Barker and Sinclair 1917, frontispiece)

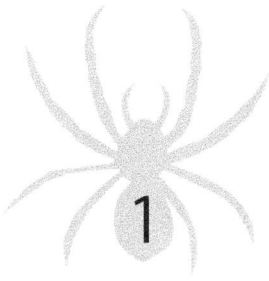

1

$\mathcal{A}$ *nansi's* $\mathcal{R}$ *oots*

The Spinner of Asante Life

THE TERM "AKAN" DENOTES AN ethno-linguistic group comprised of, among others, the Akuapem, Akyem, Baule, Asante, Brong and Fante peoples of West Africa. The Akan-Asante, the largest Ghanaian ethnic group, enjoyed cultural and political dominance in the Akan region for many centuries, and the tales reflect many elements of the Akan-Asante cultural framework. The Asante called Anansi "Kwaku" Anansi, a day-name traditionally given to males born on a Wednesday.[1] A day-name is the name given to an Asante child according to the day of the week on which a child is born (Mbiti 1969, 119). Although other animals in Akan folktales have names, none of them have the honour of having a day-name like Anansi (Yanka 1983, 6).

T.C. McCaskie's *State and Society in Pre-Colonial Asante* (1995) gives a detailed analysis of pre-colonial Asante culture in the eighteenth and nineteenth centuries. He argues that there have always been problems with the collection of data on the African continent: "It must be conceded immediately and without reservation that for large tracts of the African past conclusions are reduced to the tentative or the speculative by severe limitations in the historical record" (p. 1). Another consideration to make in research on the Asante is the nature of Asante beliefs, for although they are durable and resilient, they are also fluid, constantly adapting and changing. The Asante have continuously absorbed influences from other ethnic groups and cultures; as M.D. McLeod explains, "the history of the Asante is largely a history of change and incorporation" (1981, 14). The Californian anthropologist Noel

King describes the Asante belief system as "one round thing, no part can be separated from the other . . . [it is] an amazingly resilient system that has survived so much, and in each generation it has adapted and assimilated" (1986, 29).

This chapter will focus primarily on an analysis of the Asante folktales from Rattray's collection (1930). In 1921, Rattray established an anthropological department in the Asante capital Kumasi, which he ran nearly single-handedly and allowed him to devote himself to researching the customs of the Asante on a full-time basis. He stated that he wanted to produce a "detailed investigation into the beliefs and customs of this people", rather than rely on material produced by other officers and administrators (Robertson 1975, 54). Rattray is clearly a key figure in the collection of information on the Asante, and his research forms the main body of early-twentieth-century European writing on Asante culture. As well as using Rattray's historical research as a resource, stories from his collection *Akan-Ashanti Folk-Tales* (1930) will be examined.

Although William H. Barker and Cecilia Sinclair compiled and published a collection of Gold Coast folktales before Rattray's collection, entitled *West-African Folk Tales* (1917), its usefulness is more limited for several reasons. Barker, a geographer, collected the tales during his time as principal at a government training college in Accra. The tales were not specifically collected from the Akan-Asante, and they were written by trainee teachers at Barker's college in so-called Standard English: they are only "based" on original Gold Coast stories (p. ii). Some of the stories do share similarities with those in Rattray's collection – both texts contain narratives describing how Anansi gained all the world's wisdom and stories.[2] However, those from Barker and Sinclair's text read like English folktales, and they nearly all end with a moral message. In his introduction to the collection, Barker describes the tales as arranged for a "wider public" and provides no precise information of their origin (p. 25).

As well as translating the Anansi stories from oral narratives in Twi into English, Rattray provides detailed accounts of his collection techniques, the locations and origins of the tales and the environment in which they were told (Hartland 1917, 333–34; Rattray 1930). However, it is important to note that both these collections were complied by Europeans. As I rely on translated written, rather than oral, versions of the Anansi tales this inevitably removes me somewhat from my subject matter. In his analysis of the Akan Anansi tales, Pelton explains his own struggle with his cultural and geographical dislocation from his research: "Here I sit in the grip of Canadian winter, looking out the window at the pine trees and three feet of snow. I read the stories in English, not Akan, printed and collected, grasping them and the culture from which they rise with great intellectual difficulty" (1980, 20).

Researching the Anansi tales is not only complex in terms of one's separation from one's subject matter, but also in terms of drawing conclusions regarding Anansi's position among the Asante. Available sources are somewhat contradictory. Many claim Anansi is a god who shares some of the Asante god Nyame's power (also spelled "ONyame" and referred to as "Nyankopon" and "Odomankoma"). Barker asks, in his article "Nyankopon and Ananse in Gold Coast Folklore" (1919), "WHO is Nyankopon? Who is Ananse? What is the connection, if any, between Nyankopon and Ananse? – these are questions for which no satisfactory solution has yet been found" (p. 158). Reverend Joseph Williams, in *Psychic Phenomena of Jamaica* (1934), writes: "it is particular to Ashanti to use the sobriquet of the Supreme Being or Creator *Ananse Kokroko*, the Great Spider" (cited in Cassidy and Le Page 2002, 10). John S. Mbiti, author of *African Religions and Philosophy* (1969) also links the spider to Asante religious beliefs. He states that "among the Akan and Ashanti, the spider symbolizes 'wisdom' and for that reason, God is given the title *Anansi Koruoko* which means the Great Spider, that is, the Wise One" (1969, 51).

In Rattray's collection of Asante folktales, Anansi is described as "soul washer to the Sky-God", a description that Tanna also uses in *Jamaican Folk Tales and Oral Histories* (2000, 77). Historian and lieutenant of the West India Regiment, A.B. Ellis, in *Tshi-Speaking People of the Gold Coast of West Africa* (first published in 1887 by Chapman and Hall), explains that the subjects of his book had a traditional belief that the origin of man could be traced back to a spider-man, a hero of the Tchi (Twi) people. He writes that Anansi, the forefather of all men, "was sometimes a man and sometimes a spider, and it is probable that this tradition merely points to the existence of some early chief, who was known to his followers as 'The Spider'" (Ellis 1966, 339).

Ellis gives little evidence to support his claim, and speculations of Anansi's origins abound. Vecsey explains that the Asante see Nyame as the spiritual father of all people and Anansi as the father of the grandfathers, an ancient

Akan ancestor and possibly the founder of the Twi-speaking nations. Vecsey believes that Anansi is related to Nyame by his name "Anansi Kokuroko" or the "great spider" and that "some Akan think of the two as relatives" (1993, 112). Martha Warren Beckwith, who collected Anansi tales in Jamaica in the 1920s, writes that "the head-man on a Westmoreland cattle-pen assured me that Anansi, once a man, was now leader of the dead" in the "land of shades" (1924, xii). Other interpretations claim that Anansi had immense spiritual powers, and "that everything that happened in the world was started by Anansi" (Jekyll 1966, x).

Akan scholar J.B. Danquah, in *Akan Doctrine of God* (1944), claims that the name "Ananse" often replaces that of the Asante God, Nyame or Nyanko-pon. He quotes an Akan "ditty" in which Anansi, who he describes as "Ananse Kokuroko – Gigantic Ananse", features as one of the "holy trinity through or by Whom creation came or was brought into being" (1944, 43–44). The following poem, translated by Danquah, implies that Anansi was one of the creators of the Akan universe:

> Who gave word
> Who gave word
> Who gave word?
> Who gave word to Hearing.
> For Hearing to have told Ananse,
> For Ananse to have told Odomankoma,
> For Odomankoma
> To have made the Thing?
>
> (1944, 199)

Danquah, however, problematizes Anansi's connection to the Akan spiritual world and explains that the links made between a mythical personage named "Ananse" and the spider "Ananse" of Akan folklore are an "aetiological mistake, arising from a confusion of names" (1944, 199). He claims that Ananse was a mythical personage in the beliefs of the Sumer and Akkad from "Babylonia" (in former Mesopotamia), whose culture and language influenced the Akan. The Akan adopted from them the name of their human hero and transferred it to the spider hero "of their own tales of creation, wisdom and social life" (ibid.).

As we can see, ambiguity pervades every aspect of Anansi's identity, which makes it a challenge to draw conclusions regarding his position within the Asante world. This chapter illustrates, however, that while Anansi may have played a role in the religious world of the Asante, there is little evidence to suggest that he occupied the position of a god himself. It is more likely that he was an intermediary figure. As Ghanaian scholar Kwesi Yanka argues, Akan Anansi tales are not Akan myths as so many scholars have assumed, but rather fictional narratives with etiological features. Yanka conducted fieldwork in the Akan regions of Ghana in 1979, where he listened to and observed storytelling sessions and, when analysing the stories, drew from his first-hand experiences of the sociocultural context in which they were told. Yanka defines myth as a belief narrative; a story which is "considered to be a truthful account of what happened in the remote past" (1983, 1). He believes scholars have been too quick to categorize the Anansi tales as myths. They have been influenced, he argues, by the nineteenth-century Eurocentric assertion that animals must have a totemic significance among predominately illiterate African tribes – a stereotype created from the supposition that "primitive" peoples do not distinguish between themselves and animals (pp. 13–14).

Anansi is used to explain certain cultural and natural phenomena in the Akan world, and unlike other folkloric figures, he can both challenge and thwart the gods. Yet, as Yanka argues, it is unlikely that any of the Akan groups believed that Anansi once existed. First, the tales end with a disclaimer from the storyteller, explaining that the content of the tales is untrue. Second, there is no mention of Anansi as a divine figure in serious scholarly studies conducted on the religious beliefs of the Akan, including Rattray's *Religion and Art in the Ashanti* (1927). Third, unlike the elephant and certain species of antelope, Anansi is not venerated among the Akan (Yanka 1983, 10). Furthermore, the tales are taught and read in Akan schools as folktales, unlike Akan sacred texts, which can only be enacted by a restricted class of specialists p. 10).

The reason for the disparity in the interpretations of Anansi's origins is clear. Folktales are rarely rooted to one fixed source and the accounts of their origins are themselves steeped in fiction. But whereas reports regarding Anansi's origins are contradictory, we can find some reliable evidence regarding the function of the tales among the Asante. As we shall see, Anansi stories

are not Akan myths but vehicles through which the Akan can explain, scrutinize and question the world around them. They are also celebrations of the
intricacies and beauty of communication: Anansi is symbolic of the malleability and ambiguity of language, and the Akan delight in his use of tricky wordplay and double entendres to get the better of his adversaries (Yanka 1983,
11). For this reason, a spider design decorates the staffs of Akan royal spokes-
men, otherwise known as court "linguists" (ibid.).

It can be concluded that, from the seventeenth century to the early twentieth century, Anansi was tightly bound to Asante political, religious and social
life. Anansi did not hold a divine or god-like status among the Asante but, as
I will illustrate, his role was that of the mediator: a mediator in disputes
between tribesmen and women and, on a wider scale, a mediator between
humankind and Nyame, god of the sky (Pelton 1989, 65). Through the following analysis of the function of the tales among the Asante we gain a deeper
understanding and insight into both Anansi and Asante culture, for, as the
priest and Asante researcher Robert Pelton states, the Anansi stories "give
word, eloquently and delightfully, to the Asante understanding of human life"
(p. 61).

However, before detailing Anansi's function among the Asante, we will now
turn to a brief overview of the history, culture and religion of the Asante. The
discussion will enable us to firmly situate Anansi within this context and
examine his place in this world.

The Asante

During the pre-colonial period, the Asante sustained themselves through agri-
culture and hunting. They inhabited the fertile interior forested areas of the
region formally known by Europeans as the "Gold Coast". The Asante kingdom was formed at the close of the seventeenth century when the Asante
ruler Asantehene Osei Tutu brought together a confederation of Asante states
under his rule, transforming them into a powerful kingdom that engulfed
smaller states to the north. Throughout the first half of the eighteenth century
the strength of the Asante empire continued to grow under the leadership of
Asantehene Okpuku Ware, who died in 1750. During Ware's reign, the Asante
benefited greatly from the slave trade and the exportation of gold. They also

possessed unique skills in craftsmanship, excelling particularly in weaving (producing the famous "Kente" hand-woven ceremonial Akan cloth) and gold-smithing. As a result of the Asante's craftsmanship skills, combined with their agricultural prowess, strong military tradition and solid trade networks, Ware was able to expand, during his reign, the Asante land to cover much of present day Ghana (Isichei 1977, 60). Following the short reign of two other kings (Asantehene Osei Kwame ruled from 1777 to 1801, followed by Asantehene Osei Bonsu, who ruled from 1801 to 1824), the Asante and developed a highly organized bureaucratic system.

The kingdom of the Asante remained powerful throughout the Atlantic slave trade due to their inland location. Coastal regions, inhabited by groups such as the Fante, were weakened by European presence (Isichei 1977, 58). The Fante lived in small, disunited states and became involved with Europeans as they acted as middle-men in trading between the Asante and Europeans, excluding the Asante from direct trade and in turn controlling the export of slaves and gold from the Asante kingdom. However, the Asante reaped the benefits of the highly successful trade network they had developed, selling slaves, gold, kola nuts and ivory across the Atlantic and north across the Sahara. During the early nineteenth century, the Asante empire, which was growing rapidly, was thwarted by European intervention and the onset of colonialism. The British feared the strength of the Asante, and attempted to weaken and divide their kingdom. The Asante invaded Fante lands in 1806 and following their invasion the British supported the Fantes as allies through a series of wars between the two Akan factions (pp. 60–64).

The British used the Fante-Asante wars as a pretext to finally invade the interior of the Gold Coast in the 1870s – an action that resulted in the fourth Anglo-Asante war. In their 1874 invasion, the British sacked the Asante capital Kumasi, and troops pillaged treasures from the royal palace, which were later sold at auction in London. They then proceeded to blow up the palace and raze the entire city to the ground. In 1895 the then Asantehene Prempeh made a final attempt to improve the situation and raised enough money, through a tax on all Asante people, to send eight Asante representatives to negotiate with the British in London. The British ignored the Asante plight and Prempeh was asked to accept a British protectorate. He refused outright, claiming "my kingdom of Asante will never commit itself to any such policy" (Isichei

1977, 65). The British then sent an expedition into Asanteland that Prempeh knew was futile to resist (Pelton 1989, 65; Isichei 1977, 65–67).

In 1900 the Asante were defeated and the Asante empire was annexed to the British Gold Coast colony. The British sought to undermine the Asante by whatever means possible, and Prempeh, along with his relations and Asante chiefs, was sent into exile in the Seychelles for not paying the 60,000 ounces of gold demanded from him by the British. The Asante were dealt a final blow when British governor of the Gold Coast, Frederick Hodgson, demanded the handing over of the golden stool, the most important royal and divine object of the Asante people[3] (Isichei 1977, 65–67). The Asante refused, which resulted in further bloodshed. Following the Asantes' defeat in 1900, the British practised a form of indirect rule in the Asante colony. Only in the 1930s did they allow Asantehene Prempeh to return from exile. Finally, in 1957, the Gold Coast broke free from colonial rule and was renamed "Ghana".

Prior to British rule, the slave trade had reaped huge profits for the Asante who captured, used and traded slaves before and during the Atlantic slave trade. During the slave trade they became the main sellers of slaves on the Gold Coast, exchanging men, women and children for clothing and weapons. The Asante had a long history of keeping slaves and continued to do so into the late nineteenth century (Isichei 1977, 60–64). In Rattray's collection of folktales, "How Ananse, the Spider, Became Poor" (1930) describes how the headman of an Asante village keeps slaves. When he is notified his slave has died, he states, "you must throw him away, for I have no coffin". Anansi takes the corpse and tricks the villagers into thinking they can exchange it for a "fresh slave" (p. 259).

While the Asante state grew in strength through the selling of slaves, many Asantes were sold as slaves themselves. Many African slaves arriving on the coast to be sold had either been kidnapped, were prisoners of war or convicts, and a number of them had been slaves within Africa long before they boarded the slave ships. Although, as Craton explains, "it is worth noting that the vast majority of slaves sold on the African coast had been captured in war, or in slave-gathering raids and that Africans rarely, if ever, sold second generation slaves" (1982, 27; see also Walvin 1999, 32).

The Sacred World of the Asante

Traditional religions are still practised in Ghana today alongside Christianity and Islam. Like many other West African religions, Asante religion is primarily based around the worship of spiritual forces that structure the world and the universe. According to Asante belief, Nyame, the Great Deity of the Asante, sent his children down to earth and they bear the names of the hills and trees, the great lakes and rivers of Asanteland. They play the roles of lesser gods and are called the "Abosom" (also spelled "Obosom") (Allyene 1988, 45). Nyame has a female partner, Asase Yaa, who is often depicted as an old woman. Asase Yaa is neither Nyame's wife nor his creation. She is to Nyame what the queen mother of the Asante is to the king; she shares his power but he has no power over her (Pelton 1989, 65). Prayers are directed to both the male and female gods, with Asase Yaa representing the earth and Nyame the sky.

Anthropologist Eva Meyerowitz lived for forty years in the Bono-Tekyiman State of Ghana after the Second World War. In *The Sacred State of the Akan* (1949) she explains that "Nyame" is most likely to be derived from the word *nyam*, meaning shining, bright and luminous, for Nyame is said to have given birth to both the sun and the moon (p. 70). Asante religion is based on a belief that Nyame is present in all living things: plants, trees, rivers (special importance is placed on the river Tano that flows through Ghana) and soil. On certain types of trees, such as the fig tree, offerings were traditionally placed upon the trunks and worship would take place under the boughs. This practice was misinterpreted as tree worship by Europeans, but as Asante born author and historian T.E. Kyei points out, it was not the inanimate object itself being worshiped, but the spirit of Nyame and other lesser deities (Kyei 2001, 4). Before chopping a tree for wood, a ritual would also take place; the ritual involved the easing of Nyame's spirit and a chant pleading for the spirit not to take vengeance on the woodcutter.

The Asante believe in the presence of their dead ancestors. The dead are said to inhabit the earth among the living and it is possible for one to travel between the spiritual world and the real world (Partinder 1954, 58). The spirits of ancestors are believed to be constantly present and must be attended to in order to keep the living members of the family healthy, content and protected in times of trouble. When a person dies, the elements of the deceased's spirit remain connected for long or short periods with places and objects that belong to them, which is why carved stools, which are important religious and political Asante symbols, belonging to past relatives are used in ancestral ceremonies. The remaining elements of the dead that do not go back into the earth or remain connected with objects are either reincarnated into new children or abide with other dead ancestors (King 1986, 23).

Evelyn King lived in Ghana from 1952 to 1962, and during this period was tutored by a member of the Asante royal circle in the Asantehene's court in Kumasi. Her tutor, Madame Yaa, had been educated in a traditional Asante manner. Madam Yaa drew a diagram in the sand to explain the most important elements in Asante religion, which King recorded. In her diagram appear stools, or thrones, which represent the king and queen, as well as national social structure. Above the stools is Nyame, below them are the many children of Nyame, and in-between the world of the Gods and the world of humankind, Anansi, the intermediary, is pictured. Anansi is positioned on the male side of the illustration, along with the king, the male ancestors and the sun, while the queen and the ancestresses share their space with the moon.

Among the Asante, Anansi is not bound by the codes of the human or spirit world; he breaks all the rules of acceptable conduct, and is even able to confront and deceive Nyame. In the introduction to *Akan-Ashanti Folk-Tales* (1930), Rattray describes his surprise at the contradiction between the often potentially offensive content of the tales and what he sees as a disciplined, sophisticated and well-mannered people. He states that it is a "peculiarity presented by a people normally decorous in speech and conduct, whose folk-tales nevertheless often contain the most Rabelaisian passages, who would yet consider it highly inappropriate to relate such passages if divorced from the occasion and context in which they are nightly related" (p. ix). The reason for this contradiction, Rattray goes on to explain, is that Asante Anansi tales were a medium through which the people could criticize their superiors and air their problems. An Asante man or woman, who would have had a strict code of social conduct to adhere to, could make use of Anansi tales to scorn or reproach the elders, the Asantehene or even Nyame (p. x).[4]

Rattray describes how the storyteller would act out the tales in a comic and realistic manner. Setting the scene, the teller would expose the misconduct of powerful personages while vividly mimicking both their movements

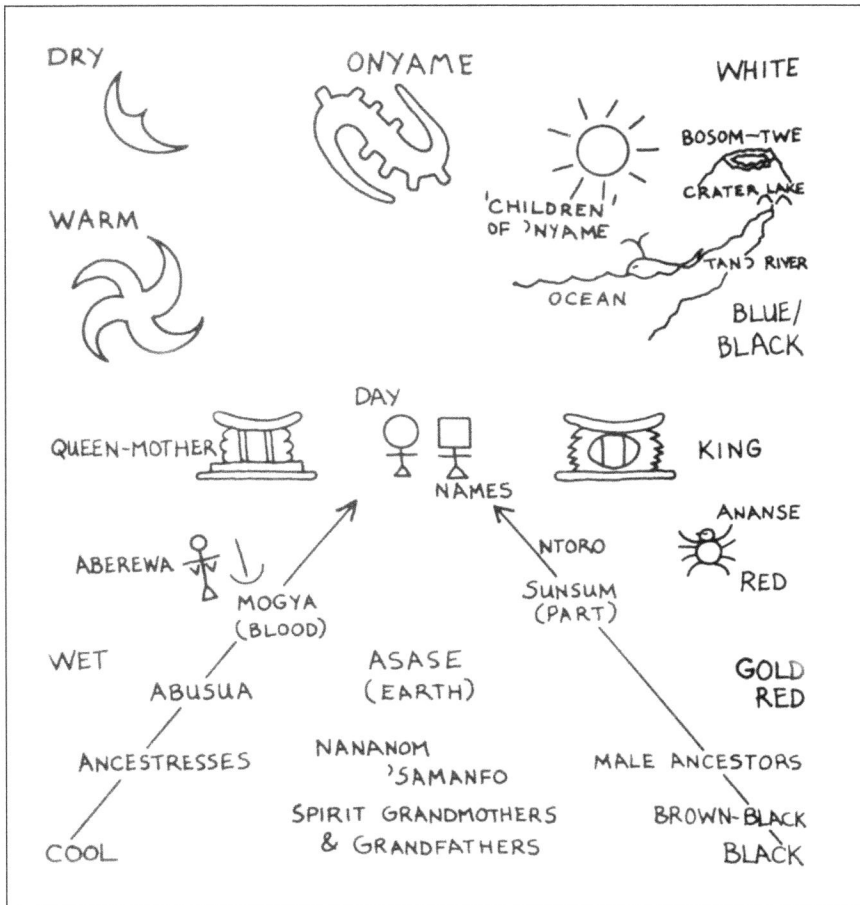

Figure 3. Madame Yaa's writings in the dust. (King, *African Cosmos*, 1E. © 1986 Wadsworth, a part of Centage Learning, Inc. Reproduced by permission. www.centage.com/permissions.)

and voices. When Rattray questioned an Asante man about the mimicry in the tales, the man explained that they were vehicles through which the behaviour of certain powerful individuals, who in everyday life could never be ridiculed, could be exposed:

> The cheating of priests, the rascality of a chief – things about which everyone knew, but concerning which one might not ordinarily speak in public. These

occasions gave everyone an opportunity for talking about and laughing at such things; it was "good" for every one concerned, he said . . . If one had a grievance against a fellow villager, a chief, or even the King of Ashanti, to hold him up to thinly disguised ridicule, by exposing some undesirable trait in his character – greed, jealousy, deceit – introducing the affair as the setting to some tale. A slave would thus expose a bad master, a subject his wicked chief [sic]. Up to a point the story teller was licensed. (1930, xi)

It is clear that the tales were used among the Asante to vent frustrations in a manner that was considered appropriate and legitimate by the state. Indeed, the Asante practised various methods of deflecting their criticism of the state and its rulers onto other things. One example can be found in the method of talking to the "shade tree" – a tree of special importance in an Asante village and synonymous with the king – and verbalizing what you would like to say to the Asantehene. Furthermore, the expression "to tear the leaves of the shade tree" is but a guarded version of "to curse the king" (McLeod 1981, 3).

There were certain rules to be adhered to if one wanted to complain about or mock the powerful in a tale that would protect the teller from causing offence. First, the tales must only be told after nightfall.[5] Second, there must be a public disclaimer made before the start and at the end of each story to show that the tales were not strictly true. In Rattray's collection, where his own comments appear in brackets, these disclaimers consist of the beginning "we do not really mean, we do not really mean (that what we are going to say is true)" (1930, 55) and the ending "this, my story, which I have related, if it be sweet, (or) if it be not sweet, take some elsewhere, and let some come back to me" (p. 59). Several tales also end with the following line: "some you may take as true, and the rest you may praise me (for the telling it)" (p. 77).[6] Rattray claims that the third method of avoiding offence was to use an animal to represent the human character being ridiculed (p. xi). It was in this way that the tales played a vital political role as a medium for members of the Asante community to air their issues publicly. This public airing could end in resolution or simply diffuse negative emotions into laughter and mockery, thus avoiding the build up of resentment and retribution.

The tales in Rattray's collection were collected on visits to Asante villages where he observed evening storytelling sessions. He would note what he con-

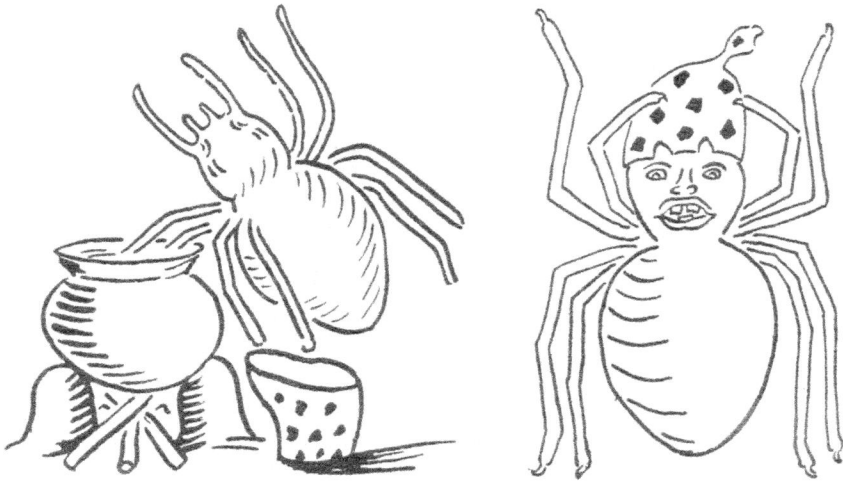

Figure 4. "Ananse putting beans in his hat" (*left*) and "Ananse caught hold of his hat" (*right*). (Illustrations from "How the Spider Got a Bald Head" recorded by Rattray [1930, 121]. By permission of Oxford University Press.)

sidered to be the "best" tale and ask the storyteller to return the next day and repeat their story. The tales would then be written down with as little editing as possible. Unlike Jamaican versions of the Anansi tales, Rattray's collection provides a name for each animal character. For example, the cat is introduced as Okra, the dog as Okraman. We also meet, among others, Akoko, the fowl; Aberekyie, the goat; Odwan, the sheep; Adowa, the antelope; and Otwe, the duyker. Anansi's family also have names: Anansi's wife is Aso, and his children are Ntikuma (which Rattray translates as "first-born"), Nyiwankonfwea ("thin shanks"), Afudotwedotwe ("belly-like-to- burst") and Tikonokono ("big-big-head").

Rattray's tales were illustrated by African artists, not all of Asante origin. He states that the illustrators read the English versions of the tales, presumably because English was the language they had in common, and illustrated the tales accordingly. Figure 4 is an artist's depiction of "How the Spider Got a Bald Head", a story in which Anansi gets his comeuppance for eating at a funeral while he is pretending to be fasting in honour of the dead. He is about to be caught eating some hot beans, so he quickly hides the beans in his hat, but loses all his hair as the beans burn his scalp as a result. This tale reinforces Asante social structure by showing the problems that can befall those who betray customs.

Rattray explains that previous European collections of Akan folktales had been compiled using the help of literate Africans who wrote down their tales in European languages at the request of Europeans. These tales he criticizes as "pseudo-African", and states that the collector's methodology was problematic (1930, vii). According to Rattray, the transcribers "ignore the African idiom, and omit apparently trivial details which stamp these tales with individuality and make them of value to students of language and customs" (p. v). Moreover, Akan "helpers" predominantly learned English through missionary schooling, which resulted in translations written in a "curious uniform standard of unidiomatic expression which is not really the spoken language of the mass of people, nor one in which these tales were originally told" (ibid.).

Rattray engages with elements of the historiographical and methodological issues relating to the production of history, and in what seems to be a reference to Barker and Sinclair, explains that "certain" European collectors of Akan tales "ignorant" of Akan languages have relied on Africans trained at "some Missionary School" for their data (p. ix). Influenced by their education, these Africans have deliberately excluded certain "improper" elements of the tales to avoid offending European readers (they may have also wanted to avoid negative portrayals of their culture when it came under the scrutiny of Europeans) (ibid.). Rattray maintains that, although he has made slight alterations to the tense in his English translations of the Anansi tales, "the originals represent the Akan language as it is actually spoken to-day in Ashanti. In this respect they are, I believe, unique among the works printed in the vernacular" (p. vi). The grammar and the tenses of the English translations reflect the original Twi language structure, and he proudly claims that any element that may appear as a "discord" in the translations will simply be "one of their chief charms and most happy claims to originality" (p. vii). It is because of his sensitivity to his sources and his cultural awareness, demonstrated here, that Rattray is a key source for this book.

Rattray explores what he considers to be three key questions in relation to the stories: the origin of the tales; the reason for their "vulgar" subject matter; and the Asante's use of animals as characters who think, speak and act like human beings (1930, vii). In applying himself to the first question, Rattray points out the impossibility of claiming that the tales are from one particular source as they bear a remarkable resemblance to other tales found "in localities far distant from the Gold Coast, and among peoples of a different race" (ibid.). The tales have been told and retold and travelled through many cultures: "a tale told in Africa may well eventually reach a remote area – remodelled; it is told and recast again and again in translation, but always recognisable in each of its many variations" (p. viii). He explains that slavery in West Africa, "both as an indigenous institution and much later in the degraded form it took under the impetus given to the trade by Europeans, was, I think, a very important factor in the dissemination of the Folk-tale" (ibid.).

As Rattray explains, with all tales told orally, characters, plots and themes are continually altered in different contexts ("local circumstances in each case influenced the telling") and modified by different groups to "conform with its own particular outlook upon life" (1930, ix). Rattray also states that as indications of "indexes of character, psychology, local customs, and beliefs of the people that narrate them . . . [the tales] mirror more or less accurately the ideas of the people and their general outlook upon life, conduct, and morals" (ibid.).

Key to Rattray's understanding of Anansi's role among the Asante is an examination of the stark contrast between the violent and overtly sexual and scatological nature of the tales and the strict moral guidelines of the Asante people. Examples of Anansi's violent, deceiving and crude behaviour can be found in "How Contradiction Came among the Tribe" (Rattray 1930, 107). Hate-to-Be-Contradicted kills those who contradict him. When he tells Anansi a lie, Anansi does not contradict him but supplies his own lie. Hate-to-Be-Contradicted lies about the ripe palm nuts that hang near his home:

> "It's in their nature to ripen like that; when they are ripe, three bunches ripen at once; when they are ripe I cut them down, and when I boil them to extract the oil, they make three water pots full of oil, and I take the oil to Akase, to buy an Akase old woman; the Akase old woman comes and gives birth to my grandmother, who bears my mother, that she in turn may bear me. When mother bears me, I am already standing there." The Spider said, "you do not lie, what you say is true; as for me, I have some okras standing near my farm, and when

they are ripe, I join seventy-seven hooked poles (to reach them to pull them down), but even then they do not reach, so I lie on my back, and am able to use my penis to pluck them." (Rattray 1930, 107)

When Hate-to-Be-Contradicted visits Anansi's home, Anansi's children are instructed to tell him that Anansi's penis has broken in seven different places and he has gone to the blacksmiths to get it repaired. Anansi and his family continue to lie to their guest until Hate-to-Be-Contradicted cannot stand it any longer and contradicts them. When he has done so, Anansi tells him that because he, who hates to be contradicted, has contradicted someone, Ntikuma must "beat him so he may die" (Rattray 1930, 109). Ntikuma does so with vigour, and Anansi proceeds to cut up his flesh and scatter it about: "that is why many persons who hate to be contradicted are found in the tribe" (ibid.). In many of these tales, Anansi scatters certain human characteristics and elements: jealousy, contradiction, wisdom, stories, diseases. It is in this way that they enter the tribe and the human world.

Another example of scatological behaviour in Rattray's collection can be found in "How It Came About That the Hinder Part of Kwaku Ananse, the Spider, Became Big, at the Expense of His Head, Which Became Small" (1930, 67–71), in which we see Anansi interact with the spirit world. Anansi refuses to heed the spirit's warning, which results in his head detaching from his body. Anansi then proceeds to take his own head and push it up his bottom – he clamps "it against his anus". Thus, forevermore, the rear end of the spider is larger than his head (ibid.).

The tales also illustrate the status and treatment of women and the importance of crops and meat in the Asante community. Although Asante society is matrilineal, and women are highly regarded within the community, females play a subservient role. Anansi's wife Aso is evidently a highly intelligent woman – she advises Anansi on how to catch Onini the Python, Mmoboro the Hornets, Osebo the Leopard and Mmoatia the Fairy in exchange for the Nyame's stories, yet she and other female characters in the stories function predominantly as cooks and cleaners, or potential wives to be won or fought over. They are background characters who are often brusquely commanded to provide food for the men, especially by Anansi (Rattray 1930, 55–59). The subservient role of women is exemplified in the tale in which Aso becomes Anansi's wife (p. 132). Aso's jealous husband is sterile, which was traditionally considered to be a sign of being an "incomplete" being among the Asante (p. 37). Following the death of a sterile Asante man or woman, burial took place in shallow graves on the peripheries of the village on what is described by McLeod as a "midden" (a place for village waste), and their corpses were mutilated and abused verbally "so their sterile spirits would not return to the world in the same sterile state" (McLeod 1981, 37). We see in this tale that the village headman has the authority to offer Aso to any villager who can impregnate her, a task which Anansi successfully performs (Rattray 1930, 132).

The centrality of successful crops, sources of water and meat in the lives of the Asante are also illustrated in both Rattray's (1930), and Barker and Sinclair's (1917) collections. The majority of the tales start with the description of famine, with Anansi in desperate search for food: "there came once such a terrible famine in the land that a grain of corn was worth more than its weight in gold. A hungry spider was wandering through the forest looking for food" (Barker and Sinclair 1917, 55). The prime focus of the Asante stories is the growing of crops and the desirability of meat – nothing seems to seduce a female character more easily than a large hunk of fresh flesh. As we shall see, like the Asante tales, Jamaican Anansi stories also start with a description of lack and suffering. Anansi, because he can always find ways to overcome the most seemingly insurmountable challenges, is conjured in life-threatening situations when food and water are in short supply, and death is imminent.

It is clear that the function of the Anansi tales in their Asante setting was to aid the harmony of the social system as a whole. Furthermore, as we shall now go on to explore, they were used as a medium for negotiation and as a temporary release from a controlled environment. The tales tested the limits of Asante codes of behaviour, but in doing so redefined its boundaries.

Liminal Anansi: Symbols of Chaos and Order

The two tales in which Anansi brings both wisdom and stories to earth have become the best-known Asante Anansi tales and have travelled around the world. They exemplify the ways in which Anansi, for the Asante, brings culture's vital elements to earth, and symbolize his immense power as mediator between humankind and the gods. In "How It Came About That Wisdom Came Among the Tribe" (Rattray 1930, 5–7), we see the vital role that Anansi plays in the human world. This tale also exemplifies Ntikuma's, Anansi's son, superior intelligence. As it is one of the most important Asante tales, I shall quote it at length.

> They say that Kwaku, the Spider, was there, and that he swept up all knowledge, gathered it together in one spot, and placed it in a gourd pot. He then declared that he would climb a tree and go and hang it on it, so that all wisdom on earth would be finished. So he took it up to go with it, and when he reached beneath the tree where he was going to hang, he took a string, and tied it to the gourd, and hung it in front of him, and he set himself to climb the tree. He climbed, and climbed, and climbed; in vain. He strove again, again he made to climb, and climb, and climb: in vain.
>
> Now, his son, Ntikuma, who was standing by, said, "Oh, your eyes have surely died (for shame), would it not have been better if you had turned round the gourd and put it on your back, then doubtless you would have been able to climb?" He (the spider) said, "Clear out, you and your old-fashioned sayings." Then he turned to climb once more as before, but once again, fruitlessly. Then he considered long and (finally) took the gourd and put it behind him. Then he set himself to climb, and mounted swiftly, Kra! kra! kra! (was the sound of his climbing); there he goes.
>
> He reached where the branches began to spread out from the stem, and he said (to himself), "I, Kwaku Ananse, by the lesser god, Afio! I might well be dead, my child who is so small, so small, so small – there I was, I collected all wisdom (so I thought) in one place, yet some remained which even I did not perceive, and lo! My child, this still-sucking infant, has shown it to me." (Ibid.)

After this revelation, Anansi seizes the gourd and smashes it, scattering wisdom across the human world.

Another of the most well known Anansi tales explains how Anansi became owner of all the stories in the world, which he won from Nyame after completing Nyame's seemingly impossible tasks. In "How It Came About That the Sky-God's Stories Came to Be Known as 'Spider-Stories'" (Rattray 1930, 55–59), Anansi asks to buy Nyame's stories. Nyame is shocked: "great and powerful towns" have asked for the tales, and here is Anansi, "a mere masterless man" with the audacity to request them. In exchange for the tales, Nyame tells Anansi he must bring him Onini the Python, Osebo the Leopard, Mmoatia the Fairy and Mmoboro the Hornet (ibid.). Anansi says he will rise to the challenge and will even add Nsia, his own mother, to the list of creatures he will bring Nyame.

Anansi consults Aso, and she suggests they trick the python into proving he is longer than a long branch of palm-tree. As Onini the Python wraps himself around the branch, Anansi takes a "rope-creeper" and ties him fast (Rattray 1930, 57). Aso then suggests he sprinkle water on the Hornets' nest. He does so, pretending it is rain, and offers the Hornets shelter in a gourd, which they accept. Anansi then closes the opening of the gourd. To catch Leopard, Anansi digs a hole. When Leopard falls in, Anansi scolds him for being a drunk – "that's why you have fallen into the pit" (ibid.) – and offers him two sticks to hoist him out. As Anansi lifts Leopard, he stabs and kills the cat with his knife.

Anansi has a clever and complicated plan to capture Mmoatia[7] the Fairy. He carves an "Akua's child", which is a "black flat-faced wooden doll" (Rattray 1930, 57), and plasters the doll's body with latex from a tree, sitting her at the foot of the odum-tree, where the fairies play. Mmoatia the Fairy tries to play with the doll and becomes angry when the doll won't respond: Mmoatia slaps her, and is stuck fast to the latex. Anansi takes his captives, along with his mother (who he wakes, drags out of bed, and carries on his back) to Nyame. Nyame consults the Asante elders and army leaders. "Very great Kings have come, and were not able to buy the Sky-God's stories," he tells them, "but Kwaku Ananse, the Spider, has been able to pay the price" (p. 59). He then addresses Anansi: "Kwaku Ananse, from to-day and going on for ever, I take my Sky-God's stories and I present them to you, kose! kose! kose! My blessing, blessing, blessing. No more we shall call them the stories of the Sky-God, but we shall call them Spider-stories" (ibid.).

This tale sets the precedent for all other Anansi tales. Here we see Anansi thwarting the existing order, and taking on the most powerful of Asante beings, through a combination of unique skills. Through his mastery of language (implemented to flatter Python, lure the Hornets, scold and deceive Leopard); his excellent practical skills (illustrated in his setting of traps, his use of the knife and ropes, his digging of holes and in his creation of rubber and dolls); his talent for cunning, disguise and subterfuge (he hides and watches his victims, striking at just the right moment, spider-style); and his ruthlessness (he sells his own mother), Anansi achieves the impossible and lures his powerful victims to meet their fates. Furthermore, Anansi is brave, confident and proud: he has the courage to challenge Nyame, boast to him and ignore his warnings. It is through the development of these characteristics that Anansi illustrates his ability to dominate powerful forces through survival and resistance tactics. These two tales illustrate how Anansi controls the fundamentals of civilization – wisdom (knowledge) and stories (history and memory) – in his tales, making him central to the very existence and survival of the Asante world.

Anansi, however, remains a multi-faceted creature. Despite bringing wonderful things to humankind, he has a sinister and violent side. Unforgiving and vengeful, Anansi commits innumerable gruesome acts for his own personal gain. Not only does he disrespect Nyame and steal from him, but in his relationships with other characters, he is often antagonistic and cruel. In "How It Came About That Children Were First Whipped" he takes great pleasure in watching his family being beaten as a result of his actions (Rattray 1930, 62). Furthermore, Anansi continually shows his disregard for the rules of society. He breaks public trust during a famine, and watches his family starve while gorging himself. In addition, if he helps humans, it is often because he will gain some form of reward. He introduces debt, jealousy, diseases, contradiction, serpents and monsters into the Asante world, and, although he brings stories and wisdom to earth, it is not through his altruism but primarily as a result of his greed (his desire for Nyame's stories) and frustration (his annoyance with his lack of climbing technique) (pp. 5–7). It is the transmission of these attributes to Caribbean society that provokes the argument for banning Anansi stories in contemporary Jamaica, as will be discussed in chapter 4.

In his spider form Anansi is an occupier of peripheries and dark places; he is linked to the world of natural forces and animal instincts. McLeod explains that the Asante were preoccupied with the boundaries between the human world (culture) and the unknown world of spirits and unfathomable forces (nature). Until the end of the nineteenth century, the very geographical layout of their villages and towns reflected this preoccupation (McLeod 1981). Obsessed with cleanliness, the Asante threw all "unclean" things onto the midden. This included not only sterile men and infertile women, but also witches, children (who were not complete beings until adolescence), and those who had died as a result of the uncontrollable forces of nature (for example, those killed by being gouged by wild animals, crushed by falling trees or struck by lightning) (McLeod 1981, 38–40). Fringe areas of the village were also used for housing menstruating women (who were deemed unclean and dangerous during menstruation), burial grounds, temples (to offer respect to the gods and also to control their entry into the human world) and village latrines. These fringe zones were viewed by the Asante as intermediary spaces in which "special conditions or entities" operated (p. 38). Beyond these intermediary zones was the bush, and "the bush and the village were strongly opposed in Asante thought" (pp. 38–40).

The Asante believed that all human activities should take place in the village; no child should be conceived or born in the bush; to die in the bush was both horrifying and disgraceful. A place of chaotic wild forces, full of spirits and superhuman beings who threatened humankind, the bush was the ultimate contrast to the carefully ordered Asante village or town. It is therefore logical that a people so focused on the opposition and boundaries between order and disorder, clean and the unclean, sacred and sacrilege, and culture and nature, should be so fascinated by the figure of Anansi, who inhabited and restructured both worlds and showed no fear in the crossing of boundaries. The intermediary midden zone that separated the town and the forest, the dwelling and the bush was "a symbolic as well as a physically distinct zone" (McLeod 1981, 40). A small low barrier of thin branches was placed around this zone for man's protection against the wild forces of the bush. This great distinction, both geographical and symbolic, between the civilized human world and the bush, not only influenced much of Asante art, but is integral to our understanding of the relevance of Anansi within the Asante community (p. 40).

Anansi is a liminal creature because he is in a continual state of metamorphosis, and he inhabits a space on the threshold between the human world and the nonhuman. From his position on the margins he tests and extends established boundaries. At this point, let us examine the term liminal. In *The Forest of Symbols* (1967), Victor Turner locates the liminal as a physical space. If we turn back to Madame Yaa's illustration of the Asante religious world, we see Anansi is physically positioned both in the middle and edge of the drawing, illustrating his role as a creature of mediation and an occupier of the margins and liminal spaces (Glazier 1998; King 1986, 23). The liminal resists straightforward definition, but it is the very complexity and intangibility of the term that makes it so appropriate in a discussion of Anansi. It is described by Jamaican scholar Diane Austin-Broos as a transitional phase in which "persons elude or slip through the network of classifications that normally locate states and positions in cultural space" (1997, 46). Pelton states that Asante Anansi's inner form is "that of the personified limen" (1989, 58).

French folklorist Arnold van Gennep was the first to document the liminal as an analytical category in 1908, when he identified a sequence that he claimed characterized rites of passage in every culture: separation (preliminal), transition (liminal), and reintegration (postliminal). During the liminal stage of a rite of passage, an individual is separated from his or her original identity and surroundings; they are "betwixt and between social categories and expectations" (Glazier 1998). Turner and Mary Douglas also identify liminal stages in rites of passage. Douglas has argued that "all social transition is perceived as dangerous. Because their status is temporarily undefined, persons experiencing transition have no place in society" (ibid.).[8]

Anansi's actions are anti-social and destructive, and his liminality lies in his ability to invert all social rules: he can disconnect his own body parts, change his sex, eat his own children, abuse his guests, unashamedly ignore the truth and disregard Nyame. Anansi has free rein to do anything he pleases. Liminality, which evidently preoccupied Asante thought, signals the reversal of social structure, yet it is the references to liminality in the Anansi tales that brought about social unity by accepting darker forces which other societies might try to eradicate. Among the Asante, it was precisely by acting inappropriately and testing the limitations of the Asante moral code that Anansi was able to set and strengthen social order. Anansi became a re-creative force in the sense that as the structure of Asante society was challenged by his liminality it was simultaneously fortified by it.

The Anansi tales can be seen as symbolic of the Asante midden, a powerful in-between space full of human waste, incomplete beings and incomprehensible forces; in essence, the gateway between culture and nature – the human and the spirit world. The preoccupation with death in the tales forms part of their regenerative essence: a celebration of a cyclical rather than linear approach to life in which the rotting corpse is linked to the pregnant mother within the life cycle. The grotesque, which would normally remain hidden in an Asante society so opposed to dirt and the unclean, when linked to laughter and mockery in the form of an Anansi tale, becomes an acceptable and amusing topic. For example, in "How Spear-Grass Came into the Tribe" we see the serious and dangerous topic of menstruation discussed in both a comic and offhand manner (Rattray 1930, 213–21). Ntikuma has brought home some yams and Anansi takes one and says, "when I have my monthly periods, I shall eat this one". Aso retorts, "since the Creator made things, have you seen a man who has monthly periods?" Anansi says nothing, but quietly goes and stays in the secluded area used by menstruating women, so he can finish off the yams, alone and in peace (pp. 213–19).

Mikhail Bakhtin's ideas on the carnivalesque shed much light on the reasons for the preoccupation with potentially offensive or grotesque themes in the Asante Anansi tales. Bakhtin analyses the carnivals that characterized the Middle Ages in Europe and Russia, up to the time of Rabelais's[9] sixteenth-century writings (Vice 1997, 150). Bakhtin explains how the carnivals of the Middle Ages played a key role in the lives of ordinary people, giving them a chance to thwart strict social rules and turn officialdom on its head. During this period people "inhabited a dual role of existence: one official, characterised by the authority of the church, the feudal system, work, and one unofficial, characterised by reversal, parody, song and laughter" (p. 150). Although in an analysis of Asante cultural practices we are dealing with completely different geographical, historical and sociopolitical contexts to Bakhtin, his ideas are relevant to this discussion. His work may be focused on Europe and Russia in the Middle Ages, but there are striking similarities in the social functions of the carnival during this historical period and the cultural practices of the Asante. Evidently, ordinary people living in hierarchical societies devise similar coping mechanisms.

Bakhtin's theory of the carnivalesque has been applied to rituals of role reversal around the world, particularly in the analysis of Caribbean carnivals. In "Carnival Theory after Bakhtin" (2004), Richard Schechner's interpretation of the role of the carnival in the Caribbean shares similarities with my analysis of Anansi's function among the Asante. Schechner applies Bakhtinian theory in his examination of the Caribbean carnival to demonstrate that it is a "cultural form which simultaneously *critiques* official culture and *supports* it": it

is an event full of the threat of the breakdown of structure – of violence, rioting and chaos – but it remains a threat and is not an open revolt or revolution
(Schechner 2004, 4).

The annual Odwira festival, celebrated from September to October by the
Asante, is analogous to the Caribbean carnival and Bakhtin's carnival of the
Middle Ages. The roots of the Odwira festival reach back to the beginning of
the Asante state. During the festival, according to observations by McLeod,
"the ordinary rules of behaviour [were] turned upside down" (1981, 37). The
Asantehene, the king of the Asante, wore barkcloth, "the garb of the poorest
slave in the realm", instead of the elaborate robes he normally wore. It was
only at the Odwira festival that those executed for being criminals were
allowed funeral rights (p. 37, p. 149).

Bakhtin described the phenomenon of the carnival as an ambivalent spectacle that involved both actor and spectator in a parody of authoritarian structures. The task of bringing down-to-earth the hierarchical institutions of a
society was one that was "achieved principally through mockery" (Vice 1997,
155). The "moral principle and beliefs were . . . turned into 'rotten cords' and
the previously concealed, ambivalent, and unofficialized nature of man and
human thought was . . . nakedly exposed" (Bakhtin 1984, 166). Allowances
were made for parodies of the powerful through humour and laughter: "much
was permissible in the form of laughter that was impermissible in serious
form" (p. 127).

Bakhtin directly links his ideas on the carnival to medieval folk humour,
which he describes as a "boundless world of humorous forms and manifesta-
tions [which] opposed the official and serious tone of medieval ecclesiastical
and feudal culture" (1984, 4). Like the Anansi tales, Bakhtin's folk forms mix
the "sacred with the profane, the lofty with the low, the great with the insignif-
icant, the wise with the stupid" (p. 123). For Bakhtin, death and renewal, both
signified by the grotesque body, are central to the carnival. He states that an
important form of the grotesque "means a coming down to earth, the contact
with the earth as an element that swallows up and gives birth at the same
time" (p. 21). Specifically, "[to] degrade also means to concern oneself with
the lower stratum of the body, the life in the belly and the reproductive organs;
it therefore relates to acts of defecation and copulation, conception, preg-
nancy and birth. Degradation digs a bodily grave for new birth" (p. 24).

As Bakhtin describes, the carnival was a time for celebration of renewal, change and rebirth in which the sacred was brought down-to-earth in grotesque form, "hostile to all that was immortalised and completed" (1984, 10). Anansi also brings everything down to a bodily level: he is a creature obsessed with his lower regions, ceaselessly preoccupied with filling his belly or satisfying his rampant sex drive.[10] The focus on the body, sex and death within the Anansi tales can be seen as part of the same regenerative cycle, with Anansi as a regenerative force at the centre. As the application of Bakhtin's theory of the carnivalesque to the Asante Anansi tales illustrates, the Anansi tales facilitated the celebration of liminality, the grotesque, degradation, death, renewal and rebirth for the Asante. The tales provided a form of social and psychological release where resentments could be aired and boundaries could be tested and extended without breaking up community ties.

Anansi's ability to challenge and disrupt human society has been discussed by Pelton (1980), Jonas (1990), Harris (1981) and Tiffin (1982), all of whom envisage him as the embodiment of creation and destruction as well as chaos and order, living perpetually on the peripheries of society. Pelton sees Anansi's role among the Asante as that of an essentially ambiguous force with civilizing and culturalizing potential. Pelton states: "Like the archaic, unconscious logic of dreams, the meanings of these stories and their links with the more conscious life of the Asante are there, embedded in the narratives, easily overlooked but open to investigation and understanding" (1980, 29).

Pelton's research is based on two main primary sources: the work carried out by Charles van Dyck for his doctoral thesis, "An Analytic Study of the Folktales of Selected People of West Africa" (1967), and Rattray's collection of folktales. Pelton describes Anansi as a centrifugal force among the Asante, whereas Nyame is centripetal. As illustrated in Madame Yaa's drawing, Nyame is at the centre of the Asante world and "the centre brings everything in order by drawing all things into a relationship with it" (King 1986, 23). Pelton states:

> There is, therefore, a double movement here. There is a movement out from the centre, bearing the power of the centre and literally redefining disorder, and there is a movement into the centre, bringing into human, social existence all those forces of nature – women, beauty, play – that, when refined, are necessary to culture. (1980, 46–47)

> Anansi reveals the Asante understanding that there can be no pure centrifu-
> gality. Just as the turning of the centre creates movement away from the centre,
> so Anansi's movement away from order creates order. He shows the power of
> liminality precisely by stressing its negation of ordinary structure. (p. 36)

Anansi is a symbol of humankind's struggle to try and define the boundaries
between nature and culture, tamed and wild, bush and village, man and beast.
He is a part of a culture in a continual state of flux where binary oppositions
are tested to strengthen the social structure. Just as there exists both a male
and female god, each with a share of divine power, "all Asante beliefs and
institutions embody doubleness so that everyday life reveals an ultimate order"
(p. 63).

Vecsey (1993) explores the significance of Akan trickster tales in his essay
"The Exception Who Proves the Rules: Anansi the Akan Trickster". Like Pelton, Vecsey sees the role of the trickster as a threat to the rules of both societal
and cosmic order. The trickster is in a continual state of metamorphosis and
throws doubt on the concepts of truth and reality. The trickster tales, through
performing a simultaneously destructive and regenerative role in society, help
a community to clarify, evaluate and reflect on their reality: "by breaking patterns of a culture the trickster helps to define those patterns" (p. 106). Jonas
sees the trickster in a similar way: "Lurking at the crossroads, around door-
ways, and in public places, Trickster is god of the marketplace . . . Associated
with inversion of social order, with deceit (fiction), and *libido* transformed
into creativity, the trickster . . . presides, godlike, over the marketplace of linguistic exchange, signifying upon authority's text in endless wordplay and
deconstruction" (1990, 11).

Vecsey explains that, in Akan thought, the community is of greater importance than the individual (1993, 118). There are strong obligations to the group,
and deviation from the norm can result in banishment, which is the ultimate
punishment for a member of such a community. Being separated from your
community is like separating from your grounds of being (ibid.). In contrast
with the Asante people, Anansi is the ultimate loner, without friends and often
even estranged from his family. He has no sense of community ties or obliga-
tion to others. As Anansi wreaks havoc, the tales portray a very well-ordered
society existing around him. While he is scheming and stealing and violating
the rules, in contrast, his neighbours are team players: they are planting crops,

cooperating and obeying (p. 119). As Anansi threatens social order, the other characters in the tales uphold it, again reaffirming a faith in the structures of the Asante community.

Furthermore, although Anansi tests Nyame's power, it remains intact or is strengthened by Anansi's challenges. When Anansi needs something, he must go to Nyame to claim it, and he often provides a service to Nyame as an exchange. As we have seen in the tales "How It Came About That the Hinder Part of Kwaku Ananse, the Spider, Became Big, at the Expense of His Head, Which Became Small" (Rattray 1930, 67–71) and "How Spear-Grass Came into the Tribe" (pp. 212–19), Anansi can suffer as a result of his actions and he normally remains subordinate to Nyame. Although Anansi can violate Nyame's rule, in doing so he reaffirms it. As Vecsey puts it: "in regard to the Akan people as in regard to Nyame, Anansi is the exception that probes and proves the rules" (1993, 119).

In conclusion, rather than having a blind faith in their social structures, through the medium of Anansi the Asante could incorporate scepticism into their belief systems, and doing so make them both more resilient and profound (Vecsey 1993, 121). We will now move on to an exploration of the first stage of Anansi's journey into Jamaican culture, and an examination of the ways in which the function and content of the tales changed in their Jamaican context.

Figure 5. Illustration by Marcia Brown, "From Tiger to Anansi". (From *Anansi the Spider Man: Jamaican Folk Tales* by P.M. Sherlock © 1956 Macmillan Publishers Limited 2011. Used by permission.)

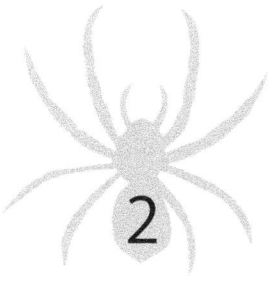

2

$\mathcal{A}$ nansi's $\mathcal{M}$ etamorphosis

Transmission and Change

Jamaica was a slave society in which the slaves heavily outnumbered the free. Personal advancement, not public good, was what counted; the exploitation of women, man, land, not responsible conduct; profits, not morality; a society totally corrupted by its perception of nine-tenths of the total population as property; as an inferior form of human being. (Sherlock 1998, 159)

THE TRANSATLANTIC SLAVE TRADE RESULTED in the largest forced migration of people in human history (Eltis and Richardson 2003, 42). Sherlock (1998) states that the slave trade began in 1415 when the Portuguese conquered Ceuta in North Africa. As the Portuguese began to explore the Western Mediterranean, they came into contact with Africans, whom they captured as prisoners and sold in Portugal. Once they realized they could barter for slaves with Africans rather than kidnapping them, the Portuguese began trading in earnest, and by 1455 were importing between seven and eight hundred Africans a year (Sherlock 1998, 118–19). In 1482, the Portuguese built the El Mina fort on the former Gold Coast as part of their aim to monopolize the trade. It was the only European fortification on the African coast until the Dutch established Fort Nassau in 1612.

Following in the footsteps of the Portuguese and the Dutch came the Spanish and the British. By the 1730s, the British were controlling the transatlantic slave trade, and half of all ships used in the trade were built in Bristol. As the British nation became more and more reliant on sweetened foods and drinks, the demand for sugar and slaves grew rapidly (Walvin 1999, 19). The British

built bases in Sierra Leone, the Gambia and the Gold Coast, and their three
key home ports were Liverpool, Bristol and London (p. 26, p. 28). Ships set
off from these ports and reached West Africa with guns, cowry shells from
the Maldives, textiles, and metal bars to exchange for slaves. Once they had
a full "cargo", they sailed the trade winds to the Americas, sold their slaves,
and returned to Britain with rum, sugar tobacco, and, in the eighteenth
century, coffee.

The exact figures for the numbers of Africans transported to the New
World have been much contested. Sherlock states that ten to eleven million
Africans were "moved by force" between 1500 and 1880 (1998, 124), and James
Walvin explains that, in total, approximately twelve million Africans were
shipped from the West African coast between the fifteenth and nineteenth
centuries (1999, 32). Walvin argues that the worst mortality rates were among
slaves in transit within the African interior. They were herded down to towns
on the coast for sale, often changing hands several times, and had to endure
brutality of African traders, starvation and thirst (p. 37). Of the slaves who
did survive the journey down to the coast and across the Atlantic, a full third
died in the first three to four years of reaching the Americas (p. 38).

So involved did African traders become in the process of enslavement and
transportation that the trade led to irreparable impacts on African economy
and society. The ever-increasing European demand for slaves affected the flux
of conflicts in the African interior and prompted African states to enslave,
kidnap and wage war on their enemies and neighbouring communities
(Walvin 1999, 29–32). Africans fought with European-imported guns to meet
the demand for slaves, resulting in the unbalancing of tribal relations, with
certain tribes (such as the Asante) increasing in power and others suffering
complete extermination.

As the demand for slaves increased, those involved in the trade within
Africa became more ruthless, and greater numbers of children were sold as
slaves (Walvin 1999, 36). After being herded to costal forts, captured Africans
were held until small ships took them to the large slaving ships that cruised
the coast in search of human "cargo" (p. 32). Although the mixture of lethal
diseases on the West African coast, to which Europeans were particularly susceptible, made it extremely dangerous to linger, traders often put all aboard at
great risk as they waited for months for their holds to slowly fill with slaves

(Walvin 1999, 32). On board the slave ships there unfolded some of the most appalling scenes of the slave trade, with Africans undergoing staggering degrees of physical and mental torture. Slaves were chained together and crammed into small spaces below deck with little air, often resulting in suffocation. The living would remain chained up with the dead, and diseases and ailments wreaked havoc. Walvin states that "it seems likely that 1.5 million Africans died during the Middle Passage and losses of up to thirty per-cent of the cargo were not uncommon" (p. 36, p. 39), while Curtin puts the mortality rate at sea at between 13 and 33 per cent (Curtin cited in Sherlock 1998, 123).

In Jamaica, the estimated population of indigenous Arawak-speaking Taino people at the time of Columbus's arrival in 1492 was between 50,000 and 60,000 (Sherlock 1998, 48). The Tainos were believed to be less skilled in warfare than the Caribs of other Caribbean islands: they are described in colonial accounts as living in democratic and peaceful communities and as having shown less resistance to invaders than their Carib counterparts (Craton 1982, 21; Sherlock 1998, 45). Following Spanish domination, the number of Tainos decreased rapidly as they died quickly from overwork and European diseases. Choosing death over captivity, many families and communities committed mass suicide by drinking poisonous cassava juice or throwing themselves off cliffs (Tanna 2000, 17). Today, numerous Taino artefacts have been found in Jamaica, including stone implements and carvings of Taino deities (called *zemis*), as well as preserved huts, the ruins of Taino villages and Taino burial sites and caves (Sherlock 1998, 44–47).

Although some sources state that the Taino population were completely wiped out in Jamaica (see Campbell 1988, 9), others claim that a number of Tainos survived Spanish settlement and, along with a few African slaves brought over by the Spanish, took advantage of the fighting between the British and Spanish and fled captivity to form autonomous communities in the island's interior. According to Craton, there is evidence to suggest that early runaway African slaves, who became known as "Maroons"[1] by Europeans, were influenced by the existing survival techniques of the Tainos and "most Maroons became effective guerrillas because they blended Amerindian with West African military methods" (Craton 1982, 63).

The British seized Jamaica (originally named by the Tainos as *Xaymaca*, meaning the "land of wood and water") from the Spanish in 1655 and established the Royal Africa Company in 1672. Within fifty years of occupation, the number of black African slaves on the island heavily outnumbered the whites. The disparity between the numbers of blacks and whites continued to grow steadily: in 1673, the population in Jamaica was 17,000 whites and 9,500 black Africans, but by 1740 the black population had risen to 100,000 while there were only 10,000 whites living on the island (Tanna 2000, 21; Walvin 1999, 15). During this period there were four hundred sugar plantations in Jamaica, and plantation conditions were harsh (Walvin 1999, 15; Sherlock 1998, 193). The average plantation slave's lifespan was little more than seven years because, as Horace Campbell explains, "apart from the physical violence, the field slave was exposed to every form of outrage and mortification to break his spirit" (1985, 17). By the end of the eighteenth century, 60 per cent of Jamaica's slaves were involved in sugar production, while others laboured as domestics, traded in the markets, reared livestock, worked as dockhands, sailors and fishermen, transported goods and people between plantations, and cultivated a range of agricultural products (Walvin 2000, 46).

Morales explains how the first enforced migration of slaves to Jamaica in the period of Spanish occupation (from 1498 to 1655) were mainly made up of Africans of Akan-Asante origin (cited in Allyene 1988, 30). Patterson states that during the period 1655–1700, "it can be said with some plausibility that the Gold Coast was the single largest source of the monopoly companies' slaves" (cited in Alleyne 1988, 41). Mervyn Allyene explains that although academics are cautious in drawing concrete conclusions as to the origins of slaves bought to Jamaica, "much evidence suggests that the Gold Coast was the main source of Jamaica-bound Africans in the formative period (1660–1700)" (Alleyne 1988, 41) (see data in the notes to chapter 1). He goes on to explain that "the languages and culture (Akan culture) of this area are highly homogenous – far more so than other slave trading areas. This is a very important key to understanding the cultural history of Jamaica" (p. 41).

Europeans employed the term "Coromantee" (also spelled "Kormantyn", "Cromantin", "Caramantee", "Koromantin" and "Cromanty") as an umbrella term for Africans shipped from the Gold Coast. Koromantyn was also the name of a slave depot and a major embarkation point for Africans from the Akan interior. The majority of Coromantee slaves were of Gold Coast Akan origin and were shipped to Jamaica where they were highly sought-after by British planters

(Allyene 1988, 167; Sherlock 1988, 134). Among the Coromantee were Akan-Asante slaves whose characteristics of defiance, organization and resilience were a result of their position as a dominant African tribe with an efficient socio-economic structure. As the most powerful Akan group, the Asante had a key role in moulding Jamaican slave culture and influencing forms of resistance. In West Africa, the Asante continued to resist the British into the Victorian era; as King explains, they "hit the Victorian British imperialists spectacularly on the head during their prime a number of times in the last century. Only in the early twentieth century did they lay down their arms" (King 1986, 20). (For further discussion see chapter 1.) No other tribe can match the allure of the image of the Akan or Asante warrior's impressive stature, as well as superior strength, prowess and bravery. All of this was imprinted on the colonial and postcolonial Jamaican consciousness. As Craton explains: "Akan-speaking 'Coromantees' were the most feared and admired of the early slave rebels, and in the melting pot of a hundred African ethnicities, aspects of the Akan culture became a focus and symbol of resistance" (1982, 57).

The Asante, along with their Akan counterparts, were often tall, well built and trained in warfare due to frequent combat with neighbouring groups. They were responsible for the organization of numerous raids and revolts both on the West African coast and in the Caribbean plantations. The many colonial accounts of their feats, written by Europeans throughout the plantation period, reveal how Europeans were in awe of their stamina and their bravery. The colonizers also took some degree of interest in their cultural forms. Planter Edward Long, who particularly hated those he referred to as "Koromantyn" slaves, wrote that their "language is copious, and more regular than any other Negro dialects; their music too is livelier, and their dances entirely martial" (cited in Williams 1934, 25). Imperial historian and lieutenant of the West India Regiment Ellis, who spent time in both Jamaica and on the Gold Coast, adds that Koromantyns "were distinguished from all other slaves by their courage, firmness, and impatience of control; characteristics which caused numerous mutinies on board the slavers, and several rebellions in the West Indies. In fact every rebellion of slaves in Jamaica originated with, and was generally confined to, the Koromantyns" (cited in Williams 1934, 26).

Due to their reputation for rebelliousness among British imperialists, a parliamentary bill was proposed in Jamaica which would force planters to pay an additional duty for bringing Coromantee slaves onto their plantations. Yet, despite their "record for intransigence", they continued to be the most expensive slaves to buy until the end of the slave trade, as they were physically adept and, often, skilled craftsmen (Craton 1982, 25). Ellis explains: "The superior physique of the Gold Coast Negroes rendered them very valuable as labourers, and this bill met with such opposition that it was withdrawn; and, notwithstanding their dangerous character, large numbers continued to be introduced to the island" (cited in Williams 1934, 26).

It is clear that, as a dominant Akan tribe, the Asante influenced Jamaican slave culture to a greater degree than their Akan counterparts. Key elements of Jamaican slave culture that can be traced directly to the Asante are evident in the presence of Asante Twi words in the language of the Jamaican slaves and Jamaican Creole[2] and the continued use of Asante day-names, such as "Kwaku" or "Quaco" (Wednesday-born), "Kofi" or "Cuffie" (Friday-born), and "Kwasi" or "Quashie" (Sunday-born) for slave children, as well as the continued telling of the Anansi tales. Joseph Williams explains that while the popularity of African day-names was not confined to the descendants of the Asante alone, "it is the Ashanti terminology that is uniformly followed in the day-names, indicating how complete the ascendancy of the Ashanti became over the entire slave population" (1979, 28). While Williams's suggestion of "complete" Asante cultural ascendancy is highly questionable, it is clear that the Asante and their customs played a central role in development of Jamaican slave culture.

As Craton describes, there was a strict hierarchy of power on Jamaican plantations. At the very top of this hierarchy was the plantation owner, who was often absent during the early stages of slavery but was forced to make more of an appearance during the turmoil of later years. Absentee owners, members of the plantocracy, were often expected to bring presents for their slaves and listen to their complaints when visiting their plantations. Known as "Massa", the owner often became a larger-than-life figure for many slaves and was sometimes offered a degree of respect, as he had power to change their conditions. He may have been perceived as occupying a similar social role to that of an African king, with his fine possessions and great house looming over the plantation fields (Craton 1982, 36).

Next in the hierarchy was the estate attorney, who was in charge of managing the plantation and organizing the plantation accounts, and then the overseer, a man often from a working-class British background who kept guard while slaves were working. Then came the slave driver, whose position was frequently occupied by a black slave selected for the post by the planter or owner. The task of the slave driver was to force the slaves to work through the use of the whip and threats. Domestic slaves working in the great house were next in the hierarchy: they frequently acted as spies, watching and listening to the whites' dinner conversation and reporting new information to the plantation slaves (see chapter 3). It was customary for the white men to practise covert and casual sex with their female domestics, who could be returned to the fields if the situation became problematic (Craton 1982, 36–45).

Below the domestic slaves in the plantation hierarchy were skilled slave craftsmen. In the early days of slavery in Jamaica those who worked as craftsmen had learned their skills in Africa. Skilled slaves were often shown some respect by both blacks and whites; they were extremely useful in the slave quarters and contributed towards keeping traditional African forms of craftsmanship alive by making masks, drums and traditional furniture. They could be paid for their work by whites, and in the later days of slavery, craftsmen and skilled slaves were able to buy their freedom using savings (Craton 1982, 45). Similar to these slaves, obeahmen and -women – slaves with knowledge of natural medicines and African beliefs – also had a degree of status in the worlds of both white and black, based on both fear and respect. However, theirs was a dangerous and secretive practice. Craton explains: "Though some whites ascribed real powers to the Afro-Caribbean Obeahman – even consulted them through their domestics – the practice of traditional medicine and religion was highly illicit, being held, with justice, to relate to slave resistance, including the arts of poisoning" (p. 46).

At the very bottom of the plantation hierarchy were field slaves. Field slaves lived in separate quarters and were encouraged to grow crops and become self-sufficient. This set-up saved whites the money usually spent on food. Paradoxically, however, it was in many ways the degree of autonomy achieved in having a provision ground that fuelled slave desire for greater freedoms and a free peasant lifestyle.

One could interpret the role of each member of the plantation hierarchy as playing a part in a carefully constructed performance of servility and superiority. It was not easy for the plantation elite to "let their hair down", so to speak, as their high status required them to live up to the expectations of both their peers and inferiors. Owners' visits to their plantations were distinguished by great pomp, ceremony and "conspicuous consumption: fine furniture, hangings and table wear, large retinue of servants, sometimes livery" (Craton 1982, 36). Even in the domestic sphere, the performance had to be maintained, particularly in the company of black domestics with watchful eyes (p. 37).

As dominant groups often have much to conceal, they like to seclude themselves. This proved difficult on the Jamaican plantations. Lower-class whites had to physically work the land and live in close proximity to slaves and other blacks. By all accounts, theirs was an "alienated existence" in which continual compromises in their treatment of slaves "were made necessary by day-to-day relationships" (Craton 1982, 38). Furthermore, house slaves were party to the private spheres of these lives and were able to observe them closely. Although the elite were continually expected to perform public roles, house slaves would catch glimpses of these whites unmasked. Slaves could read clues that might suggest what lay behind daily performances of superiority, and pass the information regarding the falsity of white performances to other slaves. As Richard Burton explains: "Massa not only saw and knew much less than he thought but was constantly seen and known, often to the depth of his being, by slaves to whom in his blindness he often denied the very capacity to see. The 'visual politics' of the plantation were in reality the very opposite of what they appeared on the surface" (1997, 50).

White working-class plantation workers further undermined the authority of the ruling group due to their close contact with slaves and absorption of elements of slaves' language and culture, as evidenced in Thomas Thistlewood's diaries (see Burnard 2004). However, cross-cultural fertilization did not only affect the working classes, but also the higher strata of white society, as elements of slave and creolized white culture became inextricably entwined. Lady Nugent, the wife of Governor General George Nugent, kept diaries during her time in Jamaica from 1801 to 1807. She was a terrible snob, and she records her shock at the creolization of the English spoken by white Jamaican "ladies":

> The Creole language is not confined to the Negroes. Many of the ladies, who
> have not been educated in England, speak a sort of broken English, with an

indolent drawing of their words, that is very tiresome if not disgusting. I stood next to a lady one night, near a window, and by way of saying something remarked that the air was much cooler than usual; to which she answered, "Yes, ma'am, him rail-ly too fra-ish." (cited in Burton 1997, 35)

This is what James Scott terms "overexposure"; for the dominant group, familiarity can "diminish the impression their ritually managed appearances can create" (1990, 13). Trevor Burnard explains that in Jamaica "the relationship between whites and blacks was fraught but involved a significant degree of close interaction" (2004, 5). In his analysis of Thistlewood's journals, he illustrates how closely some whites worked with the slaves: "during his first year in Jamaica, Thistlewood lived in a primarily black world. Between November 1750 and February 1751, he saw white people no more than three or four times" (ibid.).

Anansi's Metamorphosis

It was in this kind of colonial society in Jamaica that the role of Anansi was transformed. Certainly, in Jamaica, as in Ghana, Anansi commits acts that would often be considered taboo. In Rattray's collection we see examples of Anansi's antisocial behaviour when he tricks Aso into sleeping with him while her husband, Akwasi-the-Jealous-One, is in the same house. Akwasi-the-Jealous-One is infertile, so Anansi goes to the couple's home, telling them that his name is not Anansi but "Rise-Up-and-Make-Love-to-Aso". He is offered a spare room in the house, but insists on sleeping outside the couple's door: "I am Soul-washer to the Sky-God, and I sleep in an open veranda room, since my Mother bore me and my father begat me, I have never slept in a closed bedroom" (Rattray 1930, 133–37). Anansi poisons Akwasi, and when the poison takes effect, he wakes in the night and calls out to Anansi to open the door: "Rise-Up-and-Make-Love-to-Aso, open (the door) for me." The virile Anansi does exactly as he is bid, he opens the door, lets Akwasi out, and makes love to Aso. Akwasi-the-Jealous-One is eventually rejected, and Aso becomes Anansi's wife (pp. 133–37).

Although here Anansi breaks a fundamental societal rule by stealing another man's wife, on closer inspection the tale simultaneously upholds the social structure by acting as a warning against jealousy. It also shows the dangers of stupidity (Akwasi-the-Jealous-One's flaws), and celebrates virility, fertility, intelligence and creative thinking, as well as wit and humour. As mentioned in chapter 1, among the Asante, infertility was a great taboo: the story illustrates the necessity of procreation and the sacrifice that the individual (in this case Akwasi-the-Jealous-One) should be expected to make for the survival of the tribe. Furthermore, in the story, the order comes directly from the Nyame, who encourages another man to take Aso: "Akawasi-the-Jealous-One has been married to Aso for a very very long time; she has not conceived by him and borne a child, therefore he who is able, let him go and take Aso, and should she conceive by him, let him take her (as his wife)" (Rattray 1930, 133).

As discussed in the previous chapter, in the recorded Asante Anansi tales, where there is a testing of limits there are also always signs of the enforcement of community rules. But this is not always the case in Jamaican stories: in his plantation setting, Anansi could invert the social order without paradoxically upholding it. As we shall see, on the Jamaican plantations, Anansi had the potential to function as a character who could destroy an enforced and abhorrent social system rather than just test the boundaries of a West African society with compliant members. The terror, irrationality and amorality of the plantation environment, combined with the constant threat of violence, are reflected in Anansi's anarchic and brutal world, in which characters are perpetually in conflict with one another. The tales depict the people of the plantation, both black and white, in realistic and unsentimental terms: "their selfishness, their propensity to do anything and betray anyone for self-preservation, their drive for status and power, their basic insecurity, were all pictured in grim detail" (Levine 1977, 120). Levine adds, however, that "the trickster's art as depicted in these tales was saved for the benefit of the whites and was seldom practised upon members of his own group" (p. 131). As former slave Lewis Clarke reported in his *Narrative of the Sufferings of Lewis Clarke* (1845): "[slaves] think it is wrong to take from a neighbour but not from their master". He explains that "a slave that will steal from a slave, is called *meaner than master*. This is the lowest comparison slaves know how to use" (cited in Levine 1977, 125).

While they continued to represent West African modes of thought, resisting simplistic definitions of good and evil, Jamaican Anansi tales resonated with the ambiguity and contradictions that lay at the heart of the plantation environment. The Jamaican Anansi's actions became even more violent and remorseless than those of the Asante Anansi, and many elements of plantation life entered into the tales, such as Massa, the whip and the cane fields. However, before we analyse the changes in Anansi's function on Jamaican soil, let us examine the process of creolization the tales underwent as they absorbed elements of the Jamaican slaves' new landscapes and experiences.

In Jamaica, African characters in the tales began to be replaced with Jamaican mammals, reptiles and insects. These characters, represented as black, pit their wits against powerful, white, human figures, such as Massa, Buckra,[3] King, Preacher and even Death. We see Anansi fully adapted to his Jamaican environment: escaping the whip, tricking Buckra, stealing Massa's sheep or daughters, ambushing armies, killing the preacher, playing drums and working on his provision ground. In post-emancipation tales, Anansi is described eating callaloo (a type of spinach popular in Caribbean cooking), drinking in the rum-shop, avoiding hurricanes and duppies (ghosts or spirits), and going to church.[4] African food and drinks described in the Asante tales, such as palm-wine and palm-nuts, are replaced with Jamaican ones. For example, in the Anansi tale "Tomby" has "Miss Princess" going to market for ingredients to make a truly Jamaican feast: "little salt fish an' me little hafoo yam, t'reepence a red peas fe make me soup, quatty 'kellion, gill a garlic to put with me little nick-snack, quatty ripe banana, bit fe Gungo peas, an' me see if me can get quatty beef bone" (Jekyll 1966, 17).[5]

In Bennett's "Anansi and Sorrel" we see an example of how Anansi was employed to explain elements of Jamaican life. In this tale, Anansi is credited for the creation of a classic Jamaican drink; Anansi inadvertently and innovatively adapts the old (a hibiscus drink made in Africa) and creates something new: a traditional Caribbean Christmas drink now known as sorrel. In the story, because he has nothing to take to the Christmas Eve Morning Grand-Market, Anansi "[breaks] a long stalk of long red plant". "It pretty fi look pon", Anansi says, "I wonder wat it good for?" Anansi ends up flinging the bundle of red plants into a market seller's porridge pot, which is full of boiling water. The water turns red and Anansi, master of bluff, pretends he knows exactly what is going on. He exclaims:

> It don't finish brew yet,
> It want some sugar,
> A little piece of ginger,

A little cinnamon,
And you stir so,
And then you stir so
> (Bennett 1979, 64)

The mixture starts to smell good, and Anansi whispers to himself "how you so real, so-real, so-real?" The transfixed crowd cry "it name so-real"; Anansi brews and sells "so-real" all day: "By the end of the day, in true Jamaica fashion, so-real had become sorrel. And from that day to today, sorrel is a famous Christmas drink. Is Anancy meck it. Jack Mandora, me noh choose none!"[6] (pp. 62–64)

Representations of Anansi's family also changed on Jamaican soil. Rattray and Asante author Kyei's account of Asante Anansi's family are both very detailed. Kyei describes them as "Aso Adwoa, the beloved middle-aged wife, comforter and confidante. Ntikuma, the eldest son and 'chip off the old block'. Afu-Dotwe-Dotwe, the second son and the blue-eyed boy of the family. Nywi-Nkronhywea, the third son and problem child. Ti-Konon-konon, *kaa-kyrie*, the last born, and precocious child of Aso Adwoa" (2001, 4).

In contrast, the Jamaican Anansi tales provide us with little information regarding Anansi's family, and Anansi's son "Tacoma", also spelt "Tacuma" and "Tacomma" (derived from the Twi "Ntikuma") and his wife, referred to as "Crookie" rather than Aso, her Asante name, are the only named family members. With the exception of Anansi's wife, Tacoma is the only member of the family to share some of the limelight and often proves himself to be more rational and perceptive than his father. Anansi's other children play a secondary role, often depicted as either neglected or starved.

Jean Purchas-Tulloch states that, in Jamaica, Anansi's wife Crookie's name is derived from "Cookie"[7] meaning "the cook", which in many ways is very apt (1976, 237–38). Crookie is always preparing food and is depicted as simple, docile and submissive. Generally, female characters in the Jamaican tales fare little better than those portrayed in the Asante stories, and are either cast in the role of poor (black) housewives or depicted as the rich (white) daughters of powerful men such as the King, Massa or Buckra – status symbols to be fought over and trophies who, when won or claimed, have the potential to raise the social standing of poorer male characters (Levine 1977, 110).

In some ways Crookie is illustrative of the traditional role of the Jamaican wife and mother, with Anansi playing the part of the wayward and selfish husband. Crookie attends to the domestic sphere and tolerates Anansi's gallivanting with other women, cruelty and refusal to work, while also tending to his needs and those of the family with few complaints. Her husband is completely egotistical: he cares little about his family, will see his children starve while he gets fat and is happy to sacrifice his wife if times are tough – in the Jamaican tale "In the House Top" Anansi pushes "Mrs Anansi" down into Tiger's hungry jaws – "Anansi shove her down gi' Tiger an' Tiger swallow Mrs Anansi" (Beckwith 1924, 11; Purchas-Tulloch 1976, 238). Despite his cruelty, Anansi embodies many of the stereotypically desirable traits of Jamaican masculinity: he is strong, intelligent, a good speaker and well-endowed, with a rampant sex drive. He also is a brave survivor who can rise to any challenge.

However, in Jamaica, Anansi's powers are limited, as he is not always successful in his plans, yet just as the tales in which he wins show the benefits of cunning and intelligence, the tales in which he loses can act as a warning against stupidity and greed. Furthermore, he never gives up: Anansi is tireless in his trickery, has boundless mischievous energy and never learns from the flaws of his previous plans (Tanna 2000, 81). Anansi tales exist as separate narratives and follow no particular order, so each tale introduces the audience to a new situation. As a result, Anansi does not reflect on his previous actions but acts according to his desires in each new circumstance.

Another change in the Jamaican Anansi tales was the introduction of new mammals, insects and reptiles. Beckwith states the following: "Tiger and Monkey, with Assono (a huge unknown) are the only actors in the story not local to the island. Parrot, Black-bird (as Cling-Cling), Ground Dove, and some domestic fowls appear; of insects, Duck-ant, 'But-but' (butterfly), Tumble-bug; of reptiles, Snake, Lizard, Turtle and Old Conch the Snail; Cat, Dog and Rat have a group of stories to themselves, and Cock and Cockroach appear as protagonists" (1969, 220).

Creatures of the water, such as shark, turtle, alligator and fish, are Anansi's dim-witted victims in Jamaica, whereas the creatures of the air – bird, dove, peenywally or candlefly (a firefly), peafowl, guinea-hen, rat-bat, pigeon or chicken-hawk – are more intelligent, often avoiding falling victim to Anansi's tricks and capable of tricking him in return. Characters who live on the ground such as rat, bug, donkey, puss, pig, cow, lizard and goat are easily tricked, yet on occasion they too avoid Anansi's mischief. Interestingly, while the animals in Jamaican tales are often different to the ones featured in Asante stories, the reason for the disparity between their susceptibility to Anansi's trickery seems to be directly related to the system of Asante animal classification. The Asante classified their animals into four main categories. These were as follows:

1. Asorommoa. Animals primarily living above ground
2. Ntetemmoa. Animals primarily living on the ground
3. Nsuommoa. Animals primarily (or partially) living in water
4. Ntummoa. Animals that flew in the air

(McCaskie 1992, 221)

McCaskie states that the Asante projected a "tangled web of resemblances onto animals, often of a predictably anthropomorphic kind" (p. 221). Many animals were symbolic to the Asante because of their physical characteristics; for example, the porcupine was representative of martial virtues because of its large spines. This would explain why creatures of the water, such as turtle, alligator, shark and fish, were considered "dim-witted" in the Jamaican Anansi tales, as they are animals both frequently and easily caught and eaten by humans. Fishing was a major source of food for the Asante as it was in Jamaica, and if these water creatures had been more intelligent, they would have evaded their fates.

However, the Asante understanding and classification of animals was more complex than simply anthropomorphic. As explained in chapter 1, the Asante were a people obsessed with the division between culture and nature. Many animals of the bush, who lived outside culture, were therefore feared. As McCaskie explains, "Ontological speculation concerning animals is to be understood in relation to the parameters of this spatial and cognitive spectrum. Thus the Asante made an absolutely basic generic distinction between *fiemmoa* ('house animals', i.e. animals defined as domestic by virtue of proximity to culture) and *wurammoa* ('bush animals', i.e. animals defined as 'wild' by virtue of proximity to nature)" (1992, 228).

The Asante tried to understand animals as "beings" rather than just classify them according to their zoological features, which was the primary concern of European researchers. McCaskie states that "animal life was one body of evidence or data in the world that encouraged the Asante to intensive speculation about the nature of being" (1992, 222). While the Asante were terrified by "beings" which fell outside the parameters of culture, they were also fascinated by them; hence their preoccupation with Anansi, who existed in both worlds. As they were drawn to the unknowable, to things they could not define, they were especially concerned with animals who escaped classification. Animals which had a problematic phenomenological status and transcended the four main animal categories were believed to be very powerful and have a great deal of what the Asante termed *sasa* or *sasammoa*, which can be interpreted as meaning "dangerous spirit" (p. 231). McCaskie explains: "In some animals *sasa* was weak or pliant. But in others it situated itself . . . as the very embodiment of alien unknowing and hazardous power" (ibid.).

Animals were considered to be particularly "dangerous" to the Asante in terms of their levels of *sasa*, which was in turn based on how difficult they were to classify: "as types of being in the ontological dimension such animals combined high levels of interpretative possibility with perilous threat" (McCaskie 1992, 231). For example, the *Akyekyeretwo*, or "water chevrotain", a small hoofed mammal with similar characteristics to the deer but also semi-aquatic. It also had protruding canines instead of horns and, rather than enjoying a vegetarian diet, it fed on fish, crabs, insects and dead animals. This creature fell outside the Asante classification system and for this reason had high levels of *sasa*. Shooting it was therefore a taboo (p. 224).

Humans did not contain *sasa* but *okra*, which was the "spark of supreme being" and nothing outside culture could possess okra (McCaskie 1992, 230). Hunters, who spent their time hunting in the bush, were traditionally treated with great suspicion and needed special funeral rites to help with the disposal of dead *sasa* they obtained in the bush. Indeed, it was commonly believed that "Asante hunters were flirting with insanity" (p. 237). However, because of their knowledge of the bush, the Asante were also seen as those who harboured extraordinary knowledge, such as understanding the reasons why birds fly (ibid.).

The flight of birds was a mystery and a preoccupation to the Asante. Birds elicited a level of fear, as they mainly belonged in the realm of the bush and clearly had special powers. The Asante attitude towards birds and flight can be linked to the role of birds in the Jamaican Anansi tales, where they are depicted as so intelligent that they avoid falling victim to Anansi's tricks and can trick him in return. Similar to Anansi, scavengers like the vulture were considered liminal creatures who existed in-between two realms as they entered into the village to scavenge but belonged in the wild. Animals that lived in the human realm or were domesticated did not pose a threat. This is perhaps why in Jamaica the domestic animals ("*fiemmoa* – 'house animals'; animals defined as domestic by virtue of proximity to culture"), such as rat, puss, cow, and goat are easily tricked by Anansi (McCaskie 1992, 228). As well as belonging to the domestic world, these animals are also easily definable and easily caught and there was no taboo linked to hunting or killing them.

On the opposite end of the scale were the *wurammoa* or "bush animals"; animals defined as "wild" by virtue of proximity to nature, and the ultimate *wurammoa* was the leopard. Wild, solitary hunters, they not only existed outside culture, but because of their sporadic intrusion into the human world, their behaviour was "clearly anomalous (literally 'out of place')" (McCaskie 1992, 228). They were therefore beyond classification. McCaskie explains that, for the Asante, to take a leopard alive from nature "signalled a noteworthy triumph for culture" (1992, 228). While the Asante "cast leopard as a type of being that was alien to the project of culture", much Asante art depicts leopards, once again demonstrating the Asante preoccupation with the entities they deemed as unknowable (p. 229).

Tiger (which appears to have been used as another name for "Leopard" among colonials),[8] replaces Nyame in Jamaica as one of the powerful forces against whom Anansi most frequently pits his wits. As Tanna explains, "in Jamaica [Anansi's] . . . divine association with the sky-god had been forgotten" (2000, 77). Nyame does not appear in any Jamaican Anansi tales and in Jamaican versions of "How It Came About That the Sky-God's Stories Came to Be Known as 'Spider-Stories' ", it is Tiger, not Nyame, who is the original owner of the world's stories (Rattray 1930, 52; Sherlock 1956, 3). The replacement of Nyame with Tiger exemplifies the slaves' diminishing access to traditional West African religious doctrine. Tiger is normally depicted as a strong but slow-witted bully, unlike the clever and challenging Nyame. Nyame exerts more power over Anansi than Tiger, and punishes him more frequently. Anansi does not show Tiger the respect he shows Nyame: he rarely listens to him, bargains with him or carries out tasks for him in exchange for rewards.[9]

It is clear that Jamaican Anansi came down to earth and shifted from being assimilated into the sacred world of the Asante to become representative of the Jamaican slaves' human condition. However, Anansi's links with the divine did not die completely. Isabel MacLean, a white Christian who was in Jamaica when she wrote her 1910 account of "Black Superstitions", demonstrates, albeit scathingly, the centrality of Anansi in the lives of Jamaicans and the persistence of Asante stories in which Anansi influences both the spiritual and secular world. Regarding the "dreadful beliefs" of "Jamaican Negroes", she writes: "Most of their beliefs were very depressing and very degrading. It could not, for instance, help the children to grow into good men and women when they were told that the creator of man was a spider!" (p. 31).

One of the most popular and humourous Anansi tales featuring Tiger is a tale told throughout the Caribbean entitled "Me Father's Old Riding Horse". In this story, Anansi boasts to two pretty young ladies (or to some animals, depending on the version) that Tiger is his father's riding horse. The ladies ask Anansi, "Mr Anansi, you see Mr Tiger?" and he replies "O yes! I see Mr Tiger, but I tell you, missus, Tiger is me fader ol' ridin'-horse" (Beckwith 1924, 6).[10] Tiger is angered and asks Anansi to deny his claim to the ladies, but Anansi pretends to be ill. He tells Tiger that he will do as Tiger bids if Tiger lets him ride to meet the ladies on his back, as Anansi is too sick to move. Anansi then demands a saddle, a whip and spurs (or shoes, again depending on the version – see Tanna 2000, 63–64), so that he can stay on his back and tell him when to go fast or slow – "Anansi go tak out him saddle, Tiger say, 'What you gwine do wid saddle?' Anansi say, 'to put me foot down in de stirrup so when I gwine fall down, I weak, I can catch up' " (Beckwith 1924, 6). On arrival, Anansi, who has been pretending to be frail and sick, with his voice thin and feeble, gallops into the yard, on Tiger's back, in front of the ladies while shouting triumphantly, "Carry him in to stable, sah! I mak you to know what Anansi say true to de fac', is me fader ol' ridin'-horse" (p. 6).

In the above tale we see Anansi take control of an animal considered by humans as one of the most untameable and dangerous. Purchas-Tulloch identifies parallels to the tale in Martinique, Barbados, Guadeloupe, Suriname, Trinidad, the Virgin Islands, United States and West Africa (1976, 277–80).

Post-emancipation Anansi tales replace the figure of Tiger with Lion. Even though, for Jamaican Rastafarians, the Lion of Judah is an emblem of former Ethiopian emperor Haile Selassie, whose birth name was Ras Tafari ("King Tafari" in Amharic), Jamaican storyteller Jean Small believes that Tiger is replaced with Lion because this creature is seen as king of the jungle from a European perspective. She believes this is highly symbolic of cultural colonization and makes an interesting analogy, comparing Jamaica to Anansi and Europe to the Lion:

> These animal stories take place in the forest, and as you know the king of the forest originally was Tiger, not Lion. I think it is very symbolic that now *Lion* is considered the King of the forest. Lion is symbolic of the European colonizers. He is BIG, he *strong*, he has a golden mane. Anansi on the other hand is small, black and weak, physically weak; and *we* are economically weak in contrast with lion. (Small, interview with author, 2005)

If there is one animal in particular that perfectly illustrates the process of metamorphosis and adaptation the Anansi tales underwent in Jamaica as they became creolized and assimilated into the daily lives of the slaves, it is Assono. Beckwith, along with many other Anansi collectors in Jamaica, describes the character of Assono as "a huge unknown" (1969, 219). Most descriptions of Assono in collections of Jamaican Anansi tales describe only the creature's great size and mysterious, unidentifiable characteristics. Despite being "unknown" to many Jamaican storytellers, Assono is the elephant of West African Anansi tales recorded by Rattray and others; in Rattray's collection, Anansi tricks "Esono" and proceeds to steal slices of his bottom to eat, which parallels the Jamaican Anansi story "Annancy and Brother Tiger" (Rattray 1930, 183–87; Jekyll 1966, 7–9). Esono is persuaded by Anansi to have slices of his behind cut off in order to help him get through the undergrowth more quickly. Esono then regrets his foolishness, and sends his children to retrieve the meat, but Anansi distracts them through playing the drums and making them dance, a trick that also works on Esono when he makes a final visit to Anansi. So entrancing is Anansi's music and dance that Esono insists on purchasing the dance in exchange for his bottom. The story ends as follows: "That is why Elephant's bottom is very small; it is because of the dance which he purchased; Long ago it was not like that. This, is my story, which I have related, if it be sweet, (or) if it not be sweet, take some elsewhere and let some come back to me" (Rattray 1930, 187).

In the Jamaican version of the above tale, Tiger replaces Elephant. Anansi persuades Tiger to take off his fat to go for a swim, as it will improve his swimming, Anansi swiftly eats it, and blames the theft and gluttony on Monkey (Rattray 1930, 183; Jekyll 1966, 7). In Jamaica, Assonu became a mysterious character whose only remaining elephant feature was his great size. In the tale "Asoonah", collected by Beckwith and told by Philip Brown from Mandeville in the 1920s, the story starts with the following: "Asoonah is a big skin t'ing. When it come in you' yard it will sink de whole place" (1924, 87). In the tale, nobody can tell what "Asoonah" is, and the King offers a reward to anyone who can find out: "An' de king hear about dis Asoonah, but he couldn't tell what it is. De king say anybody can come in dere and tell what is dis, he give t'ree hundred pound." Finally a little boy finds out the creature's name and is rewarded (pp. 87–88). Here we see the metamorphosis of the Asante elephant; as there are no elephants in Jamaica, Esono loses his shape but continues to be imagined as a large, mysterious and powerful being – a "big skin t'ing".

The tale "Anancy and Assonu" that was "set down" by a teller identified as "A.S.R." in the *Jamaica Historical Society Bulletin* starts "T'ousan year ago, in de 'Shanti country'" and goes on to describe an elephant who shares characteristics with monsters of many European fairy tales, whose enormous appetite must be satisfied with "one young gal ebery morning fe brekfass" (1957, 14). Anansi sets out to kill the elephant, who will die if rain touches him, exclaiming "cunnin' betta an 'trong" ("cunning is better than strong") – a phrase which epitomizes the central theme of the Jamaican Anansi tales. Anansi gets the elephant wet, chops off his head and is rewarded with the king's daughter's hand in marriage (pp. 14–16). This is one of the few Jamaican Anansi tales in which a link is made between Assonu and the Asante Elephant. The author of "Anancy and Assonu" explains the following: "the writer set down this tale fully fifty years ago from the lips of an old man whose father had been a slave born in Africa. It should be remembered that Assonu is the elephant" (p. 14).

The interpretation of the character of Assonu in Jamaica as the "huge unknown", and the entry of so many aspects of Jamaican culture, nature and landscape into the tales are examples of the malleability of transported and transplanted oral cultures. It illustrates the creativity of the imagination of storytellers and audiences in their ability to adapt their oral traditions in a hostile new environment. It demonstrates how, when elements of their African traditions were lost or forgotten, storytellers filled in the gaps with inventive interpretations.

Numerous Jamaican Anansi tales centre on language and naming. African descendents in Jamaica, deprived of their mother tongue and forced into the adoption of a new language, were compelled to tell tales which meditated on the power of words. Through the process of creatively adapting the language of the colonizers and naming elements of a new landscape, Jamaicans living in the plantation and post-plantation world were able to take greater control of their environment and existence, and certain themes in the Anansi tales illustrate this process. In Jamaica today it is not uncommon to have a nick-name or street name, while "real" names are kept private until an acquaintance becomes a friend. Perhaps a strategy rooted in the pain of ancestors who were forced to adopt new names and a new language, many Jamaicans still keep their "real" names – names full of the power of their core identities – concealed.

A Jamaican Anansi tale which centres on the power of naming is found in Beckwith's recounting of "Cunnie-More-Than-Father" in which Anansi, on his way to his provision ground, finds a new type of fast-growing yam for which only he knows the name: "One time he work a groun' very far away into the bush, an' in going to that bush he pass a very broad flat rock. So one day a man give him a yam-plant; that yam name 'yam foofoo'" (1924, 18). When Anansi brings yams from the plant home, he tells his family, "who know name, nyam [meaning to eat]; who no know name, no nyam" and, not knowing the name, they eat nothing. His clever son Tacoma, here named "Cunnie-More-Than-Father", is desperate to find out the yam's name and eventually succeeds by making the rock near the yam plant slippery with okra – while picking a yam Anansi slips and exclaims "Lawd! all me yam foofoo mash up!" Cunnie-More-Than-Father runs home and tells the name of the yam to his whole family; "after that, whole of them say, 'Yam foofoo! Yam foofoo!' Anansi get vex, say, 'Huh! eat! nobody fin' it out but Cunnie-mo'n-father!'" (p. 29).

The name "foofoo" or "fu fu" is from the Twi *e-fufu*, literally meaning "a white thing" (Cassidy and Le Page 2002, 191). It is only through finding out the African Twi name for the yam that the family can eat; here Twi becomes a language imbued with magical powers and a gateway to a knowledge facilitating survival. Beckwith's tale "New Names" also focuses on renaming. Four friends are given new names, an act which corresponds to the renaming of African slaves by their masters: "Anansi's new name is Che-che-bun-da, Parrot new name was Green-corn-ero, Tiger name was Yellow-prissenda, Tacoomah name was Tacoomah-vengeance – the four new name" (Beckwith 1924, 18). If their mothers fail to use their new names, the mothers will be eaten. Anansi tells his mother his new name and thus she avoids this fate (pp. 18–19).

Beckwith's "Asoonah" tale is another example of the power attributed to names in the Anansi tales, in which the characters try to establish the mysterious Asoonah's name (Beckwith 1924, 87–88). Further evidence of the power of naming can be found in "Mussirolinkina", retold by Bennett, the mother of a "nice gal pickney" makes up a long name for her daughter to protect her; "an any man want her fi married to hooda haffi guess de name fuss [first]". Anansi swears that he must have "dis boonoonoonoos gal"[11] for his wife and hides by the riverside where the woman is washing her daughter's clothes. He proceeds to dirty them by crawling on them, and the mother exclaims "but is who dah nasty up me pickney *Mussirolinkina* clothes doah?" and gives the secret name away[12] (Bennett 1979, 56–57). In "Hidden Names", told to Beckwith by Eliza Barrett from Cockpit Country, there are "t'ree sister living to a house. Nobody was to know their names. An' Anansi want to hear them an' he couldn't get them" (1924, 120). Another example of naming can be found in "Anansi and Mr Able", told by Thomas White from Maroon town: "Able is a man couldn't bear to hear no one call him name; for jus' as he hear him name call, him get disturb all to kill himself" (Beckwith 1924, 120–21). Anansi eventually gets Able, who is housebound, to come outside through singing.

Singing, as well as naming, also plays a central part in the Jamaican Anansi tales, illustrating the centrality of music and song in the lives of African descendants, as well as further demonstrating Anansi's ability to manipulate language and harness its power. Anansi is able to kill, court, hypnotize and lure through playing his fiddle and singing his songs. Plantation owner and Gothic author Matthew "Monk" Lewis records in his 1816 journal: "the Negros are . . . very fond of what they call Nancy stories, part of which is related, part sung" (1999, 253). It is often through song that Anansi succeeds in his trick and lures his victims, illustrating the focus in Jamaican culture on music and melody. As Anansi sings his beautiful song, Brar Able says, "well, from since I born I never know man speak my name in such way!" and Brar Able is so moved he "[can't] stay in de house" (Beckwith 1924, 121).

During her research into Maroon music with "possible Coromantee origins", Helen Roberts argues that, in Jamaica, music "seems to bubble from the very ground itself" and it is often through the music and songs accompanying the Jamaican Anansi tales that the stories are remembered (1926, 334). Tanna explains: "the language has been retained more in song. There is something about song and rhythm – that's why the old cliché about the old-time stories that have a song – people can remember them with music; it's an amazing thing" (interview with author, 2005). Another example of Anansi using music to lure his victims can be found in "Annancy in Crab Country" (Jekyll 1966) in which Anansi pretends to be a preacher and plans to "baptize" a crab, or, in other words, kill him and eat him by dunking him in boiling water, which is a popular way to prepare crabs for eating. Crab agrees to be baptized after Anansi promises the following:

> He will have bands of music playing . . . the music will be so sweet they won't be tired walking. Anansi tell Ratta to roll the drum, an Blackbird is to rub the fiddle 'tring till it catch fire, an' Toad is to blow the flute hard as he can, an' he will be reading the tune. An he start like this:
> *The bands a roll, the bands a roll, the bands a roll,*
> *a go to Mount Si-ney. Sa-lem us Zakki-low, some a we da go to Mount Si-ney.*
> (Jekyll 1966, 71–72)

In West Africa, as in Jamaica, the success of Anansi's trick is often dependent on his music and songs, and although key West African collections by Barker and Sinclair (1917) and Rattray (1930) do not incorporate songs, we see the use of drums and dancing in the facilitation of the trick: in Rattray's version of the elephant story, Anansi tricks and entrances the Elephant Esono through playing the drums and dancing (1930, 183–87). Beckwith's (1924), Jekyll's (originally published in 1904) and Tanna's (originally published in 1984) collections,[13] to name a few, are full of tales in which Anansi facilitates his tricks using his musical talents, and all three of these contain recordings of

Figure 6. Illustration by Marcia Brown, "Anansi and the Crabs". (From *Anansi the Spider Man: Jamaican Folk Tales* by P.M. Sherlock © 1956 Macmillan Publishers Limited 2011. Used by permission.)

the musical scores that accompany the songs. While in Rattray's collection
Anansi lures Esono and her children through playing the African drum, in
Jamaican versions Anansi's instrument of choice is the fiddle (Rattray 1930,
131). In "Dancing to Anansi's Fiddle" Anansi tricks Assono, who is depicted
in this tale as Massa, through his fiddling and dancing:

> Assono a run a gang. Assono sen' one of de men for water. When he go a take
> water, him couldn't take it; Anansi play fiddle into de water-hole, "Zing a little
> ting!"
>
> T'row down de gourd an' begin to dance. Assono a come to look fe de man.
> When he come (Anansi stop playing). He call to him say, "Massa, no quarrel!"
> Him come give de massa de gourd a go fill it. Anansi begin playing, De Massa
> t'row down de gourd, begin dance. Assono dance till him drop. Anansi cut off
> him head an' tek de head make a water-cup. (Beckwith 1924, 163)

By comparing Beckwith's elephant tale to Rattray's we can see the types
of adaptations and inflections the Anansi tales underwent as they incorporate
aspects of a new Jamaican social, cultural and economic environment. The
instruments shift from African drum to a fiddle;[14] the elephant is interpreted
as another type of powerful being, Massa; and what were once Elephant's
children become Massa's servants or slaves – his "gang" of working men. Furthermore, the Jamaican tale amalgamates two Asante stories, and instead of
ending in an exchange between Massa or Elephant and Anansi, in a deeply
defiant act, Anansi chops off Massa's head and uses it as a water cup. Similar
violent acts of defiance perpetrated by Anansi form the central theme of the
Jamaican Anansi tales, reflecting the brutality, inequality and unpredictability
of the plantation environment.

Jamaican Anansi's most distinctive physical characteristics are his limp (he
often walks with the aid of a stick), his lisp and his high falsetto voice. His
shape is that of both a spider and a man. While some European collectors
have been keen to gain a fixed definition of Anansi's form, many of their
attempts have been unfruitful. Ada Trowbridge writes: "curiosity would make
me push the point with my Negro narrator and inquire: 'But was it Anansi
the *man* or Anansi the *spider*?' She would give me this reasonable and convincing reply; 'Chuh, chil'! yo' too poppesha [foolish]![15] It was Nancy, jus'
Nancy, yo' see'" (1896, 282).

Sherlock describes Jamaican Anansi as part man and part spider: "when things went well he was a man, but when he was in great danger he became a spider" (1956, 1). However, Anansi's shape remains ambiguous, and Sherlock makes a playful reference to that confusing ambiguity in an introduction to one of his collections of Anansi tales for children:

> You have heard of Brer Rabbit and so you know Brer just means Brother.
> But you may not have heard of Brer Annancy.
> Brer Annancy was a spider.
> No! He was a man.
> No! He was both a man and a spider.
> No! He was both a black spider and a man.
> No! He was both a black man and a spider.
> No! He was both a black spider and a black man.
> No! He was both a big black man and a black spider.
> No! He was both a big black spider and a black man.
> No! He was both a big black man and a big black spider.
> No! He was both a big bad black spider and a big black man.
> No! He was . . .
> Oh well! You know now, don't you?
> (Newman and Sherlock 1959, 5)

Although Anansi is part man and part spider, the question of which species of spider Anansi belongs to has only been briefly touched upon by collectors and anthropologists, and no agreement has been reached despite their attempts to identify him. Contemporary Jamaicans still call their house-spiders by his name, and Anansi is often described as carrying a bag, in which he is said to store stolen goods, over his shoulder, similar to the egg sack on the back of the Jamaican house spider (Tanna 2002, 78). Captain Smith of the Moore Town Maroons explained, "that bag Anansi carries, he carries certain tricks in there" (interview with author, 2005). In her work, Lily Perkins also mentions Anansi's sack, and makes connections between Anansi and the obeahman: "Anansi is the Ashanti word for spider and it is particularly applied to the aforesaid long typical blackish spider who carries about the big white sack, with his special movements, his venomous bite (to other insects) and his medicine bag he is the prototype of the Obeahman" (1910–77). Frederic

Cassidy and Robert Le Page also make a connection between Anansi and the obeahman; in their definition of the Creole term "Nancy-Bag" they quote Charles Rampini (1873) who wrote that the "Nancy bag" was a bag in which the obeahman kept his wares (Cassidy and Le Page 2002, 315).

In the introduction to Richard Hill's *Lights and Shadows of Jamaican History* (1859), there is an attempt to identify the particular species of spider to which Anansi belongs: "In all the West Indian Islands, 'Ananzi' is the name of spiders in general and of a very beautiful spider with yellow stripes in particular. The Negroes think that this spider is the 'Ananzi' of their stories, but that his superior cunning enables him to take any shape he pleases" (cited in Cassidy and Le Page 2002, 10). Cassidy and Le Page state that the term "Anancy" is said to refer to a species of "harmless spiders", whereas the term "spiders" and "black Anancy" refer to the poisonous variety (p. 46). They also add that "there are several different sizes of Anancy – the red-spot-belly kind is an Anancy; when he gets big he turns spider" (ibid.).

However, Pamela Milne-Home notes in her nineteenth-century collection of Anansi tales that "there is a certain large house-spider with hairy legs and yellowish stripes, quite harmless, which it is said to be unlucky to kill, commonly called Anansi" (1890, 5). During the period Milne-Home was collecting material for her collection, students from the Mico Teaching College in Kingston recorded, among other superstitions relating to spiders, that "if you kill a spider you will always be breaking crockeries [sic]" ("Folklore" 1904, 71). The students also added in the introduction to their text that they were pleased to see that the "great works of education and religion" taking place in Jamaica were starting to eradicate these "false" and "evil beliefs" born from the unchristian worship of West African "spirits and shadows" ("Folklore" 1905, 87). They would be disappointed to find out, over a hundred years on from the time of their documentation of "Negro" folklore, it is still taboo to hurt a spider in Jamaica. Fearing that a spider might be Anansi, both children and adults in present day Jamaica leave them well alone. European folklorists such as Una Wilson attribute this reverence to the spider in Jamaica as a result of residual West African beliefs and claims that "it is known that a West African tribe has to this day an Annancy spider as its totem" (1947, 1). Ellis, however, dispels these claims:

There is at the present time no spider-clan among the totem-clans of the Gold Coast, and, as the communities of the Gold Coast are heterogeneous, we cannot suppose that an entire clan has become extinct, unless the extinction took place in the remote past when communities were homogeneous; in which case there seems no sufficient reason for the memory of the totem-ancestor being preserved, after the disappearance of all those who were supposed to be descended from him. (1894, 111)

However, in her investigation of Anansi's form, Perkins quotes part of a letter by Willem Bosman, who was in the service of the Dutch West India Company on the Gold Coast in the late 1600s:

Going to my chamber at night to go to bed, I found a hideous great spider against the walls; on account of the strangeness of the spectacle I called my sub-factor and both my assistants to see it. We found his body long and his head sharp, broader in the fore than hind part but not round as most sorts of spiders are. His legs were as large as a man's finger, ten in number, being hairy and the thickness of a little finger. The Negroes call this spider Ananse, and believe that this creature made the first men. (Bosman cited in Perkins 1910–77)

As discussed in chapter 1, among the Asante, Anansi is depicted as a mediator between the gods and humankind; he is not worshiped as a god or creator in his own right. He is, however, a shape-shifter, as is apparent from the many contradictory descriptions of his form. In conclusion, then, Anansi is described as belonging to a species of spider with a large white egg-sack (Perkins 1910–77; Tanna 2000), a beautiful spider with yellow stripes (Dasnet cited in Cassidy and Le Page 2002), a red spot-bellied baby spider (Cassidy and Le Page 2002), a large harmless house-spider with hairy legs and yellowish stripes (Milne-Home 1890) and a huge and terrifying hairy spider with ten legs (Bosman cited in Perkins 1910–77). The disparity of these descriptions illustrates the ways in which Anansi defies fixity, categorization and labelling. Anansi cannot be pinned down and can be interpreted in multiple ways. This resistance to fixity reflects the instability and unpredictability of the plantation environment and the dynamic social process of an uprooted people in a continual state of flux. Furthermore, Anansi's continual state of metamorphosis posits him as an agent of change and renewal. Finally, his metamorphic nature makes him ambiguous, and it was under the cloak of ambivalence and ambiguity that Africans and their decedents were able to continue subversive cultural practices within the confines of enslavement.

I will now move on to demonstrate how, through depictions of slaves and slave masters in their Anansi tales, slaves themselves were able to criticize and subvert the Jamaican plantation power structure.

Buckra, Quashie and Dry-Bone

> Anansi became the symbolic focus of the resistance in the minds of the Africans. He was used to provide them with resilience and with modes of escape. In the plantation context he figured as a survivor. So the stories reinforced the principles of deception, guile, *tek kin tit* – take a smile to cover the pain in the heart, so you do not allow your enemy to see that you are suffering. (Chevannes, interview with author, 2005)

"Buckra" is a larger-than-life figure in Jamaican Anansi stories, as illustrated in "Dry-Head and Anansi" collected by Beckwith, a story in which Anansi, feigning illness, tricks his wife into letting him eat an entire hog as a "cure", and a character named "Go-Long-Go" (which Beckwith claims is another name for Dry-Head) tries to steal his meat. "Go-Long-Go" are the words to a song in the "Dry-Bone" tale from Jekyll's collection, which he claims refers to the abandonment of dying slaves by their masters (Jekyll 1966, 51). Go-Long-Go demands all of Anansi's hog meat, but Anansi claims that it is, in fact, Buckra's meat:

> Anansi took away the hog an' carry into a wood, him one alone. An' scrape it an' put it into a copper to cook. An' he see a wil' thing called himba [meaning wild yam], an' he dig it to cook with the meat. He saw Mr Go-Long-Go come up. Say, "Brar Anansi, wha' you do here?" Say, "I boil buckra meat, sah." Tell him mus' tak out piece of meat gi' him. Say, "I kyan' tak out fe a buckra meat, sah!" Brar Go-Long-Go say, "If you don' tak it out I 'top you mout', I 'top you breat' [I stop your breath]!" An' he take it out an' gi' him to eat. An' say, "Tak out de whole of it!" an' he tak out the whole an' put it before Brar Go-Long-Go. Eat off the whole of it!
>
> An' he said, "Brar Go-Long-Go, I no pass some plenty guinea-pea deh?" An' they went there, an' carry a pint of oil an' put him into the middle of the plant-

trash an' t'row the oil right around it, an' him light an' whole take fire. Brar Go-Long-Go say, "Come take me out!" Anansi say, "Nyam meat no gimme me no!" (Beckwith 1924, 38)

Here we see Anansi pretending to work for Buckra. Anansi evidently assumes that if he tells Go-Long-Go the meat belongs to Buckra, Go-Long-Go would never attempt to take it; this is testimony to Buckra's power over him. In this tale, Go-Long-Go is an obeahman with the power to stop Anansi's breath; he has the power to kill Anansi and Anansi is forced to feed him. Furthermore, he has no qualms about eating Buckra's meat and angering him. The tale illustrates the oppression of black Jamaicans in its portrayal of the power Buckra has over Anansi. It also demonstrates the influence and standing of the obeahman in Jamaican society, portrayed here as a fearsome and bullying force who can kill through his practice.

The character known as Dry-Bone, Dry-Head or Go-Long-Go is not to be confused with Brother-Death, but along with Brother-Death, he is the most dangerous, frightening and mysterious of all the characters found in Jamaican Anansi tales. An emaciated sinister skeleton-like figure, Dry-Bone appears in human form and is able to cling to people's backs, rendering them powerless to remove him. In Jekyll's story "Dry-Bones", Rabbit and Guinea-pig meet Dry-Bone while they are out hunting birds. Dry-Bone tricks Rabbit into picking him up and carrying him in a bag while Guinea-pig carries the birds they captured. But when "Rabbit got half part of the road he found the bag getting heavier and heavier" (Jekyll 1966, 41). Soon enough, "The bag get so heavy him begin to cry, say that him going to t'row Dry-Bone. An' Dry-Bone fasten his head an' begin to talk. He say to Rabbit – 'you take me up and you take up trouble'" (ibid.).

"Mr Annancy" comes down the road. Seeing Rabbit with his heavy load, "[Anansi] thought he would do something good" (Jekyll 1966, 41). This desire to do good is a rare gesture for Anansi, and it is highly likely that, in his presentation of Anansi as a creature of good intentions, Jekyll was thinking of his young audience and toning down Anansi's negative characteristics accordingly. Anansi then asks Rabbit if he can help him to carry the heavy cargo. Rabbit scampers off, leaving Anansi with his terrible burden and Anansi is forced to take Dry-Bone "home to his yard", where Dry-Bone proceeds to "vex Anansi" while organizing Anansi's own cockerel to spy on him and "keep him a yard", in exchange for payment. After a long while spent feeding and being bullied by Dry-Bone, Anansi finally forms a plan to get rid of him and asks Dry-Bone if he would like to go out in the yard to feel the warmth of the sun:

> An' Annancy tell him that to-morrow he will put him out a door.
>   Annancy went away an' make bargain with Fowl-hawk, that him have a man name Mr Dry-Bone, him must come to-morrow an' take him up an' carry him an' drop him, in the deepest part of the wood. An' so Fowl-hawk did do.
>   When Cock see Fowl-hawk take up Mr Winkler him sing out –
>   *Mister Wink-ler, Winkler comegivemepay.*
>   An' Annancy look up a 'ky an' sing –
>   *Carry him go 'long, An-nan-cy say so, Carry him go 'long, Me'll pay fe cock, Carry him go' long, An-nan-cy say so, Carry him go' long, Me'll pay fe cock, Carry him go' long.* (Jekyll 1966, 51)

There is evidence to support an interpretation of Dry-Bone as Massa or Buckra of the plantation period or the exploitative white boss of post-slavery Jamaica. Dry-Bone metamorphoses into "Mr Winkler" at the end of Jekyll's version and refuses to pay the cockerel for his surveillance work. Here he is depicted as an unjust master refusing to pay his slaves or employees ("when Cock see Fowl-hawk take up Mr Winkler him sing out – *Mister Wink-ler, Winkler comegivemepay*"). Furthermore, Mr Winkler is clearly an evil character, and in "Devil and the Princess" the devil is specifically referred to as "Mr Winkler" ("Devil give his name as Mr Winkler") (Jekyll 1966, 51, 148).

Dry-Bone is powerful; he is able to control Anansi. He stays for a long period in his home and even gets his own cockerel to spy on him, whose role could be seen as synonymous with that of the plantation overseer. His invincible grip on the backs of the creatures he manipulates and his talent for becoming heavier and heavier suggests the grip of the master on his workers and illustrates the extent of the master's power and cruelty. He is the load that they cannot put down; they must bear their burden silently as it becomes ever more intolerable. Tanna writes: "rather than dupe the trickster as other characters do, Dryhead forces Anansi to do his bidding through a combination of bullying, pain and fear" (1983, 26).

Jekyll makes a fascinating link between this Dry-Bone tale and the treatment of slaves by planters in Jamaica. In the following quote, note Jekyll's blinkered refusal to accept that slaves were treated cruelly by slave owners as well as his snobbish attitude towards overseers ("men of low-caste who had neither scruples nor conscience"). As an English aristocrat living in Jamaica, Jekyll seems to have felt compelled to defend upper-class English slave-owners against charges of cruelty by laying the blame on lower-class plantation whites:

> This story refers to a time of slavery. It is almost indisputable that in certain cases, when a slave was in a weak state owing to incurable illness or old age, he was carried out and left to die. To his pitiful remonstrance, "Massa, me no dead yet," the overseer made no reply, but went on with his directions to the bearers, "Carry him go along." This kind of barbarity was not practised by owners living in Jamaica. By them slaves were well treated and such a thing would have been impossible. But when the masters went away they left the control on the hands of the overseers, men of low-caste who had neither scruples nor conscience. (Jekyll 1966, 51)

Jekyll also suggests that the tune that accompanies "Carry him go long" has African origins: it is "certainly primitive" as the "short refrains" "suggest tapping on a drum" (1966, 5). In contrast to my interpretation, Patterson argues that Dry-Bone is the dying slave in Jekyll's tale, and that Anansi is cast in the role of the cruel plantation master, which he argues supports his theory that Anansi was a character the slaves both identified with and hated; a vessel into which slaves projected their self-hate at playing the "Quashie" role. Patterson states: "by identifying Anansi with the brutal white overseer (as in the Dry-Bone tale) the process was taken a step further. The self-hate, having been displaced on Anancy, was now deflected on the white master; a kind of dramatic irony of the subconscious" (1967, 253).

Patterson's theory is problematic. Anansi is bullied and abused by Dry-Bone and Dry-Bone is undoubtedly a character of superior strength. It seems more likely that the tale represents a slave fantasy in which the dynamics of power are reversed: Anansi and Fowl-Hawk treat the captured Dry-Bone, who represents the hated Buckra, in the same way that Buckra would treat a weak, incapacitated and dying slave, and throw him in the deepest part of the woods. The tables are turned and Buckra gets a taste of his own medicine.

There is another very plausible interpretation of Dry-Bone; that of the obeahman. In "Dry-Head and Anansi" from Beckwith's collection, Dry-Bone is referred to as "Go-Long-Go", and Go-Long-Go wants to eat Anansi's meat. Anansi lies and says it belongs to Buckra, but Go-Long-Go does not fear Buckra. Go-Long-Go is cast in the role of the obeahman; he has supernatural powers and tells Anansi that if he doesn't take the meat out the pot "I 'top you mout', I 'top you breat'!" (Beckwith 1924, 38).

In Sherlock's retelling of Jekyll's Dry-Bone tale, he also portrays Dry-Bone as the obeahman. He writes: "Dry-Bone was a terror to every hunter in the forest, for he had magic powers. The old skin-and-bone man could assume the shape of a bird, spreading his wings and taking pleasure in the sun's warmth" (Sherlock 1989, 77). When Dry-Bone speaks, Sherlock describes his voice as "dry and thin like the whisper of wind in a field of dry corn when there had been a long spell of dry weather and parched red dust fills one's nostrils" (p. 82). Here Dry-Bone signifies drought and barren land – the cause of long famines that so often set the scene for the Asante Anansi stories. In Sherlock's version, Anansi takes the bag from Guinea-pig and Rooster because he thinks it is full of birds that he can steal for his pot, rather than as the gesture of goodwill described in Jekyll's telling. Similar to Jekyll's tale, after Dry-Bone forces Anansi to take him to his yard he again assumes the role of the overseer or master, making Anansi a slave in his own home: "Anansi, I will get off your back for a little while, but you must work for me, bring me food and drink, look after me, take good care of me. I have asked Mr Rooster to keep an eye on you. I will pay him to do this. If you try and get away I will climb on your back and you will never get rid of me" (Jekyll 1966, 82–84).

As in the ending to the Jekyll version, Fowl-Hawk saves the day and carries Dry-Bone off with him, releasing Anansi from his enslavement. Sherlock's retelling of the tale draws from white assumptions about obeah. The ominous Dry-Bone is reinterpreted for a modern, mixed readership through the stereotype of the frightening, African-style "primitive" witch-doctor, living deep in the forest. However, putting this stereotype to one side, clearly the obeahman or -woman, in an African, plantation or post-plantation context, is a powerful, formidable and potentially threatening figure. This interpretation would account for the magical powers of Dry-Bone, his menacing appearance and his ability to frighten and conquer Anansi.

In all the Anansi tales that feature Dry-Bone, he consistently uses his power to coerce the weak through bullying, pain and fear (Tanna 1983, 26). He offers rewards – rewards that turn out to negate freedom. He holds his prisoners fast and does not let them go. He sets up surveillance systems to prevent their escape (see Beckwith 1924, 38–39; 253–54). Dry-Bone is an abuser of power, and a character through which cruel and authoritarian figures are criticized. However, like Anansi, the character of Dry-Bone resists fixed interpretation, and it is precisely through the maintenance of this level of ambiguity in their cultural forms that Jamaicans were able to covertly reference taboo subjects – the tyranny of the slave-master or white boss, the power and practice of obeah, or the suffering of the wronged slave – are all referred to in a veiled and ambivalent manner.

In "Nansi Steals Backra Sheep", recounted by storyteller Adina Henry in Tanna's collection, "Backra" is also referred to as "Whiteman" and "Massa" (Tanna 2000, 101–2). Anansi, Monkey and Rabbit in this tale represent the poor black Jamaicans, while the human characters are white and prosperous. Anansi takes the position of headman on Backra's property and starts killing sheep. When Anansi's son questions his actions he replies, "Bwoy, shet up ye mout. Look pon Backra sheep how dem nough [enough] nough nough. Ebery minute sheep a bawm [born]. Ebery minute sheep a bawm" (p. 101). Once Anansi has killed Whiteman's sheep, he stores the sheep's skins. When Whiteman becomes concerned about the theft, Anansi tells him he will find the thief and send him to Whiteman's party. Then, to avoid being caught for his theft, Anansi tricks Monkey into dressing up as a sheep and sends him to a party that Whiteman is hosting. Whiteman, when he sees Monkey dressed in one of his sheep's skins, orders his men to tie Monkey to a tree, but Monkey then evades punishment by telling Rabbit that he is tied to a tree because he is meant to marry the "yich yich [meaning rich] Whiteman's daughta" – but as he thinks he is far too poor and lowly to take her hand in marriage ("How me fe go do a ting yike dat an me so poor?"), they have tied him up to force him into it and Whiteman's men will soon return. Rabbit quickly trades places with Monkey (he is very keen to marry a rich white girl) and is consequently thrown in the fire for the theft by Whiteman's men, but at the last minute, he leaps to safety.

Similar to Beckwith's version of "Dry-Head and Anansi" (1924), this story provides a sharp social commentary on the patterns of power in Jamaica. We see the rule of the rich and landed "Whiteman", as well as an acknowledgement of a social phenomenon driving black Jamaicans, especially men, to "marry white", thus climbing up the racial ladder away from poverty and blackness towards wealth and whiteness. Frantz Fanon explores this issue in *Black Skins, White Masks* (1986). Fanon's black narrator exposes a crippling form of internalized racism suffered by black men: "I wish to be acknowledged not as black but as white . . . who but a white woman can do this for me? [The love of a white woman] takes me onto a noble road that leads to total realisation . . . I marry white civilisation, white beauty, white whiteness." Fanon maintains that for many black men, this is "a conflict that, active or dormant, is always real" (1986, 63–63).

In "Nansi Steals Backra Sheep", Anansi points out that Backra has too many sheep – every minute a sheep is born – and this justifies him killing some for himself. Anansi is the poor black man stealing from the rich white boss to ensure his survival. However, there is more than simply the drive to survive in Anansi's actions: there is revenge in his behaviour and anger in his words – "Bwoy, shet up ye mout", he tells his son irately when he questions his actions; look around you, open your eyes – Whiteman has "nough nough nough", or more than enough, sheep. Here Anansi is the medium through which the greed and discrimination at the heart of Jamaican society is criticized and acts of defiance and law-breaking against rich "Whitemen" are legitimized. In the tale "Gaulin", found in Jekyll's collection, there are similar references to the unjust privileges whiteness brings. For instance, Anansi tells Mr Monkey "as you being such a clean an' white gentlemen I think you will succeed" (1966, 73).

Both Patterson (1967) and Richard Burton (1997) argue that, in the Caribbean, Anansi functioned as a vessel into which slaves could project their self-hatred: a product of their "Quashie" role-playing. There have been many different uses of the term "Quashie". It is defined by Cassidy and Le Page as a "negro day-name for a boy born on a Sunday", "a name typifying any male negro", a "negro peasant", a "country bumpkin" or a "backward person who refuses improvement" (Cassidy and Le Page 2002, 370). While it became primarily an abusive name for blacks, academics have identified what they call a "Quashie syndrome": a type of behaviour among slaves which reaffirmed their masters' stereotypes of them, and that eventually became inextricably fused with their "real" personalities (Craton 1982, 56).

Patterson argues (and Burton supports this view) that Anansi's character traits epitomize all the undesirable aspects of the "Quashie" role because Anansi symbolized the European stereotype of the black man as dumb, lumbering and sycophantic (like the "Sambo" figure in the United States). Patterson maintains that, through Anansi, slaves could censor their self-hatred at playing the "Quashie" role without persecution and, once objectified, they could then laugh at their own despised performances and learn to accept them: "having censored this part of himself, the slave could then find it possible to laugh at it and learn to live with and accept it" (Patterson 1967, 253).

Patterson perceives the "Quashie" role as one that was shameful and debasing. I argue that acting "Quashie" was a survival technique, allowing for a certain degree of autonomy under domination, and Anansi should be interpreted as a celebration of this. Anansi is far from stupid and lumbering, yet for both Anansi and the slaves pretending to be "Quashie", such behaviour gave them more scope for devising plans against the system; a form of, as Craton puts it, "tactical manoeuvring" (1982, 54). Quashie was normally a performance, and whites responded to this performance by treating their slaves as dumb animals incapable of complex thought (p. 35). As Craton points out, playing Quashie was not as damaging as certain academics insist: "resistance has many faces", he reminds us, and "apparent accommodation is a sophisticated response to the inevitabilities of power, the means by which subject peoples are most likely to succeed in retaining at least a shadow of independence" (p. 56, p. 28).

Feigning intellectual inferiority would lower the planters' expectations of their slaves and invariably reduce suspicion and watchfulness, giving them room for resistance: an Anansi tactic of "play fool fe catch wise" (Campbell 1985, 22). Campbell exposes these techniques and cites a "white commentator" who "gained the confidence of the slaves" and observed them "outside the shadow of the whip". The white commentator describes the end of a days work in the slave quarters: "One has to hear with what warmth and volubility and at the same time with what precision of ideas and accuracy of judgment this creature, heavy and taciturn all day, now squatting before his friend tells stories, gesticulates, argues, passes opinions, approves and condemns both his master and those who surround him" (p. 23). Anansi may play the "smile-and-shuffle role with Whiteman", but he does so only when he has a trick up his sleeve (Tanna 2000, 79). The tales celebrate the ingenuity of Anansi's subversive performance, and should be seen as a source of empowerment, celebrating trickster tactics, rather than a means in which slaves dispelled feelings of self-hatred.

Anansi's ability to manipulate the powerful through self-abasement is evident in several Asante and Jamaican tales. In the Jamaican version of the Asante tale "How It Came About That the Sky-God's Stories Came to Be Known as 'Spider-Stories'", it is primarily through performing the sycophantic aspect of the "Quashie" role that Anancy is able to complete impossible tasks such as convincing Snake to stretch himself across a long bamboo to prove he is the longest animal in the world. Sherlock, who recorded the story in 1954, has Anansi apologizing to Snake in a mock cringing manner and then lying to him and praising him:

> "Oh snake I beg your pardon, I beg your pardon," cried the terrified Anansi. "What you say is true. I did try to catch you, but I failed. You are too clever for me."
>
> "And why did you try to catch me, Anansi?"
>
> "I had a bet with Tiger. I told him you are the longest animal in the world, longer even than that long bamboo-tree by the side of the river". (1989, 45–56)

In Rattray's version, Anansi pretends to be arguing with his wife, Aso, and he makes sure that Python overhears their staged disagreement. He tells Python his wife is a liar, as she thinks Python is smaller than a long piece of palm branch (note that this changes to a bamboo cane in Jamaica) (1930, 52–58).

The Jamaican Anansi tales highlight the usefulness of lying as a means of undermining the power of dominant groups, and, as the diaries of white colonials reveal, lying was indeed used as a subversive tool in plantation Jamaica. For example, Thistlewood, a yeoman farmer's son from Lincolnshire who kept several journals when working as a plantation overseer from 1750 to 1786, became paranoid and frightened when a slave threatened to lie about him to his master.

Thistlewood worked on the Egypt plantation in 1752. After four months of sick leave due to a bout of several venereal diseases (as a result of his sexual exploits), Thistlewood describes in his journal how a slave claimed that he "intended to mount some great lie, and go and tell his master to get [me] turned away". This slave, known for directing "veiled sarcasm" and "other forms of insolence" towards Thistlewood was, ironically, named Quashie. Thistlewood writes that Quashie also said "his master would believe a Negro before a white man and gave an Instance of the same" (cited in Craton 1982, 41). The verbal threat is followed by Thistlewood being physically assaulted by a slave named Congo Sam. Thistlewood starts to fear for his life, especially after he overhears slaves talking about him: "[I] have also reason to believe yt [*sic*] many of ye Negroes as Quashie, Ambo, Phibbah & Sam had an Intent to Murder me, when we should meet, by what I heard them speak one day in ye Cook Room, when I was ye Back Piazza reading" (cited in Craton 1982, 42).

Like Anansi, the slaves used words as a verbal weapon with which they threatened their adversaries. Adam, a slave who Lewis both respected and feared – and failed to punish after he had been suspected of both obeah and poisoning – caused near chaos on the plantation through rumour and lies. On his return from a trip to Britain, Lewis finds his whole estate "in an uproar about Adam", who has been telling fellow slaves that Lewis's leniency was proof of his power and prestige (Terry 1999, xxx).

"How Crab Got a Hard Back", collected by Sherlock, offers an example of Anansi's verbal skills. Here Anansi is a master flatterer, and outwits Crab by dressing up as a girl and polishing his ego. In this tale Anansi once again plays the obsequious "Quashie" role, hiding his performance to manipulate the powerful. Interestingly, however, here Quashie's sycophantic characteristics are combined with stereotypes of feminine fragility and charm:

> "Oh what a pretty gentleman," said Anansi in a voice like a girl's.
>
> "You like me girl?" asked crab. No girl had ever called him a pretty gentleman before.
>
> He was very pleased. "You like me girl?" he repeated.
>
> "Yes sir," said Anansi. And smiled at crab more with her eyes than with her lips, like a girl.
>
> "Yes sir, what a real dandy man, sir! Do you travel far?"
>
> Crab was very happy, hearing how the girl in the white dress with the pink spots praised him. He began to boast a little. "Yes girl," he said, "I travel all over the world." (Sherlock 1989, 86–92)

Anansi's mimicking of women and his ability to transcend gender boundaries is another transgressive feature of the Anansi tales, illustrated in this tale and found in several others. Anansi is sometimes referred to as "she" in both Jamaican and West African tales; in the Asante tale "How Spear-Grass Came into the Tribe" (Rattray 1930, 213–19), Anansi pretends to menstruate, and in several Jamaican tales Anansi changes his voice to sound feminine and dresses like a woman – see "House in the Air" (Beckwith 1924, 21), "Anansi and Dora" (Bennett 1979, 59), and "Anancy and Fee Fee" (p. 65). In Tanna's "Fee Fee", Anansi dresses like a girl to enter a race at a fair – "Bowy, dat little girl is like lightening" exclaim the crowd (Tanna 2000, 103–5).

Several riddles in Jamaica centre on "Little Miss Nancy". The ambiguous Anansi, with his love of playing with words, is the ideal subject of riddles, which essentially function through ambivalence and the manipulation of language. In Perkins's collection of material on Jamaican folklore she records numerous "Miss Nancy" riddles. For instance, "riddle me riddle, riddle me dat, guess me this riddle and perhaps not, Little Miss Nancy tore her beautiful yellow gown and no one could mend it. Answer: the skin of a banana." Also, "as Little Miss Nancy was going upstairs, she dropped her handkerchief, and no one was able to give it to her again. Answer: a bird dropped a feather and no one could put it in its place again", and "Little Miss Nancy with a white petticoat and a red night cap. Answer: a candle."

Here Anansi becomes "Little Miss Nancy" and metamorphoses into an upper-class (perhaps European) girl. Instead of a hairy spider, we have a type of "Little Miss Muffet", who wears beautiful gowns, petticoats and night caps, and carries a handkerchief. The age of this collection is evidenced in the other riddles assembled; for example: "my father has a set of niggers, all white and one red. Answer: teeth and a tongue" and "my father had a whole Guinea ship full of people and every one of them come out with red coat and black head. Answer: ackees" (Perkins 1910–77).

Although Jamaican society has been, and still remains, patriarchal and intensely homophobic, it is evident that even Anansi's sexuality continues to be represented, as it was in West Africa, as fluid. He can assume a traditionally weaker and more submissive female role to attain his goals. The tales in which he pretends to change gender are celebrations of the ingenuity behind a performance of subservience and an illustration of the falsity of that performance. Furthermore, it demonstrates how Anansi, like other trickster figures, is permitted to change shape, sexuality, identity and gender without having to offer any form of explanation or justification – his actions are entirely based on his current needs and circumstances.

The portrayal of gender fluidity in a patriarchal, homophobic society is another subversive element of the Anansi tales, signalling a breaking of boundaries and a role-reversal similar to that of the Caribbean carnival, during which, at certain times, men dress as women. Finally, it is important to remember that although "Quashie" became a derogatory term during slavery, it was originally an Akan day-name for a male born on a Sunday and considered exceptional – its original meaning is "born to lead". Craton beautifully summarizes the role: "Quashie, then, can stand for the slave-driver or ordinary toiler – who, in the complex dialectic of the slave plantation was both obdurate and subtle in his resistance, the preserver of African traditions who could yet survive and adapt in a changing world, biding his time" (1982, 54).

Bungo, Obeah and Brother Death

Anansi's predominant character traits in Jamaica are those of lewdness, slothfulness, cunning, deceit and greed. Among the Jamaican slaves, Anansi came to symbolize aspirations for physical contact, a break from relentless labour and a desire for plentiful meals. He is obsessed with food, has a huge sexual appetite and is exceptionally stubborn, showing an incredible persistence with his plans and schemes, and doing anything to get his own way. Although the desire for high-status women often motivates Anansi and many of his fellow creatures, it is the need for food that dominates plans. While the West African tales tell of times of terrible drought and famine, the Jamaican tales see Anansi risk his life for fruits, plantain, the Jamaican dessert of Duckanoo, or fresh meat.[16] Slaves in the Americas at times experienced extreme hunger, as a former slave from North Carolina reported: "They didn't give us nothing to chaw on. Learned us steal, that's what they done. Why, we would take anything we could lay our hands on, when we was hungry. Then they'd whip us for lying when we say we don't know nothing about it. But it was easier to stand when the stomach was full" (cited in Levine 1977, 122).

Jamaican Anansi is motivated by his stomach and will steal from his own children to feed his insatiable appetite. Through Anansi, the act of stealing food from Massa, or perhaps even other slaves, could be legitimized. Jamaican Anansi also hates physical exertion and loves nothing more than to sit back and relax while he gains from another man's labour. He is customarily described as a *ginnal* (also spelt *ginal* and *jinal*), meaning a clever, crafty con-man or trickster; a term which also "has overtones of a connection to Obeah" (Cassidy and Le Page 2002, 247). Jamaican storyteller Brother Martin,[17] otherwise known as Alexander Parker, summed up Anansi's main characteristics:

> I say Anansi is man him look like *tief*. A robber. Him like a man who walk and stir up mutiny! Anansi have about ten legs, five a this side and five a that side. Him can a shake them out and you can see all of them, or hold them in.
>
> Anansi is brave man. And him is man him have *techniques*. He is a man him have *intelligence*! Anansi is a man who *tief*! You can't find a bigger tief than him.
>
> Anansi is a very, very dangerous weapon. Anansi is a man who make trouble, and take himself out of it, and make you gwan in there. Understand? Him *ginnal* man. (Interview with author, 2005)

Representative of the slave reversing the structure of an abhorrent system, Anansi became extremely relevant to the enslavement experienced by African descendants on Jamaican soil. The skills used by Anansi to thwart his rivals were ones slaves could use to their advantage in their daily lives. When asked about the history and function of the Anansi tales, Brother Martin explained the ways in which Anansi could teach survival tactics in times of oppression, as well as be a reminder of African roots:

> It will show you that you can defend yourself in every *capasibility* [meaning capacity and capability together] that you can. Because it will help you a get out o it, you see?
>
> Them stories come straight from Africa. Because in days gone by when slave master did a rule slave, African could not speak to African like me ayou go aspeak together. Them a *ketch we, and beat we and tie up* and *rob* and a *beat* we, so we can't a talk each other. Because if we talk to each other we will form law 'gainst *dem*!
>
> So Africans get together and them a talk Anansi story, and when them a talk some of the story have *great meaning*. Dem a tell you what fee happen and how to do things, but they talk it a story, so nobody know. You understand? So it hap-

pen, right here and true. Whole heap a story, whole heap a meaning; through them you know what happen to the African. (Interview with author, 2005)

In Jamaica, Anansi is represented as talking with a lisping falsetto voice (he has particular problems pronouncing his "r" and "s" sounds), sometimes whispering and whining, at other times squeaky and child-like. Roger Abrahams explains that the Anansi storyteller "talks broad" which is "explicitly connected to Compè Nansi's[18] inability to talk properly". In his tales, Anansi, Abrahams explains, "not only speaks as the animals do, in conversational Creole, but his speech is even more *broke-up*, for he lisps, stutters and whines" (1982, 395). Jamaican Storyteller Small points out the possible origins of Anansi's lisp: "Anansi . . . speaks with a lisp; *ehe eh eh*. I heard a very interesting interpretation of that from one of the Professors at the university. A spirit coming back from the dead, who walks backwards . . . his voice is very *ehhh ehhh*, and that is why Anansi speaks like that because Anansi is a spirit" (letter to author 2006). Perkins offers a similar explanation for Anansi's distinctive voice: "We are also told that in West Africa Anancy is represented as speaking through the nose as the local demons are said to do, and here the idea still survives as is faithfully carried out in the telling of the tales. The nasal snuffle being combined with a sort of lisp or in local parlance 'tie tongue'" (1910–77).

Cassidy, however, has an even more insightful interpretation and explains that Anansi's lisping speech is termed "Bungo talk" in Jamaica: "Jekyll has him saying *yeddy, fooyish, byute, yitty* for 'ready', 'foolish' and 'brute' and 'little'. In explanation he is said to be tongue-tied, but it is really something else: 'Bungo talk'. When we consider the Twi language for example, there is no 'r' sound . . . it seems very likely that this feature is a relic of Africanism" (1961, 41–42).

In colonial Jamaica, "Bungo-talker" became a term encompassing all the supposedly negative traits of African people, which perhaps led to the association of Anansi's speech with that of an African devil or spirit, as Small and Perkins both suggest. It was used as a term to describe poor, uneducated peasant characters, often stereotyped as foolish, backward and bumbling. Cassidy and Le Page explain its Jamaican usage as signalling a "nincompoop or country bumpkin". The term, they explain, is "often also applied to one of unprepossessing appearance . . . very black; ugly; stupid, African" or "African in the sense of a descendant of slaves whose civility is minimally mediated by European mores" (2002, 80).

With his lisping "Bungo-talk", Anansi came to both assume the "parodied features of the Jamaican peasant" and represent "the ghost of the African slave past" (Tanna 2000, 80). In a statement highly applicable to some Jamaican attitudes towards Anansi, Fanon claims that "in the man of colour there is a constant effort to run away from his own individuality, to annihilate his own presence" (1986, 60). In post-plantation Jamaica, Anansi, with his connotations of Bungo, symbolized an identity many black Jamaicans came to ridicule and despise as they internalized the racist ideology and prejudices of whites, proof of which can be seen in the reluctance of late-nineteenth- and early-twentieth-century Jamaicans to tell Anansi tales to whites. This is evidenced in an article that appeared in the *Daily Gleaner*: "The people are very reticent about the subject [of Anansi] before grown-up persons. When appealed to they refer to the stories as 'foolishness' and they say they have no time nowadays to pay 'tension to such matters' and so forth" (4 February 1899). Another contributor to the *Gleaner*, who remained anonymous, argued that the Anansi stories "have naturally evolved from out of the confused ideas of a people still in a low stage of mental evolution". With regard to the role of the tales in West Africa, the contributor stated that to believe, "that they were the result of observation and imagination is to gift savages with developed mental powers which they do not possess" (4 July 1903, 9).

Collector Milne-Home wrote of her exasperation of "Negros" who "fear ridicule" for telling Anansi tales, for they are asked to tell a story, and they exclaim: "dat foolishness; wonder Missis car to har dat [care to hear that]" (1890, 2). She comments that "probably the same old woman will keep the children quiet with these tales, and the small white *buccra* sitting by its nurse will have a flood of folk-lore wasted on its entertainment" (ibid.). Una Jeffery-Smith (who used the pen name "Wona") stated that "there has grown up among the Negroes themselves a strange, almost inexplicable feeling, somewhat akin to shame, which prevents their relating these stories, even in the privacy of their own huts, as they once did" (Jeffery-Smith 1899, preface). For Jeffery-Smith it was the ugliness of patois that was the greatest cause of embarrassment:

Now-a-days, the nurse is scarcely to be met with who, when asked to tell an Anancy story, will not promptly answer "don't know none"; for the average Negro woman, like the average woman everywhere, dreads being laughed at. She knows that her dialect is not a beautiful one and that "Missus" won't like to hear it from the lips of her darlings; so even if she does know one, she remains silent. (Jeffery-Smith 1899, preface)

In 1926, when collecting material for her analysis of "Possible Survivals of African Songs in Jamaica", Roberts remarked that she found it difficult to obtain Anansi tales in places where there was a strong church influence "because he belongs in the category of old-time heathen and 'temporal' things which the church and government alike are trying to stamp out" (1926, 244). Even in the mid-twentieth century, Perkins records how Jamaicans still felt embarrassed about sharing Anansi stories with outsiders:

The majority look on them as something childish that their race has outgrown. They are diffident about telling them and seem on the whole rather ashamed to admit any knowledge of them. It requires a good deal of persuasion and tact to get an Anancy story told to one in these days. You are always met with the reply "me don't know none" or "me quite forget". There is a difficulty in getting the teller going. (Perkins 1910–77)

She adds that these are tales "of a race that in growing up, is putting childish things away". "And yet," she continues, "the things of childhood may be very appealing to grown ups sometimes, so let us preserve what is left of these tales while yet there is time" (1910–77).

Una Wilson collected Anansi tales in Jamaica in the 1940s, although one wonders why she was attracted to her subject matter. She maintains that Anansi has "so many traits that we deplore" because the tales came from the "mysterious continent" of Africa, and if he was indeed a chief there, it would further explain his outrageous actions, as they could only be "commendable to the primitive mind". She continues: "It will be noted in these stories that the qualities exhibited by Anancy are those that would be acceptable to a primitive people. He has no standard of truth and honour. He is undoubtedly clever, but he gains his ends by cunning. Lying and stealing are the outstanding traits of his character" (1947, 6). Wilson continues her bigoted musings and wonders whether Anansi was really once a man or a part of "the imaginative creations of a people still in lower states of civilisation who, like little children, believe in the possibility of Tigers and Monkeys, birds and fishes holding converse with one another" (p. 5).

As well as signifying the "uncivilized", "uneducated", very black peasant, "Bungo-man" was a name for a practitioner of obeah in Jamaica. During the late nineteenth and early twentieth centuries, the practice of obeah, with its African roots, carried the same negative connotations associated with Anansi tales and Creole (or "Bungo-talk") – too African, too primitive, too black. With their knowledge of plants and herbal medicines, the obeahman or -woman, like Anansi, was connected to the bush and, living alone outside the village, he or she operated in society's margins (Abrahams 1982, 403–4). Obeah was particularly central to the lives of Jamaican Maroons, who, living in the bush away from the community of the plantation, were occupiers of the margins and inspired dread in both slaves and whites. Trowbridge writes on the folk practices of "the Negroes of Jamaica", and when describing an African-influenced Jamaican funeral ceremony, echoes the prejudiced attitudes of Jamaican whites towards African religious practices: "When a Negro becomes civilized and Christianised up to a certain point he considers himself above this heathenish custom, and looks with no small degree of scorn upon those brothers who still cling to it as a soul-saving rite" (1896, 280).

However, as with the term "Quashie", certain African expressions of respect became racist insults when used in a Jamaican context. May Jeffery-Smith explains that the derogatory term "Bungo" may have originally meant "superintendent", signifying someone in control and in a position of power. She states that the "Obeahman calls himself 'Bungo man' and is a corruption of the Asante 'bunkun' meaning 'superintendent'. Now the term 'Bungo man' is still used for Obeahman, but the expression 'Bungo Nayger'[19] is used for a very ignorant, illiterate Negro" (1965, 5).

Anansi, linked to obeah and Bungo and perceived as uncomfortably reminiscent of a supposedly heathen African past, is still associated with supposedly unchristian practices in Jamaica today. As discussed in the final chapter, it is Anansi's perceived amorality that has urged certain contemporary Jamaicans to call for the banning of the folktales from being told in Jamaican schools. Tanna, who spent nearly ten years collecting Anansi tales in the 1970s and 1980s, always felt Anansi was at odds with her Christian faith. In an interview, she explained that because she was "raised in a Christian tradition" she "never really cared that much for Anansi" but preferred "the old-time stories . . . the ones that really, in my eyes, had some morals". She went on to describe the issues that the evangelical churches had with Anansi: "You will find that people have had to stop telling the stories because the evangelical churches said to them that this is an evil creature and it is against the religion to do this. Churches view Anansi in this one particular way, whereas others view him as a survival figure; it all depends on who is telling the story" (2005).

Jamaican storyteller Brother Martin also explained that some Christians still feel uncomfortable about Anansi, but that the duality of good and evil can be found everywhere: "You can't tell some of the [church] people Anansi stories! But every footstep of the way you have good and evil. Good man and de bad man. You have some man in the house of God and they bad people! They try and cheat the poor. In everything you have good and you have evil" (interview with author, 2005).

Although Anansi's interactions with the divine world of the gods all-but-disappeared in the Jamaican tales, they continued to represent aspects of the African spiritual world not only through their continued link with obeah, but also through their use at wakes or "nine-night" ceremonies. Originating in Africa and practised throughout slavery, the nine-night ceremony is still found throughout the modern Caribbean, in particular in Jamaica, Suriname, Trinidad and St Vincent, where the tales are told at night festivals for the dead (Purchas-Tulloch 1976, 285). On the ninth-night of a wake there is a final "set-up" or "sit-up" at the home of the deceased in which music (traditionally the playing of drums) and dancing take place and the mourners are entertained with Anansi stories to ensure nobody becomes melancholy. Milne-Home explains that Anansi stories were "related at local gatherings of black people, such as weddings or funerals, the latter being, like wakes in Ireland, equal occasions for festivity as the former" (1890, 1).

At a nine-night, visitors "spend the night with music, singing, clapping of hands; alternated with periods of eating and drinking and telling stories" (Perkins 1910–77). Europeans, as well as creoles who had been influenced by Euro-Christian values, looked upon the practice of nine-night with disdain. Trowbridge writes: "a more grim or grotesque spectacle cannot be imagined, or music more discordant or weird" (1896, 279–80). The practice of nine-night is still popular in Jamaica, and the final night will often provide the weekend's entertainment for young and old alike. It is worth noting that in Jamaica today the tales are more likely to be told at nine-night when an old person dies, as the life of a deceased youth would be celebrated with a more modern, sound-system event.

Despite the variety of interpretations of the role of Anansi stories in the nine-night ceremony, the weight of evidence suggests that Anansi tales are used to fend off or entertain the ghost or "duppy" of the deceased. Storyteller Small explained that "all the noise, the gaiety, the domino playing, and the dinky-minny dancing" at nine-nights is "orchestrated to unburden the mourners of their sadness" (interview with author, 2005). She said that Anansi stories are told for their humour, because there must be no sadness, and no one must speak ill of the dead; if you do, "the 'duppy' will surely follow you" (ibid.). Other interpreters claim that Anansi tales are told at nine-night not to entertain the mourners but rather the spirit of the dead. The stories are meant to help the departure of the "duppy" to the other side and ensure that the dead will not rise and pester the living (Herskovits 1958, 182).

During the nine-night, Anansi tales are accompanied by, according to Abrahams, "rude activities carried out rudely" such as outrageous actions, games, songs and dances (Abrahams 1982, 399). Like his role among the Asante, Anansi is used as a medium through which participants can test the social structures in an explosion of behaviour that in everyday life would be regarded as disruptive, rude and unacceptable. A "structural inversion" takes place in an energetic eruption of mockery, play and nonsense. As Abrahams explains, this "crossroads" behaviour "becomes a cultural resource for the family and community in their encounter with death" (ibid.).

Abrahams observed Anansi storytellers at a Vincentian nine-night and explained that they facilitated a celebration of "in-betweenness" – not only did the storytellers share Anansi's marginal social status (they were young men who lived alone, were considered selfish by the community and also stuttered), but, in addition, they broke down the boundaries between the social space of the street and the private sphere of the home. By bringing bawdy, playful street activity into the house – through Anansi, the "lord of nonsense" – the nine-night revellers eroded many elements of the community's physical and psychosocial barriers (1982, 404).

The celebration of in-betweenness at the nine-night not only diffuses the tension and frustrations of marginalized people, but helps the community come to terms with the in-between status of the deceased. The nine-night, an event focused on the crossroads between life and death, is therefore celebrated through chaotic crossroads behaviour and the crossroads figure of Anansi, who in his ability to overcome death, encourages participants "to prevail in the face of death" (Abrahams 1982, 408).

Another way in which the Anansi tales remained connected to obeah and the supernatural in Jamaica was through the continuation of a popular superstitious belief, rooted in Asante thought, warning that it was unlucky to tell Anansi tales in the daylight. Perkins writes, "to tell an Anancy story in daylight is a proceeding fraught with danger; the teller's mother will go blind or become a broomstick, and many other dreadful things are liable to happen" (1910–77). On 19 March 1900, an article appeared in the *Daily Gleaner* informing readers of the superstitions surrounding the setting in which the tales are told:

> Anancy stories are only told at night, in the gloaming, when the shadows are lengthening and the darkness is creeping in. This is an eerie time and it suits these stories best. No true Nana would venture to tell an Anancy story in broad daylight, she puts the children off by gravely saying she cannot tell a story in the daytime. If she did their mother would turn into a broomstick, or some other dreadful or absurd catastrophe would happen. Now these stories are printed the spell of night is broken, for who can prevent them being read in the broadest daylight.

It seems that the idea that daytime tellings are dangerous is directly linked to the practice of telling Anansi tales at wakes or nine-night ceremonies. Melville Herskovits explains that, in the "New World", the belief that it is dangerous to tell folktales in the daytime (as "the spirits of the dead will come and take away the soul of the teller") derived from the use of folktales at wakes, where "the tales fulfil the role of amusing the dead" (1958, 182). On a practical level, taboos against telling the tales in daylight can also be linked to maximizing work-time. To sit down and tell Anansi tales during work time could be interpreted as an act of laziness. Societies in both West Africa and the Caribbean therefore created the taboo to ensure productivity. There are examples, however, of tales being told during the daytime by Maroon men, at certain times of the agricultural year, while the women were at work, which further develops the link between story-time and work-time, as the men chose a time to tell the tales when they were free from their normal work duties. Here the taboo was only broken because story-time is not impeding productivity (Beckwith 1924, 292).

As explained in chapter 1, among the Asante, Anansi occupied a liminal position, existing on (and continually testing) the boundaries between the human world and that of the spirits. He was a harbourer of the great and unfathomable forces that structured the Asante universe. Although in Jamaica he became more representative of the Jamaican slaves' human condition as his connection to Nyame was severed, he continued to occupy a liminal space, at the crossroads between the secular and the spiritual. Anansi's continued liminality in Jamaica was not only exemplified by the part he played in Jamaican superstitions, creation myths, obeah and nine-night ceremonies, but also through his relationship with the powerful and sinister character Death.

In Jekyll's interpretation of "Brother Anansi and Brother Deat", Anansi is too clever to be tricked by Death, who wants him to drop from the ceiling into his hands: Anansi says he is too fat and Death must get a barrel of flour for him to drop into. However, "Deat' never know that this flour was temper lime. Deat' bring the barrel an', just as he fixing it up under where Annancy hanging, Annancy drop on Deat' head and Pum. An jam him head in a temper lime an' blin him" (Jekyll 1966, 34).

Anansi is not so fortunate in "Anancy Meets Bredda Death", recorded by Jeffery-Smith, in which Anansi tries to steal Death's livestock. A man warns him "him smart fe true dat kyan teef fram Deat" (any person who can steal from death must be very smart). Anansi ends up being burned to death, while his wife, "Crooky", in an act of defiance and cruelty which is particularly out of character, looks on, laughing (Jeffery-Smith 1899, 71–77). Before his unfortunate end, Anansi calls Death a "true Backra gemman [Buckra gentleman]"; another subversive statement that is indicative of the hatred many Jamaicans felt for "Backra", the white boss.

In Jeffery-Smith's recorded tale, Death is described as even worse than Dry-Head: "Dry head had been bad but this dreadful being, as silent as the grave, promised to be worse" (1899, 75). Similarly to death, the aforemen-

Figure 7. "The Spirits splashing the stream". (Illustration from "How It Came About That the Hinder Part of Kwaku Ananse, the Spider, Became Big, at the Expense of His Head, Which Became Small", recorded by Rattray [1930, 69]. By permission of Oxford University Press.)

tioned ominous and mysterious Dry-Head or Dry-Bone is one of the few reoccurring characters who has power over Anansi. I would like to return to a short examination of this character to demonstrate the ways in which the Anansi tales were modified and transformed in their Jamaican context. Cassidy and Le Page describe Dry-Head as "a character never clearly delineated, but dangerous, having magical powers (he is hard to get rid of), and prob [sic] to be visualised skull-like" (Cassidy and Le Page 2002, 161). Brother Martin described him as "an enemy, like a scientist. Him a man can blow fire out of him mouth. A magic man" (interview with author 2005).

Dry-Head, along with Buckra, King, Massa and Preacher, is one of the few characters depicted in the tales in human, albeit skull-like, form; the only similar characters in the Asante tales are the Spirits in "How It Came About That the Hinder Part of Kwaku Ananse, the Spider, Became Big, at the Expense of His Head, Which Became Small", mentioned in chapter 1 (Rattray 1930, 67–71). The Spirits, like Dry-Head, are imposing creatures of another dimension who can dominate Anansi. In both Asante and Jamaican tales,

Anansi is put in his place by those who gain their powers from unearthly forces. In this particular story, Anansi finds the spirits using their skulls to remove water from the stream so as to improve fishing conditions. On request, they help him do the same, but warn him that if he sings their song, his head will become detached permanently. Anansi does not pay heed, but when the warning becomes true he takes his head and "clap[s] it against his anus", which is why the spider has a small head and big body (pp. 67–71).

Maroon Isaac Bernard recounted one of the most well-known Jamaican Anansi tales which features Dry-Head:

> Anansi and Tacoma, they have a field, they work a field, and Anansi and Tacoma on the top of the field, one up top one down below, and they make a pledge to say nothing bad about one another. If anyone say anything bad about him, him going to drop down dead. Now Dry-Head him have no hair upon him head. And them look and see Dry-Head coming up. Anansi him say "My *God, look* at that – Dry-Head head *dry*!!!" And him drop down dead [*laughs*]. So Tacoma just nyam [meaning eat] him off [*heavy, snorting laughter*]. (Interview with author 2005)

This tale is clearly an adapted version of the Asante tale "How Contradiction Came Among the Tribe", which features Hate-to-Be-Contradicted (examined in chapter 1), and is likely to have been retained to a greater extent in its African form among the Maroons, who experienced little European influence in their autonomous communities (Rattray 1930, 107–11). Another version of this tale describes how Anansi works a small patch of rock on which nothing can grow. In response to the questions of passers-by who are interested in his reasons for trying to cultivate rock, he tells them he is growing food. They fall down dead if they contradict him. Dry-Head passes by, and when Anansi asks him where he has been, he tells him he is coming back from a visit to the hairdressers. Anansi contradicts him, as he has not a hair on his head, and Anansi falls down dead.[20]

Although Dry-Head or Dry-Bone is only depicted in a few Jamaican tales, he appears to be one of the most fascinating and memorable characters. Jamaican novelist and academic Velma Pollard recounts how even her grown-up children still remember him: "The other weekend we all got together, and I heard them talking about Anansi and Dry-Bone; now as soon as you say 'Anansi', they think of 'Anansi and Dry-Bones'" (interview with author,

November 2005). In the tale recorded by Jeffery-Smith, Dry-Head, like the stereotypical obeahman, is described as living deep in the forest; he is "an apparition frightful and terrible", an "uncanny creature" who makes Anansi "shudder visibly" (1899, 45–47). However, while both Death and Dry-Head/ Dry-Bone can overpower Anansi, he is also able to evade or challenge them, a skill which pays homage to his Asante past as a creature of two worlds.

These tales clearly demonstrate that Asante Anansi tales were adapted to absorb and reflect the experiences of enslaved Africans and their descendants on the Jamaican plantations. In his inherent ambiguity and transgression of the boundaries between life and death, his ability to subvert hierarchies of power, and his continued connection to West African practices, Anansi both challenged and resisted European cultural dominance in Jamaica. The following chapter will demonstrate the ways in which Anansi could be implemented as a resource for resistance among Jamaican slaves and Maroons in their struggle for survival and fight for freedom.

Figure 8. Illustration of Anansi in Pamela Colman-Smith's *Annancy Stories* (1899, 26).

3

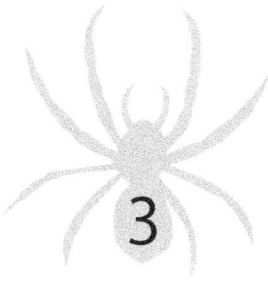

Anansi Tactics

A Resource for Resistance

African-Jamaicans somehow found within themselves the obstinate strength to reject, and to continue to reject, slavery. They did so by Maroonage, sabotage and sporadic outbursts of violence. (Sherlock 1998, 193)

WHILE IT CANNOT BE CLAIMED that the demise of slavery was the direct result of slave resistance, through their perpetual struggle against their enslavement, Jamaican slaves undoubtedly hastened the abolition of the British slave trade. With its high concentration of slaves, large numbers of new African imports, absentee owners, wild terrains and brutal plantation regime, Jamaica experienced more slave rebellions than any other island in the Caribbean (Heuman 1994, 34). Without the slaves' continual display of frustration and contempt, Jamaican planters may have been able to successfully persuade the British government that slaves were resigned to their enslavement. The British government, however, were forced to question the legitimacy of slavery in the early nineteenth century. Violent and non-violent resistance may not have toppled slavery, but it undeniably speeded up the process of emancipation (Matthews 2006, 8).

In this chapter I explore Anansi's role in plantation Jamaica through an analysis of "Anansi tactics"; a term I have coined to describe Anansi-style approaches and actions used by Maroons and slave rebels, which are illustrated in the Anansi tales. Anansi-style tactics took on a variety of forms in plantation Jamaica. Often aimed at hitting Massa in his pocket book – "where it hurt" (Burton 1997, 49) – they included lying, stealing, cheating, working slowly, self-mutilation, wilfully misunderstanding instructions, breaking tools and machinery or setting fire to the fields before harvest time (Burton 1997, 48–49; Sherlock 1998, 128). Expressions of dissatisfaction also took the form of direct acts of revenge; spitting in or poisoning Massa's food and the ultimate acts of self-protection and defiance (or protection of kin), suicide, infanticide and abortion (Burton 1997, 49).[1]

Jamaican storyteller Brother Martin described Anansi as a "very, very dangerous weapon" – a character with "techniques" who could "stir up mutiny" (interview with author, December 2005). In support of Brother Martin's interpretation, I argue that Anansi tales were mechanisms of survival and sources of wisdom or knowledge, which could, in certain contexts, translate into resources for resistance and play a part in fuelling slave revolt.

For the purposes of this chapter, it is vital to analyse the implications of the terms "survival" and "resistance". Jamaican author Velma Pollard maintains that Anansi stories were, for plantation slaves, ultimately tales of survival against the odds, which could at times inspire resistance strategies, but only if slaves were already in "resistance mode":

> I would say survival rather than resistance. The two are linked; one is a half way house to the other. I would say *always* survival, *sometimes* resistance. I think that the morals are survival morals. You would already have to be in a resistance mode. The stories are not going to turn anyone into freedom fighters. If you are already in that mode you can look at it and interpret it in that way. (Interview with author, October 2005)

While I maintain that Anansi was a resistance figure for the Jamaican slaves, I agree with Pollard when she points out that although survival and resistance are linked, they also differ. One must survive in order to resist, and at times techniques of survival are techniques of resistance. However, while resistance always implies acts *against* the system, survival can at times result in a compliance *with* the system. This chapter demonstrates how the Anansi folktales had the *potential* to encourage acts of resistance through their depiction of the deployment of "Anansi tactics" key to the survival of rebels and runaways. However, I also point out the differences between survival and resistance and examine how acts of survival, such as those used by the Jamaican Maroons, can occasionally *undermine* slave resistance. I acknowledge the problems involved in the interpretation of Anansi as a resistance figure, demonstrating that Anansi's relationship with power is both complex and ambiguous. The alliance and apparent collaboration of the Maroons with the British illustrates the problems involved in interpreting "Anansi tactics" as techniques of resistance. For both the Maroons and Anansi, the drive for survival and freedom can result in the oppression of others.

As well as examining Anansi's role in slave resistance, this chapter explores the inspirational role played by other Jamaican resistance heroes, mythological and real, in the struggle against the colonial order. Craton explains that "Anansi, the spider-trickster of West African and Afro-Caribbean folklore, was as significant a hero to the slaves as were the real life heroes of Cudjoe, Nanny and Tacky" (1982, 16). In Jamaica, the stories of the feats of these resistance figures centre on their triumph over dominant forces through bravery, intelligence and strategy. Indeed, as De Souza argues, "Anansi stands as the epitome of resistance to the given order . . . coming from the forested countries of West Africa, Anancy becomes a trope of *marronnage*, escaping plantation life for the wooded hinterland of folktales" (2003, 353). Storyteller Jean Small also makes connections between Anansi and the Maroons:

> I think it is [Anansi's] ability to adapt and recreate and his cleverness that captivates. The African slaves did that in the exigencies of their circumstances. Especially when they came to the Caribbean; in Maroonage, they had to adapt and recreate. That is what Maroonage is. The Maroons had to recreate their lives; they want to make a drum, but the trees were different. A different wood. They don't sound the same, but they make music all the same. (Interview with author, November 2005)

Away from European influence, the Jamaican Maroons developed a culture deeply rooted in West African traditions. Tanna writes that "the Maroons are one of the few groups who have consciously guarded their oral traditions" (2000, 54). Due to the prevailing influence of Akan cultural forms on Maroon society, as well as continued emphasis and reliance on oral history and storytelling, Anansi tales played a central role in Maroon culture throughout the plantation period, and, indeed, into the present day. Furthermore, due to the relative isolation of Maroon society, many of their Anansi tales remain closer to their African versions. Beckwith interviewed numerous Maroon storytellers while researching her collection *Jamaica Anansi Stories* and explains that they shared unique tales with her: "especially in the Cockpits, old tales were told to me by Maroons that I did not hear elsewhere on the island" (1924, 221). Beckwith describes how the Maroon men (while the women were presumably attending to domestic and family duties or working in the fields) would break the taboo of telling Anansi tales in the daytime and spend "a whole morning or even all day telling stories, first one and then another taking his turn and each making way for the other with a fine sense of fair play" (p. 292).

Anansi and other resistance figures, both real and fictional, formed part of a multitude of cultural resources used by slaves and Maroons in their struggle for freedom. Through song, music, dance and folktales, Maroons and slaves preserved their humanity and their heritage: they challenged the system of their oppression and kept alive faith in the possibility of freedom. On a more practical level, these cultural forms played a didactic role, teaching techniques of survival and resistance that could be implemented within the confines of their enslavement or as escapees. Stick-fighting dances trained slaves for fighting; defiant and secret messages were communicated through instruments and song; and the Anansi folktales illustrated the "Anansi tactics" implemented on plantations, as escapees, or in open revolt (Burton 1997, 30).

Anansi Tactics: Jamaican Maroons

> [Animal trickster tales] were not merely clever tales of wish-fulfillment through which slaves could escape from the imperatives of their world. They could also be painfully realistic stories which taught the art of surviving and even triumphing in the face of a harsh environment. (Levine 1977, 115)

Although Maroon communities developed on several Caribbean islands including Haiti, Suriname and St Vincent, the Jamaican Maroons specifically were considered the greatest threat to the colonial forces. The following section provides an overview of Jamaican Maroon history before moving on to demonstrate the links between the survival techniques used by Maroons and those employed by Anansi. There are inevitably gaps in the historiography of oral cultures, and the historiography of the Jamaican Maroons is no exception. Before the Maroons signed treaties with the British, invisibility, secrecy and stealth were key to their survival. Documentation of pre-treaty Maroon society therefore remains fragmentary. The collection of data on Maroon political and social organization really begins in the 1730s when British expeditions, aiming to capture and eradicate the groups, generated written reports (Kopytoff 1978, 298). Existing historical accounts conclude that the first Jamaican Maroons were slaves who had escaped under the Spanish regime,[2] who were later joined by slaves taken from the Gold Coast by the British. "Coromantee" or Akan rebellions started by slaves from the former Gold Coast were frequent in the late seventeenth and early eighteenth centuries and Maroon numbers were augmented by these rebellions (p. 295).

As discussed in previous chapters, slaves imported from the Gold Coast were named "Coromantees" by Europeans. However, Cassidy and Le Page explain that the umbrella term "Coromantee" was not only used to describe Akan slaves but, "in Jamaica, those who escaped and joined the Maroons, came to dominate them and gained a reputation for fierceness" (Cassidy and Le Page 2002, 131). The term also refers to what was considered "the secret language of the Maroons" (ibid.). There is some evidence to suggest that the "secret language of the Maroons", based on Twi language structures, is still alive in Jamaica today, and Isaac Bernard, from the Maroon community in Moore Town, claims to speak it.[3] As chief *abeng* player of the Moore Town community, Bernard is undoubtedly a man in touch with his Maroon traditions. The abeng is a cow or goat horn used by Maroons to pass information on to one another, and the code for the horn signals is apparently "never divulged" to outsiders (p. 2). When asked how he had learned what he called the "Coromantee" Maroon language, Bernard explained it had been passed on to him by the spirits of his ancestors:

> **Isaac Bernard**: It is gift. A gift. Your ancestors who are died and gone they just pass that over, you are just born in it, a gift. And you learn the word by yourself. By the spirit.
>
> **Emily Zobel Marshall**: By the spirit of the ancestors that live within you?
>
> **Isaac Bernard**: [*Nods in agreement*] Uh huh, uh huh. Anything that is far away from you they bring it to you. And tell you. (Interview with author, November 2005)

Figure 9. Maroon *abeng* blower Isaac Bernard, Comfort Castle, Jamaica. Before showing me his abeng, Bernard spat on it with white rum, to appease the spirits of his ancestors. (Photograph by the author, 2005.)

In 1739, the Jamaican Maroon communities signed treaties with the British who promised them semi-autonomy on the condition that they would hunt and return runaway slaves. After pledging they would aid the British in the capture of runaways, the Maroons became a formidable force in the policing of escapees. They turned the hide-outs in the forests and peaks of the Blue Mountains and limestone craters of Cockpit Country into dangerous terrain for those on the run. While slaves both feared the Maroons and admired their achievements, friction grew between the two groups, as Craton explains: "Though envious of the Maroons' practical freedom and style of life, slaves resented the savage efficiency of their policing activities and the arrogant way they swaggered through plantations, making free with slaves' provisions, stock and womenfolk" (1982, 66).

Evidence suggests that there was a drop in the numbers of runaways after the signing of the treaties, and that members of small bands of runaways who had not joined the Maroons were so fearful of Maroon capture they committed suicide or returned to the plantations (Campbell 1988, 158). However, Gardener wrote in 1870 that there were still 2,555 (non-Maroon) runaways at large on the island, some of whom were operating as roaming gangs and others who formed small villages in the mountain regions of the island (cited in Campbell 1988, 158). Nevertheless, it seems that few of these runaways survived up to emancipation, largely, as Mavis Campbell explains, "because of co-opted Maroons' activities against them" (1988, 158).

Jamaican Maroons formed two separate communities on the island, the Windward and the Leeward. Both communities developed political institutions outside the influence of colonial society, which were undermined after signing treaties with the British. The treaties imposed a uniform administration on the communities with superintendents posted in every settlement, making each less distinct from the another and undermining their traditional military organization. The early years of political development were therefore eroded by a treaty aimed at ensuring independence, but which ultimately led to the disintegration of the Maroons' sociopolitical cohesion and autonomy (Kopytoff 1978, 307).

The post-treaty Maroons were an ambiguous force within the power structures of plantation Jamaica. Some historians argue that they did not keep to the stipulations of the treaties, and that they helped runaways escape while at the same time pretending to pursue them. Reflecting this argument, James Lockett states "there were indications that Maroons discharged their responsibility in a half-hearted, far from satisfactory manner" (Lockett 1999, 7–8). It seems, however, that this was far from the case, and they exercised their role as slave-catchers with alarming efficiency. Like Anansi, the Jamaican Maroons, regardless of their awareness of the terrifying experiences faced by a runway, turned on the vulnerable to ensure their continued existence.

Jekyll's version of "Wheeler" (1966) and Beckwith's recording of the same tale, entitled "Fling-a-Mile" (1924), are good examples of how Anansi, having experienced something dreadful himself, is willing (or even keen) to subject others to the same fate. In Beckwith's version, the story starts with Anansi going to catch fish from the river and discovering a mysterious hole. He puts his hand inside and something holds him fast: "Who hold me?" he asks. "Fling-a-mile", comes the reply. Anansi says: "Fling me a mile mak I see." "The t'ing wheel Anansi, wheel him, an' fling him one mile from the spot. When Anansi drop, he nearly knock out his senses." Anansi then "went an' get six iron fork an' six wooden one an' stick up at the place where he drop" (Beckwith

1924, 43). Anansi takes several unsuspecting animals along to the hole – hog, goat and dog – who, when flung a mile (or in Jekyll's version, "wheeled" [1966, 152–55]), are dashed to pieces on his well-positioned spikes and stakes: "the t'ing fling Dog whee'-a, whee'-a, whee', an' dash him one mile on the stake. Dog drop on the stake dead. Anansi tak up Dog, put him in his bag an' said, 'A well wan' you fe eat long time!'" Monkey eventually stops the grisly slaughter by tricking Anansi into putting his own hand into the hole; "Monkey tak off him hat an' run half way an' stop where he could see when Anansi drop. Anansi drop on de fork an' belly burst 'tiff dead! An' Monkey take him an' put him in his bag, take him go eat him" (Beckwith 1924, 43–44). Here we see Anansi, in his unending search for food, deciding to avoid pitting his wits against the powerful and instead annihilate weaker animals. In one of the few tales where Anansi gets his comeuppance, we see how "Anansi tactics", exemplified explicitly by the tactics implemented by Jamaican Maroons, are used against the vulnerable in the drive for survival.

This legacy is an uncomfortable one for Jamaicans and Maroons today. When asked her position on Maroon involvement in the capture of runaways, Maroon community worker Linnette Wilks explained that "personally I have no problem with that, they were the first police and [capturing runaways] is the job of the police" (interview with author, November 2005). However, she added:

> It was horrible but it was also a ploy, because nine out of ten times nobody was captured. A lot of runaways found refuge with the Maroons, because the Maroons knew when that treaty was signed that it was not worth the paper it was written on. If this is what is going to get us freedom, then so be it . . . but you're a fool to think I am going to work for you.

Campbell refuses to apply revolutionary political theory, such as that of Marx or Fanon, to her interpretation of Maroon history. Maroon societies not only captured slaves but kept slaves themselves, and while they should be respected for their "independent spirit", Campbell states that they cannot be seen as "true revolutionaries or even reformers, seeking to transform the society from one of servitude to freedom" (1988, 13). Unlike Jamaican plantation slaves who, as we shall see in the course of this chapter, aimed for the total freedom of all slaves and the establishment of a black leadership during several rebellions and plots, the Maroons did not strive for collective action or the upheaval of the plantation power structure.

Despite the complex historical legacy of the Maroons, they are still celebrated in Jamaica for their incredible feats of survival and resistance. On numerous occasions, small groups of Maroons with few weapons were able to triumph over large bands of heavily armed British soldiers. They outmanoeuvred the British not only through guerrilla tactics but through their awareness of the plans and movements of whites which were gleaned via advanced communication networks and intelligence systems established within the plantations (Sherlock 1998, 137). In his eighteenth-century study of the Maroons, R.C. Dallas explains the success of the tactics they used against the British:

> [Although] some may be inclined to think a Maroon insurrection a petty warfare of unskilful Negroes . . . Officers who served in this campaign will allow that the events of it, and the tactics opposed to them, if not so grand as those that fill the Grecian and Roman pages of history, were at least some of the most singular and embarrassing . . . Negroes defied the choicest troops of one of the greatest nations in the world and kept an extensive country in alarm. (Cited in Campbell 1988, 7)

The Maroons employed psychological techniques to intimidate their enemy: terrifying soldiers with taunts, urging blacks and Indians among the militiamen to desert their ranks, and bragging about the quality of life they enjoyed in the bush. One militiaman reported that the Maroons made "hideous and terrible" noises to intimidate them, which made the soldiers "imagine their Number and Strength much greater than it really was" (cited in Craton 1982, 84).

The Maroons may have been guilty of collaboration, but Campbell believes that their story "represents another chapter in the history of the human struggle for the extension of freedom – with all the contradictions" and that writing and understanding the history of the Maroons is a matter "of practical importance" (1988, 13).

Of the two distinct groups formed by the Maroons, the Leeward community had the strongest sociopolitical structure. It was based in the north-western parts of the island on the fringes of Cockpit Country, which was described by the Earl of Balcarres, when fighting the Maroons in the 1790s, as "a Country of Rocks beyond description – wild and barren into which no white person has ever entered" (cited in Campbell 1988, 219). The Leeward community was dominated by escapees from the Sutton uprising of 1690, involving five hundred slaves, most of them of Akan origin, who had escaped to the mountains in their hundreds (Craton 1982, 77). An eighteenth-century manuscript reports that the runaways joined forces with the existing Maroons and "a common Akan heritage may have provided a special bond for the new and larger group that emerged" (Kopytoff 1978, 293). The Leeward Maroon leader, Cudjoe (born circa 1700 and of Akan heritage), developed a highly autocratic system which Craton explains was "cemented in kinship in the style of the Asante" and organized into central chiefdoms (1982, 77).

The Windward Maroons, based in the north-eastern parts of the island, lacked the homogeneity of the Leeward Maroons and are described by Barbara Kopytoff as having a political system which was "shallow" and "weakly institutionalised" (cited in Craton 1982, 77). They formed settlements in the Blue Mountains, and intersecting John Crow Mountains, and are described by historians as more ruthless and violent in their interactions with whites than the Leeward group (Kopytoff 1978, 290).

The Leeward and Windward Maroon societies developed autonomously from one another as they were geographically separated by British settlements. There was an element of rivalry between the two groups, which continues to exist (albeit in playful form) today (Kopytoff 1978, 290; Craton 1982, 214). When interviewed in 2005, Captain Smith of the Windward Maroons stated that "naturally, no doubt about it, Moore Town – it is the *number one* Maroon community in Jamaica" (interview with author, November 2005), and Bernard claimed that it was the "most *witty* Windward Maroons" who developed the Jamaican Anansi tales. However, the Leeward and Windward communities now join together in shared cultural celebrations. As Bernard explained: "from Moore Town, Charles Town, to Scots Hall to Accompong to St Elizabeth. Different tribes, but we all are Maroons, we celebrate together" (interview with author, November 2005).

Kopytoff states that the Leeward and Windward Maroons both had approximately five hundred members by 1739, with one major settlement and several minor outposts in each community (Kopytoff 1978, 301). Craton, however, maintains that, by the mid-1720s, they were said to number "no longer in the hundreds but in the thousands" (Craton 1982, 81). Each Maroon group initially struggled to keep their communities thriving due to the lack of female members and reliance on new recruits to make up their numbers. As competition for women caused problems, both developed different laws to deal with the issue – among the Leeward Maroons women were allowed several partners, whereas among the Windward, a man could be killed for "lying with another man's wife" (Kopytoff 1978, 301–3).

Among the Leeward Maroons, women played subordinate roles, and those stolen from the fields of the plantations were treated in the same way as slaves. Craton explains that gender divisions were based on those of the Asante: the men were warriors and, while they roamed the hills and hunted, polishing the arts of "concealment and ambush, marksmanship and subtle communication over long distances by means of drum, conch shell and cow horn (*abeng*)", women attended to the domestic sphere and the growing of crops (1982, 78).

Cudjoe, described by Sherlock as a "short, powerfully built man with a humpback" (1998, 136), enforced a policy among the Leeward Maroons of dealing with whites that involved "minimal provocation" (Craton 1982, 82). Although his Leeward Maroons were highly skilled in the use of firearms, he prohibited the killing of whites. Furthermore, in an effort to maintain his policy, he imposed strict limitations on the raiding and plundering of property and plantations (Kopytoff 1978, 196, 297). Cudjoe also enforced the speaking of English in his community, possibly in an effort to eliminate any ethnic rivalries among his people. Kopytoff argues that it was as a result of the high levels of organization and strict laws of governance enforced by Cudjoe that the Leeward Maroons were better able to protect their territory than the Windward group (1978, 324–27).

The Maroons kept numerous West African cultural and religious practices alive, among them the practice of obeah, discussed in chapter 2. Obeah was practised by both men and women, and was central to the lives of both Maroon communities. Obeahmen and women were counsellors and soothsayers who helped prepare their warriors for conflict with ceremonies, spells and charms (Kopytoff 1978, 298). An Englishman who visited Cudjoe's Maroons in 1743, after the signing of the treaties, reported as follows: "they were very superstitious having during their State of Rebellion a Person whom they called Obeahman whom they greatly revered, his Words Carried the Force of an Oracle with them, being Consulted on every Occasion" (cited in Kopytoff 1978, 298).

Although Maroon women were generally expected to attend to the domestic sphere, in the Windward community, the legendary, eighteenth-century obeahwoman named Nanny occupied a position of considerable power. Nanny, described by Sherlock as a great tactician, was believed to have been of Asante origin and to have cut a formidable figure which struck fear in the hearts of British soldiers (1998, 137). Around her wrists and ankles she is said to have worn bracelets made from the teeth of the white soldiers she had slain. One Englishman, sent to facilitate a treaty with the Windward Maroons, described her thus: "The old Hagg . . . had a girdle round her waist, with (I speak within compass) nine or ten different knives hanging in sheaths to it, many of which I have no doubt, had been plunged in human flesh and blood" (cited in Craton 1982, 81).

Nanny played an inspirational role among the Maroons and numerous legends tell of her incredible feats. She is said to have had magical powers; she caught the bullets or cannonballs of the British in her vagina, backside, or petticoats (the tale changes depending on both storyteller and audience) and would fart them back out at her enemies, annihilating them. This is a tale that has strong African parallels, and, coupled with the centrality of the role of an obeahwoman in the Maroon community, it demonstrates a strong African influence at this stage of Maroon development (Craton 1984, 81). Nanny, like Anansi, used her intelligence to overcome her opponents. Bernard pointed out the similarities between the two folk-figures: "You see Nanny was like Anansi too. She was tricky. She used her brains. She use *science* [obeah]. When them shoot her with the gun, she took them an' catch the balls in her behind. Science. She kill thousands of them" (interview with author, November 2005).

Despite sparse historical evidence of Nanny's existence, she is celebrated as one of Jamaica's seven national heroes. There is a memorial dedicated to her in the Maroon community of Moore Town. In National Heroes Park, located in central Kingston, Nanny's statue stands alongside monuments dedicated to Alexander Bustamante, Norman Manley, Samuel Sharpe, George

Figure 10. Maroon security guard "Rocky" beside Nanny's memorial in Moore Town, Jamaica. (Photograph by the author, November 2005.)

William Gordon, Marcus Garvey and Paul Bogle. Like Anansi, Nanny is a resistance figure, famous for her trickery in outwitting the British and a heroine of the underdog. The Windward Maroons I encountered during the course of my research perceived both Anansi and Nanny as emblematic of Maroon bravery and intelligence. Jamaica's seven national heroes could all be described as resistance figures, while Samuel Sharpe, Paul Bogle and Nanny were rebel leaders during the plantation period, reflecting Jamaica's continued celebration of, and fascination with, individuals who have challenged the dominant colonial order.

Nanny organized her people into three settlements and fostered an aggressive attitude towards the British among her followers (Craton 1987, 81). Bernard displayed a respect for Nanny which is still echoed throughout the Windward community today: "British could not conquer her. They made them sign a treaty but they could not conquer Nanny. Countryman send them to sign a treaty with the Maroons, [she] say 'alright', [she] sign the treaty, but they never defeat [her]. She not defeated. She full of tricks" (interview with author, November 2005).

During the eighteenth century Nanny's Windward Maroons formed a cooperative federation famous for its ruthless raids on whites. Her Maroons frequently descended from the mountains armed with knives and cutlasses to attack the settlements below. As they lacked the strong, centralized organization of Cudjoe's group and "the institutions necessary for subtler and less destructive systems of social control", death sentences were implemented regularly to control the members of the community (Kopytoff 1978, 299–324). The rigidity and severity of the Windward Maroons' methods of dealing with deviant behaviour is reflected in their captain's attitude towards discipline today. Captain Smith lamented the loss of the principles of respect in his community and remembered a time when a young man caught whistling (a sign of disrespect) in front of an elder (a "big man") would be severely beaten:[4]

> And if he allowed that big man to catch him up the big man would hit him and hit him, if it's a young guy, you hit him again, and that small guy couldn't go home and tell his father, because his father would have to hit him again. And if the big man was very offended he go and hit the father too. This is not a joke! It is respect; that was one of our principles. (Interview with author, November 2005)

As well as glorifying survival strategies, the Anansi tales reflected the prominence of violence in the lives of slaves and Maroons. Anansi is often depicted as brutal and merciless, as evidenced in "Tiger's Death", a classic Anansi tale of bloodshed. Anansi and Monkey plan to kill Tiger, Anansi's sworn enemy and Monkey's godfather. Anansi prepares some fish for their breakfast and Tiger steals it and eats it all. Monkey and Anansi start to challenge Tiger, and Puss gets involved, saying, "Come, make we beat him off to deat." "Puss catch up a fire 'tick, an' Annancy catch up a mortar 'tick, an' they never cease murder Tiger till they kill him" (Jekyll 1960, 136). Peafowl watches from a tree as they then skin Tiger and salt him. Puss, Anancy and Monkey bribe Peafowl with gold to ensure he doesn't "talk that they kill Tiger" and then devour Tiger together (pp. 135–37).

Puss's easy comment, "come, make we beat him off to deat" and Tiger's murder at the hands of a gang who bludgeon him to death, cold-blooded and relatively unprovoked, suggests a familiarity with violence and death. Although numerous societal rules are broken – Monkey kills and eats his own godfather – the law continues to operate, as the animals must bribe Peafowl to stop him "talk that they kill Tiger". In a cruel act of defiance, the small creatures overcome Tiger, the "big man", and are rewarded for their law-breaking with a feast, food being essential to their existence. This tale could be interpreted as implicitly illustrating the brutality in the lives of slaves and Maroons, and the violent strategies they implemented to survive.

Two major wars were fought between the British and the Maroons, which proved to be a major drain on the colonial authority's resources. Due to Cudjoe's policy of avoiding antagonizing whites, coupled with his leadership qualities, the colonial authorities held a "cautious respect for Cudjoe and his band" and tried to first eradicate the Windward Maroons, who had a more aggressive policy (Craton 1982, 82). The first Maroon war took place in 1734 and was an attempt by the British to disperse Maroon settlements and re-enslave their occupants. After a five-day battle and weeks of attempts to capture the Windward Maroons' villages, Nanny Town was secured by the British and completely destroyed. The network of three villages, which once stood on the highest ridge of the Blue Mountains, soon became a ghost town. Nanny is believed to have led a large group of refugees eastwards to eventually establish "New Nanny Town", eighty kilometres away from the original Nanny Town (renamed Moore Town in the 1760s), and others joined Cudjoe's band (pp. 81–96).

Following the capture of Nanny Town, fighting shifted leeward and increased in ferocity, resulting in Cudjoe's signing, on 1 March 1739, after ten days of negotiation, the famous Maroon treaty. The terms of the treaty with

Colonel Guthrie were as follows: peace was promised forever, the Maroons pledged service to the governor in the event of foreign invasion, and they were to return any runaways and maintain the roads in the surrounding area. Furthermore, they must report to the general once a year; the colonial governor would choose future leaders of future generations of Maroons; two white men would live permanently in the Maroon settlement and the Maroons would, if called upon, serve against rebels. Their judicial process was to follow more-or-less the colonial order, and any plantation runaways who had joined their band within the last two years were to be returned to their masters (if they were willing) and would then be granted a full pardon. Only those taken during 1739 would be returned unconditionally. In exchange, the Leeward Maroons were granted 1,500 acres of land laying between Trelawny town and the Cockpits, on which they could grow crops (apart from sugar) and raise stock and sell them at market. They could also hunt, provided it was not within three miles of a colonial settlement (Craton 1982, 81–96).

In July 1739, the Windward Maroons were persuaded to sign a similar treaty with a few, but significant, differences: instead of standing ready to help police rebels and runaways, they were to form parties to capture runaways whenever required, while recruits who had joined their community within the last three years were to be returned to their masters. Each village would be under the command of a white man, and they were also obliged to "cut such roads as the governor shall order, and that they immediately cut a road, so as to be rideable, the nearest way possible to a plantation" (cited in Craton 1982, 92). It was through these two treaties that the British bound the Maroons to their military, economic and judicial systems and denied them their independence (Craton 1982, 85–91).

The second Maroon war started in 1795 and involved three hundred Trelawny Maroons (who formed a part of the Leeward group), two hundred runaways and fifteen hundred British troops. In the course of the war, the Trelawny Maroons successfully "outfought and outwitted" British forces for over eight months (Craton 1982, 211). Craton explains that the events of the second Maroon war have all the elements of a classic tale: "a desperate cause, a heroic fight against odds, and a tragic outcome deeply discreditable to the winning side" (p. 211).

The Maroons had long been considered a threat by white planters; their seemingly continued state of independence was viewed as a "dangerous abnormality" (Craton 1982, 211). Furthermore, from their geographical vantage point, they controlled the movements and communications of the island's interior. The fears of planters and the colonial government were further exacerbated by rumours of slaves and Maroons being infiltrated by French agents aiming to begin an insurrection on the same scale as the rebellion taking place only a day's sail away in St Domingue, which played a central part in inspiring slave revolts across the Caribbean.

Between 1791 and 1804, slaves in St Domingue, led by Toussaint L'Ouverture, had succeeded in overthrowing French colonialists. Taking advantage of the tension between colonial whites and creoles on the island, the disturbances and new ideologies in revolutionary France, and the disruptions of war between France and the European powers, the slaves of St Domingue successfully rebelled and created the first independent black republic in the Americas. St Domingue provided an example of a successful revolt for slaves across the Caribbean, and rumour of their achievement spread quickly (Craton 1982, 164–212). Whether or not there were agents at work in Jamaica, there is little doubt that these events offered encouragement to rebelling slaves and Maroons, who were to an extent aware of the impact of the French Revolution and the revolt in St Domingue on the colonial powers (p. 211).

The Trelawny Maroons were frustrated by land shortages; the 1,500 acres they had been allocated during the treaty were not proving to be enough space to accommodate a growing population. Their frustrations were compounded by the illegal flogging of two young Maroons in Montego Bay (found guilty for theft) by a slave (which they considered an insult and an injury to their pride), and the introduction of a disagreeable new superintendent into their settlement, who they decided to eject. When considering the Maroons' complaints, local magistrates offered to negotiate, but the Maroons refused, fearing a trick. The general, Alexander Lindsay, Earl of Balcarres, overreacted to the news of Maroon unrest, and martial law was declared on 29 July 1795. All Maroon passes were guarded and the settlements surrounded (Craton 1982, 211–18). As British troops insisted upon their surrender, the Trelawny Maroons burned their own houses and crops, and sent women and children to emergency provision grounds deep in Cockpit Country. Fighting continued, and the militia were ambushed. This resulted in the loss of thirty-four men. With an intricate knowledge of the inhospitable terrain, and sharply honed skills of guerrilla warfare, the Trelawny Maroons were able to pick off the remaining soldiers. After several months there was still no evidence of Maroon fatalities, and they had recruited two hundred male slaves from nearby estates to join their number (ibid.).

Meanwhile, the Windward Maroons refused to show their loyalty to Earl of Balcarres, escalating fears of an island-wide Maroon insurrection. Balcarres had placed officer George Walpole in command of field operations, and Walpole decided the best tactic to use against the Maroons was to cut off their food supply. Balcarres wrote the following in 1795: "as long as the Maroon . . . holds the charms of Food and Freedom, so long will the Negro look up to him. But the matter is entirely changed when the Maroon throws himself on the Negro to be fed" (cited in Craton 1982, 217). The importance of provision grounds is stressed in the Anansi tales, as these small patches of cultivated land ensured the survival of both the Maroon and slave communities.[5]

Implementing the Anansi tactics of bluff and bragging, the Maroons passed "effortlessly" from one estate to another (cited in Craton 1982, 218). At the same time, they turned to plantation slaves for help, appealing to shared cultural and ethnic bonds and painting an idealized picture of Maroon life free from "Backra" law. In a court hearing after the conflict, a slave reported that the Maroons told him that blacks all over the island were just waiting to join the Maroons and that the Maroons, in due course, would kill all those who did not join the rebellion (ibid.).

On 10 October 1795, Maroon captain Leonard Parkinson descended from Trelawny to the Amity Hall Estate with twenty male warriors, four women and three girls and killed a bookkeeper. In addition, as an ultimate act of defiance, he burned the plantation owner's great house and its surrounding buildings. In "Devil's Honey-Dram" (Jekyll 1966), Anansi, like Captain Parkinson, burns his enemy's house. Anansi fights the Devil after his family is threatened, overcomes him by using his intelligence, and then takes his place. The story starts with Anansi's son who keeps getting drunk on the Devil's "honey-dram". The boy is caught by the Devil's mother, but Anansi sends the woman to sleep with a song. While she sleeps, "Annancy (the clever fellah) took his son out an' light Devil house with fire. An' when Devil in the bush look an' see his house is burning he t'row down his gun an' 'tart run in his yard" (Jekyll 1966,

69). The house burns to the ground, the Devil has a heart attack, "An' Annancy take Devil honey-dram for himself an' build house in Devil own place, an' from that day Mr Annancy becomes the smartest man" (ibid.).

The *coup de grâce* in the second Maroon war was put in motion by Balcarres who, impatient to see the end of the drawn-out conflict and its ensuing destruction of lives and white property, sent for one hundred bloodhounds and forty-three handlers from Cuba. His intention was to use the dogs to hunt down the Maroons. On their arrival, the dogs, which had landed in Kingston in December, attacked and killed several people and horses. After hearing news of this imminent threat, the Trelawny Maroons started negotiations with customary stealth and caution: "they sent forward only one or two envoys at a time while the rest of the men kept guard and women and children remained hiding" (Craton 1982, 221). On 28 December, Balcarres gave the Maroons an unrealistic deadline of three days to surrender, but most of them, suspecting deception, decided to continue negotiating. Eventually, five hundred Maroons surrendered on 14 January 1796, forty in February and a final thirty-six in March. On 26 March 1796, Balcarres announced the end of the war with the Maroons: "a People, which Historians assert, were not to be overcome, but would ultimately acquire the Domination of the Island" (cited in Craton 1982, 222). So keen were the island's whites to see the back of the Trelawny Maroons, it was decided that those who had not surrendered within the deadline, and even those who had, were to be deported at the cost of the colonial government. Five hundred and thirty-eight Maroons were deported on two packed ships from Port Royal to the inhospitable Canadian province of Nova Scotia and then, after three and a half years, to Sierra Leone, where they went on to form a semi-aristocratic "creole" elite whose descendents hold positions of significant power in the country today (Craton 1982, 211–22; Lockett 1999, 8, 12; Campbell 1988, 216–19).

In her brief comparative analysis of Jamaican Anansi stories and West African oral literature, Marian Stewart (1982) argues that Maroon communities provided a favourable environment in which Anansi tales and other African cultural forms could be maintained. Stewart states that "folklore is still today the area in which the strongest retention of African features may be observed" (1982, 4). She goes on to argue that the tales were not just a medium for psychological release but had a "practical thrust" (ibid.). For

Maroons as well as plantation rebels and runaways, Anansi stories could provide a form of mental training, illustrating tactics which could be implemented in the field – the arts of cunning and disguise, spying and surveillance, hiding and subterfuge. It is for this reason that the Maroons still see Anansi as representative of the skills that made their survival possible.

Captain Smith of Moore Town explained that storytelling was central to Maroon life when he was a boy. He described the setting in which the Anansi tales were told in his community when he was young:

> An Anansi story, with the parents, is after everybody cook and eat. We used to have pretty moonshines, so you can sit outside when the time is dry. You can sit outside on the veranda like here, and grandma and grandpa would take you up in an Anansi story. When they told the stories you would have children coming from other homes to come and listen. And that would last for late night, and some children after hearing some story they afraid to go home. (Interview with author 2005)

The Maroons interviewed during the course of this research remembered more Anansi tales than other Jamaican participants, and many could recount several tales from memory with remarkable rapidity. On a visit to the Leeward Maroons in Cockpit Country, Roberts recorded four songs from Anansi tales. She analyses these in her article "Possible Survivals of African Song in Jamaica" (1926), stating that it is in "Maroon country" that the "unusually clever exploits of that none-too-scrupulously-honourable spider, Anansi . . . are told and hearted with unfeigned delight" (Roberts 1926, 345).

Roberts recorded the music that accompanied the Anansi tales "Goolin" (told her by Maroon Thomas White and also recorded in Beckwith's collection), "Ya Ya Osa", "Wild Bear in the Wood" and "Anansi Ma Beau". She explains that many "primitive features" of the songs, such as the repetition of the same phrase over and over again, could prove that they are of "Koromanti" origin. She goes on to describe how many fragments of African song have been preserved through their incorporation into Anansi stories, with the characters in the song changing over time, as animals in the new Jamaican environment replaced those found in Africa (1926, 356).

Roberts explains that the "Koromanti" music, which follows the most "orthodox procedure", is the music which accompanies the song in the Anansi tale "The Dumb Wife", also called "Goolin". It is a burial song repeated four times in the story; Beckwith explains that the whole point of the story lies in the constant repetition of the burial song. Anansi tricks the "Dumb Wife" to sing the song by pretending her husband, Goolin, is dead:

An' wife sing now,
Goolin gone, t'de-e-e,
Goolin gone, Goolin gone,
Goolin gone home t'dee-e-e!
          (1924, 124)

Unfortunately, in spite of her rigorous musical analysis, Roberts is left frustrated by the Maroons who, "poor negroes", are in "such a muddle" because their ideas are passed down to them through "gleaning here and there from the experiences through which they have passed", as well as the "tales and religions of various people with whom they have had some contact, slight as it may be". In her view, this inevitably means that "seldom one finds complete logic in any of their explanations and often, as in this case, apparently, none at all" (1926, 358). Roberts, although inspired by Maroon culture, is typically Eurocentric in her thinking and her need for logical, unambiguous explanations, which seems to have denied her a full appreciation of the rich and complex oral culture and history of the Maroons.

Key to the success of Anansi's tricks is his manipulation of language. With his lisping "Bungo talk", described in the previous chapter, and through his use of verbal trickery, Anansi is able to overcome stronger forces. Anansi wins Aso, his wife, from Akwasi-the-Jealous-One by tricking him into saying "Rise-Up-and-Make-Love-to-Aso". With his lies, his bluffing and bragging, his guessing of secret names and use of magic songs, Anansi can both hypnotize and kill with words (Rattray 1930, 133–37; De Souza 2003, 357–58).

The Maroons, like Anansi, specialized in linguistic as well as practical tricks. During the first Maroon war British militiamen reported how the Maroons would taunt their party, urging the black slaves among them to come and join their ranks: "Desertions of Negroes, though they were few, were of great military value to the Maroons, for the defectors took with them plans and tactics of the English. They were not only welcomed but sometimes actively solicited by Maroons who called out to them from the bush during battles, inviting them by artful expressions to quit a slavish life" (1722 letter from Ashworth to Hunter, cited in Kopytoff 1978, 294). Another document underlines this Maroon tactic: "They call'd to our Negroes and Inquir'd after their Wives and acquaintances; and bid them tell them how well they live and if they will go to them they shall live so too, at the same time asking Our Party Negroes to come to them persuading them not to fight for the White Men" (1733 letter from Daper to Hunter, cited in Kopytoff 1978, 294).

Maroons implemented verbal Anansi tactics of boasting, lying, pleading and persuading, as well as becoming masters of disguise, spying and sub-terfuge. Like Anansi high on his web, from their mountainous hideouts Maroons could watch the movements of the whites below them. For example, in the tale "Man-Crow" it is through hiding and watching from a tree that Anansi sees the "yawzy fella" Soliday[6] kill Man-Crow and is able to claim the victory himself (Jekyll 1966, 54–57). As Campbell states: "Maroon spies during warfare were everywhere, and very effective, commanding, as they did, the plains below from their eminence" (1988, 217).

The Maroons also became experts in attacking and ambushing their ene-mies at night, camouflaged and silent. Rupert Kenton, a Maroon from Maroon Town, explained the origins of the name of the area known as "Jagoon Hole" in Maroon Town: "When the soldiers reach to jagoon hole, the walking bushes who is the Maroons who have thatch aroun' their bodies just nip off de sol-diers head of de horses . . . They found dat there are walking tree in de bushes, they couldn't understand it so de rest turn back to Falmouth a dats how de Maroons kept where they live from de white soldiers in Maroon Town" (Grant 1967–69, Ms. 1947). "Jagoon" may originate from the Jamaican Creole term "jag-jag", which Cassidy and Le Page describe as meaning a "large bundle of briars" on which "African influence seems probable" (2002, 240).

On my visit to Moore Town, Isaac Bernard explained how Anansi's skills inspired Maroon survival tactics: "That is a plan of the Maroon you know. Is these tricks of the Anansi. Now, you coming for a little Anansi story. But you're gaining *bigger* than that! Because you want to know *how* Anansi started to talk his story. Through *we* Maroon. We get in de bush. And we *ham-bush*! And is anyone passing through, we a scare them right *there*!" (interview with author, November 2005).

Anansi uses the type of tactics employed by the Maroons in the tales

"Tracking Anansi" or "House of Air", told to Beckwith by Simeon Falconer, who lived in the Santa Cruz Mountains in the parish of St Elizabeth. Here we see Anansi living in a high hidden refuge from which he descends to steal from people: "Anansi live into a tree with wife and children, then go about and robber the others and they can't find where he live" (Beckwith 1924, 20). Even when pursued by his enemies, "Tiger and Bredder Tacoomah dog him and see when he send down the rope and swing up whatever he provide for the family" (notice "Bredder Tacoomah" here is seen as an adversary rather than a son), they fail to catch him. Anansi is too clever for them: "They couldn't eat Bredder Nansi at all; him was the smartest one of all" (ibid.). Here Anansi's tactics reflect those of Maroon raiding parties who descended from the Cockpits to the farms and plantations below to steal slaves and livestock.

A Maroon Anansi tale, which features Maroon survival skills, is "Tiger Catching the Sheep-Thief" (Beckwith 1924, 9–11). Beckwith explains that the "story of the sheep-thief and the disguised watchman is popular in Jamaica", especially in the Maroon parish of St Ann. She observes that numerous Anansi tales are based on a "compensation motive" in which a "rascal" takes advantage of "aristocratic wealth" – a theme which Beckwith claims is unique to the Jamaican Anansi tales and not found elsewhere (p. 237). In "Tiger Catching the Sheep-Thief", Anansi steals sheep from Mis' Madder's flock of twenty. Mis' Madder enlists Tiger to catch Anansi. Tiger eventually traps him and throws him into the sea, but Anansi survives by running under the water: "An' from dat time you see Anansi running under water" (ibid.).

Another tale which centres on watchmen and stealing produce from the more affluent is Jekyll's version of "Annancy and the Old Lady's Field", first recorded in 1904. Anansi tries to make the old lady's watchman steal and eat from the field he is guarding. The watchman refuses, as he knows that if he eats the produce he will fall ill – a reference, Jekyll explains, to a poison used in Africa to protect gardens from thieves (1966, 53). Anansi is eventually able to lay claim to the field after playing a tune on his flute, which kills the owner: "An' when the old lady hear the sing she beguns to dance an' wheel until she tumble off the rock an' dead. An' Annancy becomes the master of the field until now" (p. 51–53). Webster Sutherland, from the mountain village of Hay-field in St Thomas, explained that he believed the Anansi tales taught

Maroons and rebels, like Paul Bogle, practical lessons in survival: "[Through Anansi] they learn ways of surviving; through the story they learn how to hide, and when they hide, what to do . . . This is a Maroon part you know. Even Paul Bogle. When Paul Bogle go down that way you know, the horse him ride, him shoe him *back* way. So anytime him gone through hill, you feel like him gone back" (interview with author, October 2005).

As Sutherland illustrates, Anansi has remained emblematic of Maroon and rebel resistance, as well as survival in modern Jamaica. In the late 1960s, Jamaican artist Michael Auld created a comic strip based on stories of Anansi and Maroon resistance which was printed in Jamaica's afternoon paper, the *Star*. The comic strip that appears here focuses on Anansi's role in the second Maroon war. The cartoon places Anansi at the heart of Maroon resistance, and although light-hearted, illustrates the direct parallels drawn by Jamaicans

Figure 11. Michael Auld's *Anansesem* comic strip. Here Auld imagines Anansi's role in the second Maroon war. (Reproduced by permission of Michael Auld.)

between the tactics used by Maroons and those practised by Anansi. Here Anansi eavesdrops, spies and hides in an effort to help Maroon "friends" against Governor Balcarres and his men.

Not only were Maroon resistance and survival strategies reflected in the Anansi tales, but the tales aided an understanding of the new and confusing world in which new runaways found themselves. For the first generation of escaped slaves, born in Africa and surrounded by the unrecognizable fauna and flora of an unknown territory, the Jamaican bush would have seemed an unsettling and threatening environment. For Akan-Asante peoples, used to living in a village community that stressed a dichotomy between the human and natural world, and viewed the bush as a dangerous place full of roaming spirits and threatening forces, the Anansi tales would have offered a degree of comfort and reassurance. African tales could be manipulated to explain how the new environment came into existence, as well as the reasons behind the unfamiliar behaviour of unknown animals and insects. Furthermore, storytelling was a communal activity, bringing the group together in the evening as the skies darkened. After a day of work, through storytelling, members of the community of all ages could relax, be entertained and enjoy the company of others. For Maroons born in West Africa, it is probable that sharing stories functioned as a reminder of home. One could imagine that, through such stories, Maroons and slaves gained a sense of security and control in the "New World", as well as keeping the memories and traditions of Africa alive. As Levine states: "The didacticism of the trickster tales was not confined to tactics and personal attributes. They also had important lessons to teach concerning the nature of the world and the beings who inhabited it" (1977, 120).

For example, in "Tumble-bug and Anansi" the characteristics of the Jamaican "tumble-bug", which rolls into a motionless ball when threatened, are explained. Anansi is outwitted in this tale after he argues with Tumble-bug over a "bunch of plantain and a keg of butter" and then "boxes" the bug: "Tumble-bug fawn dead. Anansi get frightened, said 'Hi! Tumble-bug, the least bit of fun I make with you, you dead?' Tumble-bug never wake. Anansi run, leave the butter an' the plantain an' everything, take to the woods for it. Tumble-bug wake up an' eat up the plantain an' the butter. After that he fly away after Anansi now" (Beckwith 1924, 46). Tumble-bug finally catches up with Anansi and "Anansi start running an' Tumble-bug after him. He run out to a place call 'Dead man country', get among the dry trash, and that's where he live ever since" (p. 46). As well as providing explanations for the Jamaican environment, stories like this, in which Anansi is outwitted, acted as a warning, encouraging caution and aptitude: if you leave yourself open to trickery, these stories implied, you will be undone. Another implicit warning in "Tumble-bug and Anansi" is that sight is not necessarily the most dependable of the senses. Tumble-bug was not really dead, and for his hastiness and errors of judgement, it is Anansi who must live in "Dead man country" – another lesson in survival in a conflict situation.

For the Maroons, the arts of stealth and silent communication were reflected in the names they gave the areas surrounding their communities: Watch Hill, Land of Look Behind, Wait-a-Bit, Quick Step, Me No Sen You No Come, Don't Come Back and Come See (Sherlock 1998, 133, 142). Popular Maroon Anansi tales focused on illustrating when one must stay silent and when one must speak; for example "Dry-Head at the Barbers", told to Beckwith by Maroon storyteller Charles Thomson. This tale was recounted to me by two of my Maroon interviewees[7] and is a Jamaican version of the Asante tale "How Contradiction Came Among the Tribe" (Rattray 1930, 107–11). The Asante tale is didactic; those who do not like to be contradicted should not contradict others. As well as focusing on silence and stealth, the Maroon version warns against disrespect and untrustworthiness – codes of conduct stressed by the Maroon community – and is one of the tales in which Anansi is killed and eaten. This is Charles Thomson's version:

> Once Anansi and But [Butterfly] made agreement that they wasn't to talk one another. Anansi went to a road and But went to one. Part of the day, Dry-Head [who is bald] was passing where Anansi was working and complain to Anansi that he going out to a ball to-night and he going to a barber-shop to get his hair barber. And after he gone Anansi say, "Pardon me, me Lord! whe' Brar Dry-Head get hair on his head to go to de barber-shop to barber?" An' Anansi fell down an' died, an' But went back an' pick him up an' eat him. (Beckwith 1924, 42)

Another folktale told among the Maroons that focuses on silence is "The Dumb Wife", previously mentioned and told to Beckwith by Thomas White from Maroon Town. The story starts, "Deh was a man name of Goolin. He had a wife. He married him wife fe so many years dat de wife turned dummy

– she couldn't speak to nobody" (Beckwith 1924, 124). Anansi advises Mr Goolin on how to make his wife speak again, telling Mr Goolin that he must pretend to be dead and fake his funeral. The wife starts to sing as she mourns, and once again song is portrayed as a powerful and magical medium of expression. It is also noteworthy that in this tale Anansi asks Mr Goolin if he "had a mountain groun"; this is another reference to the crop-growing provision grounds in the mountains used by both Maroons and ex-slaves.

Similarly to Jekyll's "Tiger's Death" (Jekyll 1960, 135–37), the Anansi tale "Shut Up in the Pot", found in Beckwith's collection, told by Simeon Falconer, illustrates the brutality of survival tactics (Beckwith 1924, 20). Beckwith explains that "this common African story is not popular in America in this form, either because the idea is repulsive or because it is too simple to make a good story" (p. 242, notes). The story starts as follows:

> There was a very hard time, no food whatsoever could they get, so Anansi him family well fear. So when Bredder Tiger and Bredder Tacoomah go see him, he tell them for last three or four days his wife and children didn't eat bread. Say they will go back home and send him some of 'em food, and the two go back from Nansi yard and just dodge him now and hear his wife call, "Heah! dinner ready!" (p. 20)

It turns out that Anansi and his family do have food. He tells Bredder Tiger and Bredder Tacoomah (who is an adversary here rather than Anansi's son) that they can share his food if they follow his instructions closely, and instructs them to get in a big pot on the fire. He then shuts them up in it, putting a heavy weight on top: "An' he went right outside and tell him wife mus' shove up the fire, mak the fire bigger an' bigger. An' when him come back, them was properly cooked, they gwine eat now, he was tuning up his fiddle, *I got them now! I got them now! Them think they got me, but I got them now!*" (Beckwith 1924, 20). Here Anansi deceives and then eats Tiger and Tacoomah, who were willing to share their own supply of food with him and his family.

Despite the ruthlessness of some of Anansi's tactics, emphasized by his modern critics who fear the rise of violence, trickery and crime in Jamaica, Anansi tales are viewed by present-day Maroons – who are perhaps in a better position to understand and forgive his merciless actions – as a source of Maroon wisdom. Captain Smith of Moore Town told me: "When you think about Brer Anansi and the story and what he has done – how he use his wisdom, I call it wisdom . . . it helps you to improve". He further explained: "Anansi make mischief, but the mischief that he make, it's a merit, it's something that can help" (interview with author, November 2005).

Similarly to Captain Smith, Rocky, from the Moore Town community, described how the Anansi tales used to teach the young people in the Maroon community to think for themselves and reflect on their morals, as well as teaching survival strategies: "because he is very crafty . . . he can get you down into a hole, and he can take you out" (interview with author, November 2005). However, while he insisted that storytelling was still alive in his community, he lamented the decline of the tradition: "Up here in the culture we are African descendants and we have storytellers, if you have some old people dem a tell you some stories you a gon laugh, dem very interesting . . . whole heap a dem dem know still, but true you no hear dem long time because within these modern times we kinda push away dem things behind de television" (ibid.).

As Lynette Wilkes, a cultural and community activist living in the Maroon country, pointed out, Anansi must be placed in his historical context to be properly understood. There are selfish tricksters in every society, she explained, but for her, Anansi is a character "who is creative, who is a thinker, and a planner". She saw the Anansi tales as a medium through which the history of Jamaican people could be passed down to their children, and she called for a resurgence in traditional cultural forms to help Jamaicans deal with the problems of the present. Like Captain Smith, she interpreted the Anansi tales as a "form of wisdom":

> We have to go back. Once ago you had grandparents who passed on their traditions to their children. Today you have a host of young people who are having children who know nothing at all about themselves in terms of their history. So they have nothing to pass on. They can't tell their child an Anansi story. But they can tell them about a soap that has been going on for twenty-five years on TV. You can pass down your family oral history through the tales. It is a form of wisdom. (Interview with author, October 2005)

Anansi Tactics: Rebel Slaves

During rebellions against the colonial regime, slaves and Maroons, already deeply locked into a survival mode, fought the system of their oppression through overt displays of resistance. Resistance against the regime began before the arrival of African slaves to the Americas. African-born slaves attacked European buyers and traders on the West African mainland, on the coast and the Middle Passage, exemplified by their seizures of the trading ships *Thomas* (1797) and the *Amistad* (1839) (Craton 1982, 24). According to Walvin, 10 per cent of all slave voyages across the Atlantic experienced some type of slave resistance or attack (Walvin 1999, 40). As Craton explains, "Few voyages were ever completed without the discovery or threat of slave conspiracy, and no slaving captain throughout the history of the Atlantic slave trade ever sailed without a whole armoury of guns and chains, plus as many white crewmen as he could recruit and keep alive to act as seaborne jailers" (1982, 24).

On the slave plantations, the stories of the courageous feats of Nanny, Cudjoe, Bogle, Tacky, Sharpe and others were a source of encouragement and strength to slaves, as were the tales of Anansi. Sherlock's tale, "From Tiger to Anansi" (1956, 3–10), another Jamaican version of the Asante tale "How It Came About That the Sky-God's Stories Came to Be Known as 'Spider-Stories'", demonstrates the way Anansi had the power to overturn the structured hierarchy of his environment (Rattray 1930, 52–58). The story starts with Tiger being introduced as the strongest animal of the forest and Anansi as the weakest:

> At evening when all the animals sat together in a circle and talked and laughed together, snake would ask:
>
> "Who is the strongest of us all?"
>
> "Tiger is the strongest," cried Dog. "When Tiger whispers the trees listen. When Tiger is angry and cries out, the trees tremble".
>
> "And who is the weakest of all?" asked Snake.
>
> "Anansi," shouted dog, and they all laughed together. "Anansi the spider is the weakest of all. When he whispers no one listens. When he shouts everyone laughs". (Sherlock 1956, 3)

The weakest and the strongest animals of the forest come face-to-face one day and Anansi asks Tiger a favour – for all the stories told in the forest to bear his name. Tiger likes the stories and wants to keep them as Tiger stories, so he sets Anansi a seemingly impossible task – to bring Brer Snake to him alive. Once Anansi has completed the task, by using Snake's pride against him: "never again did Tiger dare to call these stories by his name. They were the Anansi stories ever after, from that day to this" (p. 10).

While there were numerous rebellions in the history of colonial Jamaica, slaves also continually practised small and covert acts of resistance against the colonial powers. These tactics helped slaves not only survive physically, but also emotionally, aiding the welfare and preservation of their pride and humanity. Interactions between slaves and their white "masters" were infused with a multiplicity of forms of duplicity and trickery. Ambiguous folktales, riddles and proverbs, rude and scorning songs and jokes, and plantation gossip all created space for psychological resistance to a dominant ideology. Anansi's behaviour reflected the need to become experienced actors and devious manipulators of the system when faced with the constant brutality of the plantation environment. It is clear, as Levine explains, that the Anansi tales were used as a medium through which slaves could learn and celebrate these methods of subtle subversion: "The trickster's exploits, which overturned the neat hierarchy of the world in which he was forced to live, became their exploits, the justice he achieved, their justice; the strategies he employed, their strategies. From his adventures they obtained relief; from his triumphs they learnt hope" (Levine 1977, 114).

While the Jamaican slaves implemented strategies of subversion under the noses of planters, real freedom came at an enormous cost, as revolt or escape could lead to devastating repercussions. Slaves discovered plotting or captured during violent uprisings would be tortured, killed, or forced to endure the murder of family members or loved ones. Covert Anansi tactics were safer than a direct challenge to the system and could take numerous forms, such as non-cooperation (working and walking slowly), vandalizing machinery and stealing. Furthermore, as Craton explains, "within the plantations slaves discreetly preserved their private integrity, exploiting the planters' fear of rebellion with constant threats, which cost the slaves less than actual revolt" (1982, 16). While covert tactics were used throughout the plantation period, overt challenges to the colonial authorities mainly occurred during the decades at the beginning of the plantation period, when the system was not fully established, and at the end, when slaves believed abolition to be imminent (Burton 1997, 48). However, as Craton maintains and evidences throughout his text, at every stage of the plantation period "there was far more planning and calculation that any whites recognised" (1982, 15).

The diaries of Europeans living and working in Jamaica during the plantation period offer the researcher insights into the dynamics of daily life during slavery, and the impact and extent of slave resistance. This is perfectly illustrated in the diaries of Matthew Lewis, written between 1815 and 1818. During his first few months on his plantations, Lewis seems to have been playing the proud role of "paternalistic master", but his slaves soon made a mockery of him, and he became an unwilling participant in a never-ending game of Anansi tactics of trickery, duplicity and deceit.

Even before his visit to Jamaica, Lewis, a liberal-minded young man new to the plantation environment, was filled with doubts regarding the ethics of slavery and sympathetic to parliamentary initiatives in Britain concerned with its abolition (Terry 1999, xv). In 1812, he made his first journey to the two Jamaican plantations he inherited after his father's death, namely the Cornwall plantation in the far west of the island and Hordley in the far east (p. xiv). Lewis was welcomed with overwhelming warmth and enthusiasm by his slaves, who rejoiced loudly for several days and nights following his arrival. His slaves had cunningly spread the rumour that Lewis was going to set them free: "that Good King George and good Mr Wilberforce have given me a paper to set the negroes free . . . but that the white people of Jamaica will not suffer me to show the paper" (Burton 1997, 55).

Lewis became keen to live up to the image of the generous and kind liberator that his slaves had created for him, and thus enacted the self-satisfying performance of the paternalistic master. The slaves responded with a performance of gratitude and eagerness, not only because they thought that Lewis held the key to the improvement of their situation, but also because they wanted to take revenge on the cruel plantation managers who had mistreated them in his absence. Burton comments on this role-playing: "all the time that Lewis has been acting out his roles as provider, protector and righter of wrongs, his slaves have been pursuing their own individual agendas"

(p. 56). By acting naively and pretending that Lewis was something akin to a demigod, they could create more scope for forms of resistance and non-cooperation, thus improving their lot on the plantation.

Although Lewis infantilized his slaves, he appeared to have secretly admired their rebellious spirit. He was in awe of Adam, a creole and former chief slave driver (which was a position of considerable power) of the Cornwall plantation whose narrative is the longest in the Lewis journal. Adam was accused of poisoning twelve slaves and had "been long and strongly suspected of having connections with Obeah men" (Lewis 1999, 92). Lewis goes on to describe him as "a most dangerous fellow, and a terror to all his companions", but a man "unfortunately, clever and plausible" (ibid.). Lewis does not get rid of Adam, who is nicknamed "Bonaparte" due to his leadership qualities, but on his second visit to the island, he finds Adam causing chaos. Adam has been fighting and attempting to poison and murder other slaves while claiming that Lewis was a soft touch and would give him his old job back as chief governor (chief slave driver) (Terry 1999, xxviii–xxxiii).

Adam's behaviour may have been caused by personal disputes, or it could be interpreted as an attempt to create an atmosphere of disorder and confusion on the estate, thereby undermining the system while displaying dissatisfaction and anger. Lewis states that Adam had "a decided talent for hypocrisy" (1999, 223). He possessed the trickster's gift of being able to convincingly perform a role of servility and subservience while simultaneously challenging the system. This ability is demonstrated by the description of Adam's distinctly docile manner and behaviour between Lewis's two initial trips to the estate and during his court hearing. According to Lewis, Adam "begged [him] to order a little daughter [of Adam's] to be instructed in needle-work" (1999, 145).

In the reports of Adam's court hearing, we see him pandering to the court officials' morals and sympathies, telling them he has been learning to read with the "sole purpose of learning the Lord's prayer" (Lewis 1999, 223). After several obeah items were found in Adam's home (which may have been planted there), he was finally evicted from Lewis's plantation. Yet far from displaying any anger towards Adam, Lewis goes out of his way to make sure that Adam is transported rather than hanged, and ends the narrative: "He is a fine-looking man between thirty and forty, squarely built, and of great bodily strength and his countenance equally expresses intelligence and malignity.

The sum allowed me for him is one hundred pounds currency, which is scarcely a third of his worth as a labourer, but which is the highest value which a jury is permitted to mention" (pp. 223–24). As Judith Terry succinctly summarizes, in her introduction to Lewis's diary, "Adam's narrative is that of a dissident and thwarted leader, and Lewis's sympathy, reluctant, unacknowledged, may be gauged by his last words on Adam, the most recalcitrant slave on Cornwall" (p. xxxi).

Lewis documents the daily forms of resistance and trickery (veiled in performances of servility and respect) carried out by his slaves. He mentions how slaves would reopen old wounds and rub dirt in them and continually chat to passers by to avoid work. He also reports that they not only stole, but also performed simple tasks ineffectively, after which he would find them "sauntering along with their hands dangling" (cited in Burton 1997, 56). The excited celebrations led by the slaves on Lewis's arrival gave them the scope and space needed to perpetrate acts of covert defiance on his plantation. We find out that during the festivities the pen-keeper "accidentally" let the cattle escape and trample over Lewis's best canes (p. 57). Lewis's cattle "trustees" – his drivers, his watchmen, his domestics, and even his "little servant boys" – passed the night "in play and rioting" (Lewis 1999, 127). He complains that "although they were perfectly aware of the detriment which the cattle were doing my interests, not a negro could be prevailed upon to rouse himself and help to drive them out" (ibid.). The slaves' actions are examples of "Anansi tactics" – covert acts of defiance implemented by the dominated weak through "Quashie" role-playing, trickery, duplicity and deceit. Lewis reflects bitterly on the cattle incident in the following quotation, as his best cane pieces were severely damaged: "And so much for negro gratitude! However, they still continue their eternal song of 'Now Massa come, we very well off'; but their satisfaction evidently begins and ends with themselves. They rejoice sincerely at being very well off, but think it unnecessary to make the slightest return to Massa for making them so" (ibid.).

Lewis's journal is littered with evidence of these types of "Anansi tactics" carried out by slaves. Incredibly, he remains, for the most part, completely flummoxed regarding what he considers to be strange and confusing behaviour: "the attempt to make them correct a fault is fruitless; they never can do the same thing a second time in the same manner", he complains (2005, 182).

Lewis goes on to explain how his cook, if praised for a dish and asked to cook it again, "is certain of doing something which makes it quite different" (ibid.). When he asks her to cook salt meat, she cooks nothing but salt meat, and when he complains that there is nothing fresh to eat, she cooks nothing but fresh items. She also cooks erratic quantities of food, and when told there is not enough on the table, "the next day she slaughters without mercy pigs, sheep, fowls, ducks, turkeys and everything that she can lay her murderous hands upon, till the table absolutely groans under the load of her labours" (ibid.).

One slave named Cubina is a master of Anansi tactics. According to Lewis's journal, cats are getting into his home, causing chaos. Cubina is asked to shut all the windows. He assures Lewis that he is shutting the windows tight every night, but still the cats cause havoc in the house. Only when pressed does Cubina tell Lewis that one of the window panes is broken: "[Cubina] had continued to turn the cats out of the door with the greatest care, although he was perfectly conscious that they could always walk in again at the window in [sic] five minutes after" (Lewis 2005, 183).

Another prime example of Anansi tactics, which Lewis presents as another example of "curious" slave behaviour, is Cubina's mode of dealing with the pigeon-house. Cubina, Lewis describes, creeps up on the pigeons and then suddenly pokes his head through the door. Inevitably all the pigeons fly out: "[Cubina] has now no resource but entering the dove-cot, and remaining there with unwearied patience for the accidental return of the birds", which often does not take place "till too late for dinner and Cubina returns empty-handed" (2005, 183). Lewis takes pity at Cubina's "embarrassment" and fits sliders over the holes to keep the birds in the pigeon house, but Cubina "fails" to close one side of the sliders, and the pigeons again fly away (ibid.). After being alerted to his "mistake", Cubina closes the slider, but does so when the pigeons are out, and the pigeons cannot return home. Cubina sits and waits "with exemplary patience, but without success" (ibid.). Having effectively ruined Lewis's practical plan, Cubina is able to abandon the sliders and continue his old routine – undoubtedly looking forward to numerous afternoons spent "waiting" (or resting) in the pigeon house, free from all duties.

Lewis informs us that one of his girl slaves, whose job it is to open the doors in the morning, "never fails to leave three or four closed" and Nicholas, his carpenter, when ordered to make a box for sweetmeats, makes a box "so small that it would scarcely hold a single jar, and then one so large that it would have held twenty" (2005, 184). At last, Nicholas makes a normal size box, but, while it is still empty, he nails it closed "so effectually . . . that on being directed to open it . . . he split the cover to pieces" (ibid.). "Yet", Lewis concludes woefully, "among all my negroes, few are equal to Nicholas and Cubina in adroitness and intelligence. Judge then what must the remaining three hundred be!" (ibid.)

Towards the end of his journal, we see Lewis becoming more and more aware of the tricks his slaves are playing on him; they have turned him into a liberator figure (a "soft touch"), and news of his leniency has spread to slaves across the island. Slaves begin to come to him from other estates with grievances concerning working conditions and unfair treatment at the hands of their masters, and he is bombarded with visits. Plantation production on his estate falls dramatically, as the slaves work less, yet when Lewis broaches the topic he explains that his slaves always have a story for him. A slave will sympathize profusely with his problem and "having said so much, and said it so strongly, that he, convinced of its having full effect in making the others do their duty – thinks himself quite safe and snug in skulking away from his own [work]" (cited in Burton 1997, 57).

Lewis eventually begins to understand that he is being manipulated and even, towards the end of his journal, describes his slaves as "persevering tricksters" (cited in Burton 1997, 61). It is apparent, however, that Lewis is to some degree complicit in this trickery and, perhaps unconsciously, he lets himself be tricked. There are signs that he may have partly understood the performances that he and his slaves were playing from the very beginning of his visit but did nothing to change the situation. This is evidenced in his knowledge and documentation of the slaves' challenging behaviour, and his refusal to exact the expected discipline and punishments. While he believes that "their satisfaction evidently begins and ends with themselves'" and is aware of the insincerity of their displays of affection towards him ("so much for negro gratitude!"), he takes no action (Lewis 1999, 127). Lewis, as we can see from Adam's narrative, had a certain admiration for his slaves, as well as a concern for their welfare. He questioned the very ethics of their enslavement, and was therefore unwilling to continually threaten and punish them. Even less lenient

owners and masters knew that violence and threats could not be used continually, and the constant surveillance of each slave proved difficult.

The centrality of Anansi tactics to slave life are excellently illustrated in
the saying commonly used by slaves in South Carolina: "De bukrah [whites]
hab scheme, en de nigger hab trick, en ebry time bukrah scheme once, de
nigger trick twice" (Scott 1990, 163). Moreover, Beckwith explains that
another name for "trickster tales told by Negroes" was "neger ['nigger']-tricks":
"To all . . . story-telling, as to riddling and song, the name of 'Anansi story' is
applied – an appellation at least as old as 1816, when Monk Lewis in his journal describes the classes of 'Nancy stories' popular in his day among the
negroes as the tragical witch story and the farcical 'neger-trick'" (1924, xxii).
This direct link made during slavery by both blacks and whites between the
Anansi tales and "neger-tricks" offers an indication of the extent to which the
stories reflected the Anansi tactics used by slaves in their daily lives.
De Certeau discusses the connections between storytelling ("theory") and
action ("practice"). He explains that the art of storytelling is a form of
rehearsal for a particular mode of thinking (1980, 35). Indeed, the Anansi tales
could be described as a type of toolkit or form of mental revision. As James
Scott states, the slaves' trickster tales were "ambiguous and coded" versions
of the hidden transcripts[8] of resistance, which had the potential to inspire
rebellion (1990, 19).

As Beckwith points out, Lewis records "Nancy Stories" and "Neger tricks"
in his journal, some of which are told by the "picturesque" storyteller Goose
Sho-Sho "with her little sable audience squatted round her" (1999, 194, 254).
He believes that the stories "resemble our quaint old *nursery* tales" and refers
to them with a mocking tone, explaining that he enjoys the simplicity of such
"specimen[s] of negro facetiae" (p. 254, p. 261). Although Anansi is not the
subject of the tales Lewis recorded, and they are full of European motifs,
Goose Sho-Sho's "*nursery* tales" (emphasis added) turns out to be rather more
ambiguous than Lewis had hoped; he comments to his friend Margaret Baron-
Wilson in a letter from Jamaica (dated March 1815) that the "expected moral
of the tale" *must* have been superseded by the storyteller's desire for the "rum
and backy" she expected from him, and he feels obliged to condemn the tale's
apparent commendation of lying (pp. 160–61).

Thistlewood's diaries, written sixty-five years earlier, provide a more chilling account of plantation life in Jamaica than Lewis's journals. The Thistlewood diaries offer an insight into the thoughts, emotions and experiences of lower-class plantation workers, and the strange and corrupt society they formed in Jamaica. It seems that, on an island rife with disease and under the constant threat of slave uprisings, activities such as copious drinking, over eating, degraded sex and violence were often ineffectual remedies to feelings of isolation and alienation. The roles of lower-class plantation workers were those of brutalizers, and their existence appears to have been often lonely and unfulfilling (Craton 1982, 38).

Thistlewood was twenty-nine when he arrived in Jamaica and was given employment overseeing forty-six slaves at a livestock pen called the "Vineyard". While waiting for employment, Thistlewood describes the punishment of runaways: pepper, lime and salt is rubbed into the fresh wounds of a ruthlessly whipped runaway and a dead runaway is dug up, decapitated and his head stuck on a pole as a warning to potential escapees – apparently a common practice on the island (cited in Craton 1982, 39).[9]

Thistlewood soon had few qualms in cruelly asserting his authority as an overseer. Within his first working week he tied his driver, Mulatto Dick, "to an Orange tree in ye garden and whip'd to some purpose (given Near 300 lashes)" (cited in Craton 1982, 39). He went on to have numerous sexual encounters with slave women; during his first year on the island he had sex with eleven of the eighteen women working in his pen. He learned about the lives of his slaves as he talked at length with his partners and socialized with them, details of which are recorded in his journals. He learned that despite the differences in ethnicities, African slaves often became close to their shipmates during the Middle Passage and formed relationships on board which continued onto the plantations. Slaves at the Vineyard Pen told him about the horrors of the Middle Passage and explained how members of their group who had been shipmates had planned a shipboard revolt: "it was agreed to rise, but they were discover'd first" (ibid.).

Thistlewood's diaries penetrate the private lives of the slaves as he regularly entered into their "private" spaces; into their quarters, dances, celebrations and beds. As Burnard illustrates, his diaries portray the details of the slaves' daily lives: "The forty slaves at Vineyard educated Thistlewood in Jamaican and African ways. Dick, the slave driver, introduced him to gungo peas (which were used in soup and served with rice) and slave medicinal remedies. Other slaves taught him how to cure sores and comfort irritated eyes. They told him about Jamaican plants and animals and adaptations of African recipes they had developed in enslavement" (2004, 6). Thistlewood left the Vineyard Pen after getting wind of plots to poison and murder him in revenge for his sexual activities. But before leaving, he paid for a house to be built for one of his regular partners, Marina. He writes in his diary entries in 1751: "At Night gave Marina, Some Sugers, 4 bottle of Rum, some Beef and Pepper Pott, with 10 points of Corn made with Fingo, to treat ye Negroes, and specially her Ship Maters withal, at her house warming – They was very Merry all Night. Sang and drum'd, Guy and Charles, Phibah & Wanicker danc'd Congo . . . Marina herself got very drunk as well as Many others" (cited in Craton 1982, 40).

Edward Long's writings also give us a unique glimpse of Jamaican plantation life and the strategies of resistance used by slaves. His work carries the stamp of racism derived from his firm belief that black people were repellent and inferior beings. Long came to Jamaica in 1757 as the owner of the Lucky Valley Plantation and went on to become lieutenant governor. Craton explains that Long hated Coromantee slaves "with a venom inspired by fear", as they were seen as the instigators of rebellion (1982, 127).

Long recorded the events of one of the most famous and bloody Jamaican slave revolts, known as Tacky's Rebellion. He describes how it involved mainly "Cromanty slaves and very few others", and he goes on to list many examples of non-Coromantee or creole slaves who had stayed faithful to their masters throughout the revolt (cited in Craton 1982, 127). Tacky's Rebellion began on Easter Day, 7 April 1760, while the British were embroiled in the Seven Years War with France and Spain, which, as the slaves observed, had put visible strains on the British armed forces (Heuman 1994, 35). Fifty to one hundred Coromantee slaves stole muskets and gunpowder from a store, killed the storekeeper and advanced to the overseer's house with a Coromantee "yell of war" (cited in Craton 1982, 129). The reason the revolt started in the parish of St Mary, according to Long, was due to the parish's higher concentration of Coromantee slaves and lower concentration of whites than anywhere else on the island. The leader of the rebellion was an Akan slave named Tacky, who, like Nanny, was a religious leader with alleged magical powers (p. 131).

According to Long, the rebels demanded "the entire extirpation of the white inhabitants" and "the partition of the island into small principalities in the African mode; to be distributed among the leaders and headmen" (cited in Craton 1982, 127). Tacky was eventually captured. Long writes that the British troops found him "tricked up with all his feathers, teeth, and other implements of magic, and in this attire suffered military execution by hanging" (p. 131). News of Tacky and his men's bravery spread rapidly and Long states that "the fame of Tacky, and the notion of his invulnerability, still prevailed in the minds of others and continued to inspire revolt" (p. 131). Plots continued to be discovered, as an excited atmosphere of revolt swept the island. Slaves celebrated the revolt in a traditional Akan mode: a wooden sword was found in Kingston that was used among Akans as a signal for war. After hunting down the source of the object it was discovered that Akan slaves had raised a female slave named Cubah to the rank of royalty and named her "Queen of Kingston". Long reports that "in their meetings she had sat under a canopy, with a sort of robe on her shoulders, and a crown upon her head" (p. 132). Craton states that a woman's participation in the centre of a conspiracy was likely to be a "genuine re-enactment of the West African practice, with Cubah assuming the role of the Queen Mother of the Ashanti" (p. 132).

The bravery of an Akan rebel captured by the British is documented by Bryan Edwards, a leading member of the colonial assembly who defended planters against William Wilberforce's criticism of slavery. He describes in *History of the West Indies* (1798) how the British sought to make an example of the revolt's Coromantee captives. Edwards describes an incredible final act of defiance:

> [He] was made to sit on the ground and his body being chained to an iron stake, the fire was applied to his feet. He uttered not a groan, and saw his legs reduced to ashes with the utmost firmness and composure, after which, one of his arms by some means getting loose, he snatched a brand from the fire that was consuming him, and flung it in the face of the executioner. (Cited in Craton 1982, 137)

Planter-governor Christopher Codringdon also provided an account of the resilience and bravery demonstrated by Akan or Coromantee slaves: "intrepid to the last degree, not a man of them but will stand to be cut to pieces, without a sign or a groan" (cited in Craton 1982, 100). It was in the aftermath of

Tacky's Revolt that a legislative committee proposed the banning of further imports of slaves from the Gold Coast but "to Edward Long's disgust, the assembly failed to enact the resolution" (Craton 1982, 139). Planters aimed to create a mixture of ethnicities on their plantations in the future and became highly cautious in accepting large groups of African-born Akan slaves (p. 101).

The Hanover plot of 1776 could have potentially been another major Jamaican rebellion, but it was thwarted by authorities. The plot started in the mountainous parish of Hanover, which had seventy-five plantations and a higher ratio of blacks to whites than anywhere else on the island, with twenty-five blacks to every white. Due to the imposition of rations following the wartime import of provisions to North America, slaves were hungry and the atmosphere of discontent could be sensed throughout the estates. The plot was discovered after a domestic slave was found tampering with his master's pistols. Following this discovery, the militia arrested forty-eight "ringleaders" and executed six of them; a further seventeen were executed following a tribunal (Craton 1982, 172–79).

During the trials, planters were horrified to discover the scale of the planned rebellion, the secrecy with which it was to be executed, and the long-terms goals of the slaves. Although the slaves' plans following a successful rebellion were confused and contradictory – with Akan African-born slaves aiming to set up Asante-style polities, Ibos wanting to live in self-contained forest villages, and Jamaican-born creoles, inspired by the Maroons, aiming for a type of peasant-creole lifestyle – planters were shocked to discover the plot involved over eighty-six hundred slaves from forty-three estates, and was planned over several months by both elite slaves (drivers, craftsmen and domestics) and field slaves of both African and creole backgrounds (Craton 1982, 175–78). The plot was discussed and organized by slaves in the town of Lucea on Sundays, when they were granted some time away from work, as well as at other gatherings such as funerals. Funerals were used as meeting points in other uprisings – on the Lyndhurst Penn estate in 1831 a planter observed and recorded "an uncommon concourse of stranger negroes to a child's funeral" and found that slaves were plotting and singing songs by the "King of the Eboes" (Burton 1997, 84).

The funeral as a ruse is a dominant theme in the Anansi tales, used by (or sometimes against) Anansi to facilitate tricks. In the Maroon folktale "Whitebelly Meks Brer Nansi Kill im Mada", told to Tanna by Accompong Maroon Thomas Rowe in 1973, "Whitebelly" (a direct reference to a prosperous white man) has more corn than Anansi. Anansi fools him into ruining his crop, and, in revenge, Whitebelly pretends to bury his mother and receive money from his dead mother's grave. Anansi kills his mother – "im pawn [grasp] the morta tick [mortar] an im lick [hit] im [her] inna de head" – to receive his own share of cash, only to find Whitebelly's mother was still alive (Tanna 2002, 86). The tale focuses on characters travelling backwards and forwards between life and death; as discussed in chapter 4, this is a reoccurring and transgressive theme in the tales.

The guise of religion and worship was frequently used to cloak illicit activity on the plantations. This is illustrated by Sharpe's role in the emancipation rebellion and will be discussed in the final part of this chapter. Involvement in religious activity offered the slaves a degree of release from the gaze and command of the planters. Again, this is reflected in the Anansi tales: in "Annancy in Crab Country", Anansi pretends to be a preacher to "baptize" Crab in boiling water and, in "How Monkey Manage Anansi", Anansi uses a fake funeral to lure his victims (Jekyll 1966, 71–72, 126–29).

It was revealed during the trials for the Hanover Plot that the slaves most trusted by planters had deceived their masters and been used as messengers and couriers, sent to all corners of the parish to find recruits. "Sam of Coromantees" testified that, after the rebellion, he was to have been made "King of the Coromantees"; Charles of the next estate was to have been made "King of Creole slaves"; and the slave "Prince" from Lucea would have been "Head Man or King of the Eboes" (Craton 1982, 175). Following a signal of the firing of guns, and smoke from burning houses and canes, the main rebels were to kill the whites on their estates, take their arms and organize a slave army to attack the town of Lucea from which they would take control of Hanover, with an aim of spreading the rebellion island-wide (p. 176).

"How Monkey Manage Anansi" is a tale illustrating key conflict strategies of plotting and spying, as well as deception and ambush. One of these specific strategies is sham funerals. In the story, Anansi wants some fresh meat, so he and his wife plot to kill Bro'er Cow, Bro'er Monkey, Bro'er Sheep, Bro'er Goat and Bro'er Hog. They discuss their plot without realizing that Monkey is in the tree they are sitting under, listening. Anansi wraps a barrel up in a sheet,

pretends it is his dead father and invites the animals in to his home to mourn.
Monkey won't go; he "was too clever for him". Anansi hides his cutlass, nicely
sharpened, behind the door and locks it after the animals enter. As they pray,
"He kill the whole lot of them. In the morning Monkey laugh, say – 'Bro'er
Annancy, If me min come in a you house you would a do me the same.'
Annancy say 'No.' Him give Monkey a piece of the meat" (Jekyll 1966, 22).

Jekyll's version of "Crab and his Corn-Piece" also focuses on spying, listening and stealing crops from the master (1966, 126–29). Crab's corns are
being stolen, and Anansi is employed as a watchman to secure the fields.
Crab, depicted as Massa, explains that he will check on Anansi in the night
to see if the job is being done properly. Anansi tries to set him up by sending
Tacoma, possibly in the role of obeahman, because he knows Crab is petrified
of him – but "Ratta was hearing Annancy bargain which he is making with
Tacoma. An' he went home an' tell Crab" (Jekyll 1966, 127). Crab discharges
Anansi and hires Ratta as his watchman, but Anansi tells Puss to go and kill
Ratta. However, "Candlefly was hearing Annancy what he is telling Puss to
do to Ratta, an' he went an' tell Ratta" (ibid.). Eventually Crab hires Cock,
who claims to be able to "watch as any solider", and Dog to watch his corn
(ibid.). Cock demands a gun but Crab only has a flute to give him and a drum
to give Dog. Cock then proceeds to lull Dog to sleep with music, catches the
thief and gains a reward (p. 129).

Just as eavesdropping undermines Anansi's plans in "Crab and his Corn-
Piece", listening and rumour were central to the Hanover Plot, and planters
blamed themselves for "far too casual discussion of political matters" (cited
in Craton 1982, 172–74) in front of their slaves, especially by those sympathetic
to Americans rebelling against British imperialism. The Reverend John Lindsay of Spanish Town wrote the following:

> In our late constant disputes, at our tables (where by the by every Person has
> his own man waiting behind him) we have I am afraid been too careless of
> expressions, especially when the topic of white American rebellion has been by
> the Disaffected among us, dwelt upon and brandished with strains of Virtuous
> Heroism.
>
> Dear liberty has rung in the heart of every house-bred slave, in one form or
> another, for these Ten years past. While we only talk'd about it, they went no
> further than their private reflections upon us & it: but as soon as we came to

blows, we find them on our heels. Such has been the seeds sown in the minds of our Domestics. (Ibid.)

Sensing a division in the colonial ranks, slaves were encouraged to rebel, and they gained inspiration from the philosophies of freedom discussed at the planters' dinner tables. Ultimately, however, it was the constant awareness of the movements and attitudes of whites, who suspected little of their slaves, which made the Hanover Plot possible.

An Anansi tale that may be thought of as analogous and demonstrates the destruction caused by rumour and listening is Jekyll's retelling of "Annancy and Brother Tiger" (1966). After Anansi has persuaded Tiger to take off his fat while swimming and eaten it, he flees to Little Monkey town and tells Bro'er Monkey that he heard a song by the riverside which went "Yesh-ter-day this time me a nyam Ti-Ger fat [*repeated four times*]" (Jekyll 1966, 9). The monkeys love the song so much that they have a ball and play it contin-uously. When Tiger comes looking for his fat, Anansi directs him to the mon-keys. Hearing their song, he thinks they have stolen his fat and wants to fight them. The monkeys call for reinforcements – "lots of soldiers" – from Big Monkey town, and "flog" Tiger and Anansi: "From that, Tiger live in the wood until now, an' Annancy in the house top" (ibid.). It could be argued that this tale not only focuses on the power and rapidity of rumour (Anancy's song), but also makes reference to British troops (Big Monkey soldiers) and planta-tion discipline (flogging). Furthermore, the animals – Anansi and Tiger – must go into hiding, like the Maroons.

Craton believes that the Maroons were perhaps the greatest influence on the Hanover plotters, as the aims of the majority of slaves were shaped "by the Maroons' example as they perceived it" (1982, 177). Although slaves' feel-ings towards the Maroons were ambiguous – they captured runaways and were known to raid provision grounds – the Maroons represented freedom. Whites across the island realized the influence of the Maroons on the spirit of rebellion. One planter wrote of "the very high Idea the slaves entertain of them" (cited in Craton 1982, 177). Some slaves claimed there had been Maroon involvement and support for the plot, and although the Maroons had aided the suppression of Tacky's rebellion in 1760, planters became nervous of Maroon disaffection, even after it was decided that this rumour was untrue.

This demonstrates uncertainty on the part of the planters regarding the loyalty of the post-treaty Maroon. The planters knew that the Maroons, like Anansi, could never really be trusted.

The emancipation rebellion, also known as the Christmas Rebellion, the Sam Sharpe Rebellion or the Baptist War, of 1831 has been described as the best organized and most significant of all Jamaican slave rebellions (Hart 1998, 37). Following the Hanover Plot and the crushing aftermath of Tacky's Revolt, slaves once again revived the idea of overthrowing the systems of their enslavement (Burton 1997, 83). This was a revolt based on knowledge: knowledge that slavery had been destroyed in St Domingue by slaves, coupled with the perceived knowledge that freedom had already been granted to Jamaican slaves by the king in England, but that the information was being withheld by planters in their effort to continue reaping plantation profits.

A significant factor in the emancipation rebellion was that the uprising, which was aimed at bringing about an end to slavery, was not aimed at undermining British colonial rule. As Richard Hart points out, "severance of the colonial relationship with Britain was not one of [the slaves'] demands" (1998, 36), and this limitation in the slaves' ambitions would have significant consequences for Jamaica's future (Burton 1997, 87). At this stage in Jamaica's history, slaves discriminated between the *good* British – the king, Wilberforce and the missionaries – and evil "Buckra" – the local slave owners and planters (Burton 1997, 88). The emancipation rebellion was not, therefore, aimed at creating an independent Jamaica.

Rumour once again played a central role in this rebellion. The slave trade had been abolished in 1807 in the British colonies, and so convinced were Jamaican slaves that slavery was ending, or had ended, that King William IV saw it necessary to issue a decree in June 1831 stating he had no intention of freeing the slaves. This decree was read in churches and chapels across Jamaica on 22 December and greeted with "evident contempt" by the slaves who thought it another plan by their owners to keep them from a freedom that was rightfully theirs (Burton 1997, 88).

The rumour that the king of England had freed all blacks, but the information was being kept secret by whites, was circulated by what Craton calls slave "elites" – literate blacks at the top of the slave hierarchy. Whites at the time did not underestimate the potential danger of these rumours resulting in physical resistance; the rumours "spread widely and uniformly through the mass of slaves implied not only an effective network of communication but also a degree of concurrence between elite and ordinary slaves that deeply disturbed the master class" (Craton 1982, 244). Lady Nugent records how slaves, listening intently to the conversation of whites over dinner, learned of the news of the overthrow of the slave system in St Domingue and realized that even their masters were in awe of the success of the St Domingue rebels. Some whites praised the leaders of the revolution's qualities of "superior strength" and "firmness of character" to such a degree that she reports "the blackies in attendance . . . hardly change a plate, or do anything but listen" (cited in Burton 1997, 83). Lady Nugent understood the power of rumour in inspiring defiance among slaves. In another entry in her diary, she records that the night on which it was learned that a French fleet was headed for the island, a normally submissive and subdued slave boatman looked her directly in the eye and grinned (Wright 1966, 289).

The slaves' conviction that freedom had already been granted was central to the emancipation rebellion, and Baptist leader Sam Sharpe, an educated man and skilled orator who was known to mesmerize his audience, used this conviction to stoke the fires of revolt among his supporters (Craton 1982, 301). Like Anansi in Jekyll's version of "Annancy in Crab Country", who "form himself as a minister" to lure Crab, Sharpe took advantage of his position as a preacher to mobilize the masses (Jekyll 1966, 71–72). Hart points out that it is difficult to deduce whether Sharpe truly believed the rumour himself, as he was familiar with abolitionist material from England, or if he simply used it to facilitate his plan (1998, 37). In order to spread the news of the end of slavery, Sharpe incorporated it into his sermons, took advantage of prayer meetings to gather supporters and organized free-blacks (who could move relatively freely from parish to parish) to spread the news of an uprising. Such was the extent of his planning that the rebels had their own uniforms and gave themselves British military titles, such as colonel or captain, which corresponds to the Maroons whose leaders' titles replicated those of the British army (p. 87).

Sharpe's original plan was to campaign for wages and freedom through passive resistance. It is believed all participants swore an oath not to work after Christmas and demand wages for their labour – only on refusal of these terms were they to start fighting for their freedom (Hart 1998, 37; Burton 1997, 87). Although Sharpe wanted the revolt to use only the threat of violence to achieve its aims, Craton argues that the very idea of a peaceful slave rebellion is a "contradiction in terms" (Craton 1982, 301). Indeed, Sharpe's goal was perhaps unrealistic, given the dissatisfaction of the conspirators during this period (ibid.).

Before Christmas 1831, the Jamaican assembly decided to reduce the number of days the slaves were allowed off at Christmas, which provoked anger and frustration (Burton 1997, 86). On 27 December 1831, slaves were scheduled to get back to work following their Christmas break. Thousands in the west of the island refused to do so and made their demands clear: "We won't be slaves no more, we won't lift hoe no more, we won't take flog no more. We free now. No more slaves again" (cited in Burton 1997, 88).

An estimated twenty thousand slaves were involved in the rebellion, which was recorded in detail by Reverend Hope Waddell, a Presbyterian missionary who visited estates in the parish of St James (Craton 1982, 302). Waddell records how rebels organized beacon fires which could be seen across Trelawny, in St Ann and near the boundaries of St James, Hanover, Westmoreland and St Elizabeth. The sight of the ominous beacons spread panic among the whites; Waddell writes, "the sky became a sheet of flame, as if the whole country had become a vast furnace" (p. 303). In the midst of the chaos, Sharpe travelled from one estate to another, rounding up supporters. By the end of the week, the rebels controlled the entire western interior of the island and had cut off communications (Craton 1982, 308). The troops' task of capturing the rebels proved challenging, as the rebels employed "Anansi tactics" at every opportunity: "Parties of rebels once pursued, even when surrounded, vanished into thin air – or, more accurately, into dense bush, defiles, or hidden caves. Estates were either deserted or peopled by slaves protesting their innocence, while behind and all around the troops fresh fires sprang up, like fierce will-o-the-wisps" (p. 310). Rebels were pursued into the west's high and difficult terrain; after reporting rebels in Westmoreland's "Bamboo hills" a slave named William explained to the whites: "Master you do not know what a wood is up there, the white people will never be able to get to them there, for they can kill them easy without the white people seeing them" (cited in Craton 1982, 310).

Although skirmishes between the rebels and troops continued throughout the parishes, the Accompong and Windward Maroons offered their services and slowly cordoned of the remaining rebels, many of whom gave themselves up (Craton 1982, 309–10). By 1 February 1832, the end of martial law was proclaimed. In the wake of the rebellion, all took stock of the huge damage done to the property of not only whites (around £1,000,000), but also to the provision grounds and homes of slaves (Craton 1982, 11; Heuman 1994, 35; Campbell 1988, 222).

The disparity between the amount of whites and blacks who lost their lives is staggering. Rebels killed in action numbered 214, and 344 were hanged or shot by firing squad, whereas only 14 whites were killed (Hart 1998, 37). Slaves condemned to death were reported by contemporary commentators as facing their executions with astounding calm and dignity, as "many negroes had learned to prefer death to bondage" (cited in Hart 1998, 38).

Sharpe was interviewed in prison in Montego Bay by Methodist minister Henry Bleby, who stated: "I found him certainly the most intelligent and remarkable slave I had ever met with" (cited in Craton 1982, 319–21). Sharpe was reported by Bleby to have said that he was disappointed that "the spirit of revolt, once evoked, was not susceptible of control" (p. 319; 321). It was Bleby who recorded Sharpe's final famous words, "I would rather die on yonder gallows than live in slavery", before he was finally executed on 23 May 1832 (cited in Hart 1998, 38).

Contemporary historical accounts depict the emancipation rebellion as a mass resistance on a huge scale inspired by the sense of the collapse of the power of the planters. It seems that freedom was a realistic possibility, and the rebellion undoubtedly hastened the onset of abolition. Historian Barry Higman argues that "in the political arena in which the legislative decision to abolish slavery was made . . . the [emancipation] rebellion strengthened the hand of the humanitarians and their supporters" (cited in Matthews 2006, 7).

Anti-slavery groups in Britain had been calling for a gradual end to the system of slavery, but the rebellion showed the extreme dissatisfaction of the slaves and accelerated the Abolition Act, which was finally passed in 1833 and brought slavery to an end on 1 August 1834, only two years after the rebellion had begun (Hart 1998, 36–39). Other rebellions in Barbados (1816) and Demerara (1823) had helped to convey the message to the British that abolition was an urgent matter, but the Jamaican emancipation rebellion was the "final and decisive event" leading to freedom for Jamaican blacks, although it was to prove to be a freedom both dubious and questionable (pp. 38–39).

Following the Abolition Act of 1833, the lot of ex-slaves improved little from the days of slavery. Rumours of re-enslavement and Jamaica joining the United States as a slave state, along with high taxes and the "buckra law" of cruel bookkeepers and overseers were factors that fuelled plots in 1839 and 1848, riots in 1859 and culminated in the 1865 Morant Bay Rebellion (Heuman 1994, 39). The Morant Bay Rebellion in St Thomas was an expression of the grievances of post-emancipation black Jamaicans. Ex-slaves wanted real freedom and their grievances were specific: the lack of justice, limited access to land, and low and irregular pay (p. 37). On 11 October 1865, a group of blacks, led by rebel leader Paul Bogle, marched into town, looted weapons from the police station, released prisoners from jail and attacked the courthouse. They killed eighteen soldiers and council members, which led to several minor rebellions in the area. The colonial authorities were so afraid of the rebellion spreading across the island that Governor Eyre executed 437 blacks, flogged hundreds, and hanged Bogle, along with the mixed-race critic of the colonial government, George William Gordon (pp. 37–39).

Although most British abolitionists did not initially support violent revolts, Gelien Matthews argues, in *Caribbean Slave Revolts and the British Abolitionist Movement*, that the "rebels forced British abolitionists to adopt some of the very revolutionary ideas that repulsed them" (Matthews 2006, 9). No longer could slaves be perceived as the suppliant and pitiful creatures portrayed on the famous Wedgwood ceramic medallions,[1] as presented by abolitionists to the British public. Rebelling slaves defied the perception abolitionists had of them and "stretched the angles" from which campaigners were prepared to fight for abolition, while moving the policies of abolitionists "progressively to the left" (p. 10).

During the plantation period, the Anansi tales reflected and encouraged methods of both Maroon and slave survival and resistance in a multitude of implicit and explicit ways. The telling of Anansi tales not only strengthened community bonds and helped Maroons and slaves come to terms with their surroundings, but their consistent theme of enemy defeat through "Anansi tactics" nurtured an attitude of defiance. Victories over whites using physical, intellectual and linguistic skills could be mastered and celebrated through the tales. Anansi's actions in the stories provided a resource of resistance, as they replicated and inspired the tactics slaves and Maroons were forced to adopt. The tales played a part in moulding the quickness, sharpness and guile needed to turn the tables on their oppressors. However, Anansi's actions also suggest that self-preservation is paramount, whatever the cost to others. Similarly to the survival tactics deployed by the Maroons, Anansi is willing to make use of the tools of the oppressors for his own gain.

Figure 12. Illustration by Marcia Brown, "Anansi in Fish Country". (From *Anansi the Spider Man: Jamaican Folk Tales* by P.M. Sherlock © 1956 Macmillan Publishers Limited 2011. Used by permission.)

4

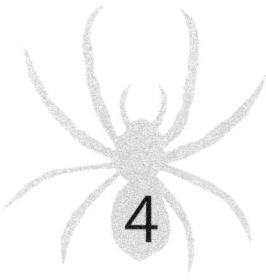

Anansi in the Modern Age

WE WILL NOW TURN FROM an examination of Anansi's capacity to inspire resistance in the eighteenth and nineteenth centuries to scrutinize his highly contested position in twentieth-century Jamaica. This chapter will offer an insight into impact of the Anasi tales' transformation from oral to written narratives and then move on to an exploration of the consequences of Anansi's metamorphosis into a twentieth-century pantomime star. The chapter concludes by questioning Anansi's legitimacy as a contemporary Jamaican cultural icon. It asks whether Anansi is a purveyor of corruption and a dangerous role model, or a source of empowerment in the face of the harsh realties of contemporary Jamaican life.

The recording of Anansi stories in written form, which started in earnest in the late nineteenth century, was a process that brought "new" Anansi's to life – unrecognizable from the plantation trickster – and simultaneously ensured Anansi's survival, leading to global popularity with Anansi stories published and translated worldwide. The earliest recording of Anansi tales available in written form are those told by slaves to overseer Thistlewood (1748–86) and plantation owner Lewis (1815–17), and recorded in their diaries. Milne-Home (1890) explains that Anansi tales were also told to the masters, mistresses and charges of black "Nannies", "Nurses" and house servants throughout the late nineteenth and early twentieth century. Jekyll writes that his tales, originally published in 1907, were "taken down from the mouths of men and boys in my employ" (Jekyll 1966, xxxix). His description of the process is as follows: "The method of procedure has in every case been to sit them down to their recital and make them dictate slowly; so the stories are *ipsissima verba*. Here and there, but very rarely indeed, I have made a slight change, and this is only because I thought the volume might find its way to the nursery" (ibid.).

However, as Scott points out, "any collected version [of a trickster tale] naturally represents a single performance – without the nuances of pacing and emphasis – and it is quite possible that these variants transcribed by slave-holding whites or outside folklorists represent the most sanitised or prudent tellings" (1990, 163). In plantation Jamaica, whites such as Lewis and Thistlewood showed only a passing curiosity in the Anansi tales. It was not until the late nineteenth and early twentieth centuries that interest in Jamaican folklore, predominantly from women of European ancestry living in Jamaica, prompted the collection and recording of numerous Anansi stories in written form. However, as Scott warns, in this initial stage, as the stories moved from the sphere of the oral to the written, the content and function of the tales changed as key elements were altered to appeal to a broader and whiter audience.

One of the first recorded African tales in the Americas is recorded in Thistlewood's journal (Morgan 1995, 70). Thistlewood was told many "Nancy Stories" by a slave named Vine, whose white "husband" was an employee on the nearby Roaring River Estate. Vine visited Thistlewood's house, and he recorded a period of ten days over which she told him "Nancy Stories" nearly every evening. The following is drawn from his entries in September 1768:

> Sunday 18th: Mr Say's Vine told many diverting Nancy stories (as Negroes call them) this evening at my house. She tells them very cleverly.
>
> Tuesday 20th: In the evening Phibbah's Coobah came here. Vine told many Nancy stories.
>
> Wednesday 21st: At night Vine and Abba told Nancy stories, &c.
>
> Friday 23rd: Vine here this evening and told Nancy stories, &c, &c.
>
> Saturday 24th: Vine here, told Nancy stories, entertaining enough.
>
> Tuesday, 27th September: Vine told Nancy stories, &c. (Hall 1999, 160)

No more Anansi storytelling is recorded after this "concentrated exposure" in Thistlewood's journal (p. 160). Douglas Hall comments on Thistlewood's apparent dwindling interest in the stories: "whether in the hearing, or in the recording, there seems to have been a declining appreciation on Mr Thistle-wood's part" (ibid.). However, on 10 May 1751, Thistlewood had already recorded "How the Crab Got Its Shell" told to him by Phibbah (one of his many sexual partners during his time at the Vineyard cattle pen) who described it as a "Coromantee story" (Morgan 1995, 70). This tale is derived from an Asante version, which Rattray also recorded, entitled "How Okoto, the Crab, Got a Shell, and Aberewa, the Old Woman, Got White Hair" (Rattray 1930, 31–35).[2]

Anansi tales were not only told in the presence of whites in plantation Jamaica, but entered the great house – the very heart of the plantation power structure and ultimate symbol of white dominance – and were recorded by its residents. Predominantly told in the great house by domestic slaves and servants who recounted them to the children they served, the telling of Anansi tales was a practice which continued into the late nineteenth and early twentieth centuries, evidenced by the title of Milne-Home's collection *Mama's Black Nurse Stories* (1890). Collector Jeffery-Smith explains that "in the old slavery days it was the custom for the Nana or nurse to tell the breathless little 'buckra pickney dem' these stories at night" (1899, preface). The irony that Anansi tales were told to entertain whites in their houses overwhelms Burton: "Here then is the first paradox of many in this universe of paradox: the Anancy story may have its origin in the Negro Village, but it can be told in the great house, and not just with impunity, but to the evident pleasure of the great house residents" (1997, 64).

The main collectors of Anansi stories in the late nineteenth century were white middle-class women such as Pamela Milne-Home (1890), Ada Wilson Trowbridge (1896), Pamela Colman-Smith (1899) and Una Jeffery-Smith or "Wona" (1899). Their Euro-Christian values unavoidably influenced the content of the collections they chose to assemble; yet as Tanna points out, a few did make efforts to present their material in a "fair approximation" of Creole or "dialect English" (2000, 22). In 1899, an article praising the work of Colman-Smith and Milne-Home appeared in the *Daily Gleaner*. The article claimed that the tradition of telling Anansi tales was dying out due to emancipation and modernization, and it congratulated the two women for preserving the tradition in writing: "It is a pity that they have never been regularly collected and recorded, for the race of the old time house slave woman who held her audiences breathless with the wonderful doings of 'Anancy', his wife 'Crooky' and his son 'Tacoma' is almost passed away" (*Daily Gleaner*, 4 February 1899).

In 1900 another article was printed praising Jeffery-Smith's *A Selection of Anancy Stories* (1899) and criticizing Colman-Smith's *Annancy Stories* (1899). The paper claimed Colman-Smith's illustrations were "not distinctively Jamaican" and she failed to capture "the Negro's dialect" in her tales, but praised Jeffery-Smith for "adding to the folklore of Jamaica even if it is in so humble a way as in Nancy stories" (*Daily Gleaner*, 19 March).

Jeffery-Smith, in the preface to her collection, describes the tales as "quaint legends or traditions of the West Indian Peasantry, which their African forefathers brought with them from the mysterious 'Dark Continent'" (1899, preface). It would seem that whites failed to recognize the ambiguities, veiled criticisms, double-meanings, allegories, metaphors, symbolism, jokes and allusions present in the stories. It was only later, in the early twentieth century, that white anthropologists and collectors started to unravel the coded and defiant messages found in the tales. However, in 1892 Abigail Christiansen did note in her collection of American slave trickster tales that the trickster represents the "coloured man" and gave the following warning: "if we believe that the tales of our nurseries are as important factors in forming the characters of our children as the theological dogmas of maturer years, we of the New South cannot wish our children to pore long over these pages" (cited in Levine 1977, 113). Englishman Jekyll, who spent thirty-four years in Jamaica, made a direct link between Anansi and "the Negro" in his early-twentieth-century collection. He dubiously commented that, for both Anansi and the Negro, language was the "art of disguising thought" and "straightforwardness is a quality which the Negro absolutely lacks" (Jekyll 1966, 53). However, as Rex Nettleford retorts, "Annancy admirers will probably reply that in order to cope with an unstraight and crooked world one needs unstraight and crooked paths" (p. xiii).

By 1900 there were around forty Jamaican Anansi stories in print in journals, pamphlets and books. Jekyll's *Jamaican Song and Story*, first published in 1904 and reprinted in both 1907 and 1966, was the first major collection of Anansi stories. The second major collection, published in the 1920s in several volumes by the American Folklore Society, was by Martha Beckwith, who was an American student of anthropologist Franz Boas. She made four trips to Jamaica accompanied by ethnomusicologist Helen Roberts. Beckwith's tales, transcribed in Creole directly from Jamaican storytellers, present the narratives as oral performances: she carefully captures the nuances of the storyteller's language as accurately as possible. The next major collections of Anansi tales were published in the 1950s and 1960s by Sherlock, who published Anansi tales in Standard English in *Anansi the Spider Man* (1956) and *West Indian Folk-Tales* (1966), and produced a number of small collections for schoolchildren.

The 1970s saw several versions of Anansi tales published as short stories in Standard English, among them Alex Gradussov's *Anancy in Love* (1971) and David Makhanlall's *The Best of Brer Anansi* (1973), *The Invincible Brer Anansi* (1974), and *Brer Anansi Strikes Again* (1976). In these Anansi tales, much of the violence found in the traditional stories is tempered and Anansi is presented as less anarchic and ruthless. For example, in *Anancy in Love*, even though Gradussov integrates a few Jamaican Creole words and phrases into his adaptations (with a list of footnotes entitled "Jamaican expressions translated into standard speech" [1971, 9]), his characters live "happily ever after", Anansi is invited to "dinner parties" and, uncharacteristically, he keeps his promises (p. 30). Although Anansi gets angry – when his rival Rooster runs off with his love interest his "anger knew no bounds" – he refrains from expressing it through destructive acts. One encounters in most of Gradussov's tales a surprisingly well-behaved and rather docile Anansi (p. 9).

However, while several folklorists and authors were publishing somewhat toned-down Anansi tales in Standard English, collections were also being recorded directly from Jamaican storytellers by researchers, all of whom made efforts to retain the tales' stylistic Creole features and remain as close to the oral narratives as possible. David Decamp collected several tales for his work on Jamaican linguistics, which he published in *Creole Language Studies,* co-edited by Le Page (1961). MacEdward Leach also recorded Jamaican songs and partially transcribed tales; these are housed at the University of Pennsylvania. There was also an extensive Jamaican folklore project (1967–1968) conducted by folklore research officer Jeanette Grant Woodham for the Institute of Jamaica (Grant 1967–68). This valuable collection remains unpublished and is housed at the National Library in Kingston (Tanna 2000, 24).

From the late 1950s through the 1960s and 1970s, several Anansi stories aired on the radio in Jamaica, most of which are now housed at the Library of the Spoken Word at the University of the West Indies in Kingston. Among them are *Folkways of the Caribbean: Anansi Stories* (1957) and *How Anansi Stories Got Their Name* and *Anansi and Dry Bone* (1970) narrated by Sherlock, *Why Anansi Lives in a Web* (1967) narrated by Trinidadian poet and academic Cecil Gray, and *The Quarrel* (1970) and *Anansi and the Alligator Eggs* (1970) narrated by Chinese-Jamaican poet Easton Lee. In the 1980s, *African Stories and Stories from the Caribbean* (1989) was also recorded and narrated by Newman and Sherlock. However, while the broadcasters attempted to bring Anansi to life for a mixed audience, their tales were narrated in BBC-style Standard English and retained little of the original flavour of classic Creole Anansi tales.

Before the independence era of the 1960s, while collections of Anansi tales were being published by folklorists and researchers, Anansi also started to be incorporated into educational material for children's literacy programmes. Again, these Anansi tales were less violent and more "accessible" to a younger audience than traditional tales.[3] As there was a drive instituted by the colonial government to push Creole out of the classroom, the stories were written in Standard English in a manner which deliberately ignored Creole stylistic features to emphasize "alphabetic and functional literary objectives" (James 2004, 4). Anansi was depicted as a rogue who changed his ways in an effort to promote Christian morals in school, and typically creole traits and language were portrayed as "laughable" (p. 5). As a result, the Anansi presented in textbooks was a trickster who continually received his comeuppance for his wickedness. However, as Trinidadian writer Cynthia James points out, even the sanitized textbook Anansi played a multifaceted role, as children could still identify with his anti-authoritarian energy, humour and scampish behaviour (p. 4).

Anansi was also used as an educational tool in Britain; in 1936, Newman and Sherlock's short collection of six Jamaican Anansi tales was published for the British primary school educational series "Beacon Library" (book 4 stage). Newman and Sherlock explain in the preface: "If we told you these stories as they are told in the lands where they belong, you would not be able to understand them. So we have to tell them in English, which you can understand, and we have had to leave out the little songs" (1959, 3). They add that readers

Figure 13. Illustration of Anansi by Rhoda Jackson from Newman and Sherlock's *Annancy Stories* (1959, 4)

Figure 14. Illustration of Anansi and his family by Rhoda Jackson from the tale "Work-Let-Me-See" in Newman and Sherlock's *Annancy Stories* (1959, 23).

"must call Annancy by his right name. Say it as if it is written 'A-Nanncy'" (ibid.).

Newman and Sherlock's collection is illustrated by Rhoda Jackson, who portrays Anansi as a black man with spider's legs. Jackson's Anansi is slightly reminiscent of a "golliwog" doll; the whites of his eyes and the thickness of his lips are over-exaggerated, and he wears a straw hat and has bare feet. In this depiction of Anansi we see traces of the "Bungo Nayger": the stereotype of the poor, uneducated, "simple", black peasant discussed in chapter 2 (Cassidy and Le Page 2002, 317). Jackson created a Jamaican peasant stereotype for a white British audience so as to represent a way of life outsiders found "charming" and "folksy" but also "backward".

The process of metamorphosis Anansi underwent as he became incorporated into tales published for educational purposes can be examined through a comparison of African and Caribbean versions of the tale "Work-Let-Me-See". In Newman and Sherlock's collection, "Work-Let-Me-See" tells of how Anansi and his family are punished for their greed by being turned into spiders. Although the violence is not tempered in this tale, the preface warns "there are many stories of Annancy. Some are good, others are not so good" (Newman and Sherlock 1959, 3). Anansi discovers a pot that magically produces food itself when he calls out "Work-Let-Me-See", and he tries to keep it a secret from his family. Anansi's smallest child hides under his bed, discovers the secret and tells "Mrs Anansi", who makes the pot produce food for the family and then cleans it vigorously. The pot refuses to make food for Anansi once it has been cleaned, and in a rage he goes to the spot where he found the pot but finds a whip in its place. The whip tells him to call out "Work-Let-Me-See". He does so, and the whip beats him ruthlessly. He takes the whip back to his home and lets his wife and children find it, and they all receive a flogging as punishment for their greed and deceit:

> The whip flogged and flogged
> Then they all changed into spiders
> A little time after
> Brer Annancy came back, he looked into his room
> He could not see Mrs Annancy
> He could not see the children
> But he saw a big, black spider
> And three other little spiders.
> Then he had to change into a spider too.
>
> (Newman and Sherlock 1959, 33)

In the Trinidadian tale "Anansi and the Magic Bowly" (1973) written by Al Ramsawack, who for over thirty years adapted Caribbean folk stories for schoolchildren, we can see an even more toned-down version of "Work-Let-Me-See" in which a moralistic Anansi repents for his actions. In Ramsawack's tale, when Anansi goes to work in the deep forest to chop wood he finds a bowl that can magically create his favourite meal (curried meat and rice) when he sings it a little chant in French, "*belle petite quibello, belle petite quibello* ['beautiful little thing-that-is-beautiful, beautiful little thing-that-is-beautiful']" (Ramsawack 1973, 12). He stops work for the day and returns home, where he builds an extension in which he hides the bowl from his family. His wife, however, soon discovers it: "this is nonsense. Each day we starve while Anansi fill his stomach with the best food in this room" (p. 14). The bowl loses its powers as Anansi's wife and children eat from it and Anansi, in a rage, returns to where he made his original discovery and finds the whip, which whips him when he sings the magic song. He then cunningly places the whip for his

family to find, "hoping to enjoy the sight". But this Anansi, with far less original flavour than Newman and Sherlock's version, repents and stops his family
from getting hurt at the last minute, promising to end his life of trickery and
greed. Particularly unusual for an Anansi tale, there is a happy ending: "He
saw his poor family scampering about under the whipping. He became sad,
and in a rage he jumped and caught the whip. He flung it to the ground and
chopped it to bits with his heavy axe, and never again did he play tricks on
them while they starved. And so they lived happily together" (pp. 21–22).

Ramsawack's "Anansi and the Magic Bowly" is, in Scott's words, an example of the "most sanitised or prudent tellings" of an Anansi tale (1990, 163). If
we compare it to its West African version, we can see how in the process of
sanitization the original meanings have been lost. In Rattray's recording of the
Asante tale "How It Came About the Children Were (First) Whipped", Anansi
finds a magic dish called "Fill-up-some-and-eat" which produces food (palm-
oil soup) (1930, 66–67). The tale follows the same pattern as "Anansi and the
Magic Bowly", but Anansi is not punished for his actions. Anansi hides his
source of food from his family during a famine and watches them starve while
he grows fat – until his son Ntikuma discovers his secret. Once the magic
powers of the dish are destroyed, Anansi finds the whip ("Swish- and-raise-
weals") and his family are whipped ruthlessly. Anansi watches and shouts "lay
it on, lay it on, especially Ntikuma, lay it on him" (p. 67). After Anansi has
made sure his family are "properly flogged" he takes the whip and "cut[s] it
into small pieces and scatter[s] them about. That is what made the whip come
into the tribe" (ibid.). The tale ends as follows: "so when it comes about that
when you tell your child something, and he will not listen to you, we whip
him" (pp. 66–67). The tale explains not only how the whip entered into the
human world, but why children should listen to adults. However, as a modern
educational tale, it would be deemed as inappropriate; encouraging the whipping of children and wives, as well as endorsing violent and greedy behaviour.

Although it was a sanitized Anansi who officially entered colonial schools
across Jamaica in educational texts, a collection of Anansi tales compiled by
Reverend Joseph Williams, author of *Psychic Phenomena of Jamaica* (1934),
and composed by Jamaican schoolchildren in the 1930s, exemplifies the continued popularity of the the Creole versions of the tales in pre-independence
Jamaica. This is a fascinating and enormous collection of just under five thou-

sand stories which were typewritten and sent to the *Gleaner* newspaper offices as entries to a nationwide Anansi story-writing competition advertised in the newspaper from 1930 to 1931. Three copies of the manuscripts, titled "Anancy Stories of Jamaica", exist – two in Jamaica and one in the library of Boston College Graduate School, Massachusetts, where Williams worked as a professor of cultural anthropology. The tales offer an intriguing insight into the ways in which Jamaican children viewed Anansi during this period, and it is clear that a comparative analysis of the impact of the different geographical locations, economic backgrounds and types of schools on the tales would lead to further illuminating insights.

Some of the tales in this collection are written in Standard English, but the majority are written phonetically in Creole, which points to the continued popularity of Anansi tales among the Jamaican general public at the time. Furthermore, despite the drive to encourage children to speak Standard English, the language choice indicates the use of Creole in schools. For example, Eric Plunkett (age thirteen) writes his story, entitled "Old Nanas of Jamaica" in a typical Jamaican patois: "Once bredda spider and his pitneys [meaning children] ben go aground fe go reap in corn. Whilst dem ben di [there] dey bredda spider nam [eat] the raast corn till him nealy dead. Night ben dey come the Pitney dem ben wan fe go home but bredda spider ben feal woser" (Williams 1930–31, Ms. 1366).

Some of the tales are invented, while others are interpretations of traditional tales. The authors age from seven to fourteen years old and their stories are all short (approximately nine to thirteen lines in length). The spelling of Anansi is, as always, varied, some children preferring "Hannancy", "Ananscy" or "Anausey" (Williams 1930–31, Ms. 1362, Ms. 1110), although most are titled "Anancy Story" and, like their Asante versions, start with a description of hard times: "Bro Anancy and him wife was living very poor" or "Anancy has a wife and twelve children. It was hard time and they could get nothing to eat" (Ms. 987; Ms. 990). Lily Waul's story follows the same theme as Rattray's "Why It Is the Elders Say We Should Not Repeat Sleeping-Mat Confidences", in which Anansi is not allowed to scratch while working the king's land[4] (Rattray 1930, 129–33). Sylvester Little (age eleven) writes a story about Anancy and the Duckanoo tree in which a tree replaces the magic pot in "Work-Let-Me-See" recorded by both Sherlock and Ramsawack (Williams 1930–31, Ms. 989).

Most significantly, the tales exemplify how the traditionally cunning and despicable Jamaican Anansi was not replaced, in the minds of Jamaican children, by his often sterile counterpart found in the pages of their schoolbooks. In another tale written by Sylvester Little (some of the children have two entries) and entitled "Sister Fowl Children", Fowl has twelve children. Anancy tempts Fowl's children with the offer of some corn: "The chickens jumped up on the mortar and put down it head for corn. Anancy quickly took his mortar stick and crushed its head and killed it". Fowl then comes looking for her children. Anansi kills her and steals her crop of coco: "she put down her head, and Anancy killed her for dinner. He had now got crop of coco for himself" (Williams 1930–31, Ms. 266). Here we see the ruthlessness and violence of the traditional stories; Anansi sets traps, kills innocent children, eats mothers and steals crops.

Some of the children's tales also provide a commentary on the social and economic injustices in Jamaica during the 1930s. Several refer to stealing Buckra's property. Maurice Discon from Warwick school (age ten) writes a version of "Anansi Steals Backra Sheep", which is also found in Tanna's collection (2000, 101): "One time Brer Anancy go thief Backra Sheep when Bra Anancy tief the sheep im begin fe sing wafe oh wafe oh put on the pot deh wan mek fe mek ten tebin [fill it to the brim].[5] De wife wash de pat put on and dem kill de ten sheep and cook them one time" (Williams 1930–31, Ms. 1153). After a good meal Anansi takes up his fiddle and sings a song blaming the theft of the sheep on Bra Monkey. "When de Backra dem yerry [hear] bout it them teck bra Monkey and try him. Dem sentence Bra monkey and try him fe life time and Bra Anancy get way" (ibid.), writes Discon. This tale highlights the divide between the Jamaican rich and poor – Anansi steals from the rich Buckra to eat – as well as the harsh system of governance which sentences the innocent Monkey for life for stealing sheep from a white man.

After Jamaican independence in 1962, the way in which Anansi was perceived changed dramatically in Jamaica and across the Caribbean. This new era saw the onset of a renewed appreciation of folk-culture. There was a revival in the documentation of folktales for children throughout the British Caribbean, which James calls "a distinct marker of the beginnings of the West Indian children's literature" (2004, 4). In Jamaica, old ideas about the inferiority of Creole and folk-culture were challenged, as Jamaicans took part in cultural celebrations inspired by independence and the Black Power movement in the United States. In the decades following independence, many Jamaicans started to call for a return to the performance of folktales in the traditional manner. Storytellers were encouraged to take to the stage and reclaim the Anansi tales as oral genres. This redefinition of folk-culture (which James believes gathered even greater pace in the 1990s) was aimed at installing a sense of pride in Caribbean people and encouraging them to celebrate their history, culture and identity (p. 8).

Anansi's continued popularity throughout the latter part of the twentieth century in Jamaica owed much to actress, comedienne, poet and storyteller Louise Bennett, who made great efforts to keep Anansi alive and introduce him to a global audience. During the 1950s and 1960s, Bennett was not only responsible for promoting Jamaican folklore worldwide but for making Jamaican Creole an acceptable medium of artistic expression. Known affectionately as "Miss Lou", she insisted on always telling Anansi tales in Creole, and her "dialect" verse established a genre of poetry that reflected the everyday experiences of the Jamaican public. Tanna explains the impact of her work: "Louise Bennett was so *so* important. When Louise Bennett published in patois in the *Gleaner* it was a huge step; few others . . . had done it before. And Anansi was a part of that, he spoke in patois; the punch line was often just Anansi saying something in patois" (interview with author, November 2005).

Bennett often worked with popular entertainer and friend Ranny Williams, and they performed Anansi tales together on stage, television and radio until Williams's death in 1980 (Tanna 2000, 24). As well as performing Anansi tales, Bennett published several collections: *Anancy Stories and Poems in Dialect* (1944), *Anancy Stories and Dialect Verse* (1950), *Laugh with Louise: A Pot-Pourrie of Jamaican Folk-Lore, Stories, Songs and Verses* (1961), and *Anancy and Miss Lou* (1979). In her performances and collections, Bennett focused on Anansi's comical side as well as highlighting his capacity to help people laugh in the face of adversity. As Rex Nettleford puts it, "humour becomes, as it were, the expression of people's will to live and Miss Bennett recaptures this will with understanding, compassion and truth" (Nettleford in Bennett 1966, 24).

Bennett reclaimed Anansi as a Jamaican resource for resistance against cultural colonialism. By popularizing Anansi tales in Creole she encouraged Jamaicans to feel proud of their cultural heritage and language. Furthermore, through the medium of Anansi, Bennett conducted an astute social commentary on Jamaican society. In "Anancy an Yella Snake" (1979, 49–50), which incorporates aspects of an Asante tale in which Anansi wins Nyame's stories (Rattray 1930, 52–58), Bennett turns Anansi into a type of black crusader, proving himself cleverer than "Yella"-skinned man (a light-skinned person of mixed ancestry) and winning the girl (Cassidy and Le Page 2002, 486). The attitude of the girl in the tale illustrates the dynamics of internalized racism in Jamaica which drives certain Jamaicans to seek light-skinned partners as a means of raising their social status: "Once upon a time, dere was a gal livin in Jamaica an plenty man did want fi married to her, but she nevah want noh black nor noh dark nor noh brown man; she dida look fi *yella* skin man" (Bennett 1979, 49). Bra Yella Snake marries the girl, but drags her into his hole saying, "Ah wi suck yuh, till yuh mumah and pupa cyaan even fine piece a yuh calla bone" (p. 50), but Anansi impedes his plans by playing on his pride:

> Anansi hear bout it, an go see him can ketch snake. Anancy cut one long juice a bamboo an walk pass snake hole. Hear Anancy loud, "Not a man don't like dish bamboo, not a man een de whole worl can long like dish bamboo." (Anancy tongue-tie, yuh know, so him call "dis" "dish"). Yella snake hear Anancy, an as him proud a him twelve-foot Yella skin him come outa him hole seh to Anancy "Ah bet yuh seh me longa." (p. 50)

Anansi ties Snake round the bamboo pole, and carries him to the girl's family. "De gal bredda shoot yella snake, an from dat day till teday man dah shoot snake. Is Anancy mek it. Jack Mandora me noh choose none" (pp. 49–50).

Another interesting element to this tale is the way it ends with the girl's brother using a gun to shoot Yella Snake: a reference to the weapon of choice for many young Jamaican men in the late twentieth century. Bennett's use of Creole in her performances and publications of Anansi tales gave great scope for humour and irony, as did the use of word play, parody, puns and local references only understood by a Jamaican, Creole-speaking audience. Many Jamaicans enjoyed hearing Creole, the language of the people, spoken publicly. Tanna believes that Anansi's "broad patois" is still one of the key reasons for his popularity with contemporary Jamaican audiences, as it ensures he is "both loved and laughed at" (interview with author, November 2005). Tanna revealed that, in her twenties, when she first came to Jamaica she found it "very odd" that Jamaicans saw the use of patois so comical. She described how, while compiling her collection and recording Anansi tales, "one of the things that made people laugh the most was when Anansi would speak in patois. People laugh as soon as they hear patois" (ibid.). In her view, because Creole was suppressed by the British and perceived as the language of the uneducated, some people laugh at its use partly out of embarrassment. However, she believes that the reasons for its comical effects are complex. She explains that Jamaican feelings towards both Creole and Anansi are ambiguous, but the ambiguity at the heart of both Creole and Anansi is key to the popularity and survival of both. Tanna states that storytellers "get a laugh" when they use patois while telling Anansi tales due to "a whole mixture of cultural reasons: denial, thinking that they should be ashamed, secretly pleased that patois is being used. So there is a duality there . . . no – *ambiguity*. Part of the ambiguity of Anansi is what makes him so enduring" (ibid.).

Today Anansi tales can be found in several hundred publications worldwide and Anansi even appears in two episodes of the Disney animated series entitled *Gargoyles*.[6] The impact of this global interest, however, has accelerated the "watering-down" of the tales and the production of extremely Westernized adaptations. Among these is David Brailsford's *Confessions of Anansi* (2004). Tanya Batson, in a *Sunday Gleaner* review of Brailsford's book, argues that "*Confessions of Anansi* has very little that would remind one of the Anansi stories as they are told in oral culture. In essence the formality of the language (not merely the fact that Standard English is used) robs the stories of the 'magic' to be found in folktales. They are told without wonder, without mystery" (4 April 2004, 6). Batson applauds Brailsford's attempt to keep the folkfigure alive and weave elements of Jamaican history into the stories (he is, however, accused of doing so in a "glaringly artificial" way), but she rightly criticizes him for depicting a "pink-faced Anansi with a straight nose" as the book cover illustration. This gross distortion, explains Batson, shows the extent to which Brailsford is "culturally removed from the tales", which results in Anansi's "confessions" being "confessed by a consciousness too removed from his own" which cannot portray and appreciate his "full *ginnalship* [trickery]" but offers "just a watered-down version". To drive this final point home, a large picture of Miss Lou is printed beside the review with the caption "Jamaica's folklore and cultural ambassador" (ibid.).

However, while "watered-down" adaptations abound, contemporary Caribbean authors are using Anansi stories for their own political and cultural purposes in response to what they see as the needs of the twentieth and twenty-first century Caribbean. Caribbean writers have begun to portray Anansi as the embodiment of Caribbean cultural resilience, renewal, cross-cultural fertilization and creativity. James sees Anansi as a "paradigm for the West Indian ethos of survival, inherent in the resourcefulness that has sustained West Indian people, regardless of particular ethnic ancestry" (2004, 3). She explains that "in this sense Anansi represents the indigenous syncretism that has evolved over centuries of Caribbean creolisation" (2004, 3).

In his essay "Jazz and the West Indian Novel", Edward Kamau Brathwaite makes connections between jazz improvisation and the Anansi stories (1995, 328–31). He explains that many Caribbean folk-forms contain elements of improvisation, creating similar patterns to the forms of improvisation used by a jazz musician. The Anansi story is "an almost perfect example of improvisation, in the jazz sense, where tone, rhythm and image come together to create a certain kind of effect" (p. 329). Brathwaite takes an Anansi story as an example of how the structure of a story can create a verbal melody. This effect is often the result of the repetition of a theme, which Brathwaite likens to a jazz "riff" (ibid.). This jazz "riff" is a "kind of collective response which marks the end of one improvisation and the beginning of the next" in music, poetry and folktales (ibid.).

Brathwaite uses the tale "Brother Annancy and Brother Death" as an example of how rhythmic elements can be presented in a narrative. In this tale Anansi lets Death marry his daughter for some eggs, but Death refuses to talk after the wedding when Anansi hassles him for more food. Anansi says: "Bro'er Deat', me son, me hungry" but "Brother Deat' no 'peak". The next time Anansi asks him the sentence is abbreviated to "Deat' no 'peak". These words are repeated throughout the story and create a drum-like rhythm, forming the structure and tempo of the tale. In his essay, Brathwaite continues to develop this idea and argues that it can be used as an ethically grounded aesthetic model for literature: he explains that any West Indian writing in this form will "absorb its rhythms from the people of this community" (p. 330). This, he maintains, is a step towards an integrated creole culture and a creole world-view, which starts with the preservation and adaptation of folk forms that reflect both the culture and history of Caribbean people.

Andrew Salkey's work is an example of the kind of writing Brathwaite describes. His poems and novels are inspired by Caribbean oral traditions, and they often play with the rhythms and structure of Creole and Anansi narratives. Jamaican-born Salkey created two volumes of his own versions of Anansi stories, *Anancy's Score* (1973) and *Anancy, Traveller* (1992). In *Anancy's Score*, Salkey creates a unique vision of Anansi, portraying a politicized freedom fighter, a symbol of resistance and hope who guides his people through a troubled history but remains confusing, contradictory, complex, ambiguous and tricky. Salkey describes his Anansi as one who "holds no reservations; makes only certain crucial allowances; he knows no boundaries; respects no one, not even himself, at times; and he makes a mockery of everybody's assumptions and value judgements" (Salkey 1973, author's note).

Salkey's volume addresses global political issues of war and nuclear power in "Vietnam Anancy and the Black Tulip" and "Anancy and the Atomic Horse". In "Political Spider" Anancy's friends call Anancy "Hope", "which, as you know, is a green thing" (p. 31) and his speeches start with "Me name is Anancy is spider is Hope is a green t'ing" (p. 37). As the reader follows this Anansi on his journey through time and space, he reveals the complexities of the history of the Caribbean people. Salkey's Anansi may be untrustworthy, but he is a guide, a solver of problems and an emblem of change and regeneration. He is caught in a web between two worlds – the old and the new – and tries to help his people to come to grips with the difficulties of the past, present and future Caribbean. This Anansi has been reworked according to new conditions; Salkey uses him as a medium through which to embolden working-class black Jamaicans and encourage their radical political development.[7]

Anancy's Score contains vivid and abstract illustrations of Anansi drawn by Jamaican artist Errol Lloyd in black ink (see figure 15). Both Salkey and Lloyd were highly politicized Jamaicans, influenced by the ideas of radical black Caribbean anti-colonialists such as C.L.R. James and John La Rose. These influences affected their conceptualization of Anansi. Lloyd's illustrations have an unsettling, dream-like quality: Anansi is often lurking in the corners

Figure 15. Illustration by Errol Lloyd in Andrew Salkey's *Anancy's Score* (1973). (By permission of Errol Lloyd.)

of the image, disguised as another object, or in his web, surrounded by fragmented forms and shapes. Lloyd depicts a figure so central that all other
images on the page absorb the attributes of the spider and his web.

This illustration accompanies the tale "Political Spider", in which Anansi is
deeply involved in Jamaican politics. He transcends boundaries between rich
and poor, leading the poor to complain about his "bad buckra complex" since
he dresses like a dandy and talks to "those who come from a different class of
ideas an' life" (Salkey 1973, 32). He leads starving crowds of spiders, fleas and
leeches to the great houses of the rich on North Hill, promising them wealth,
but then steals their belongings, "making a brazen sale to Brother Tacuma, the
world-famous travelling merchant" (p. 37). They are then appeased by Anansi's
music, and he teaches them a lesson about greed, showing them the downfalls
of coveting wealth and trying to "get something for nothing" (ibid.).

In Lloyd's illustration, we see Anansi addressing crowds of black people. A
sinister figure holds Anansi's head in their hands: perhaps a rich white man
by whom the people feel Anansi is being manipulated. The dejected, seemingly pregnant woman in a headscarf to the left of the image is suggestive of
the suffering and pain of black Jamaicans, while the mouths of the houses of
the rich on North Hill hang open and hungry, waiting to devour the struggling
populace.

Similarly to Salkey, Wilson Harris depicts Anansi as representative of an
artistic link between black culture of the "old" and the "new" worlds. For Harris he is symbolic of regeneration and forms of creative resistance in the face
of enslavement and colonialism. He makes a connection between Anansi and
the "limbo" dance he claims developed on the slave ships of the Middle Passage. Harris believes that the limbo originated from the need for the slaves to
contort themselves into spider-like shapes due to lack of space. As Harris
watches modern-day limbo dancers crouching, like Anansi, close to the
ground, he sees their movements as representative of the creation of something positive from something terrible (1981, 378). For Harris, the limbo
dancer passing under the obstacle is like the slave passing thorough a gateway
or threshold into a new world. He calls the metamorphosis of African culture
into the New World the "Limbo-Anancy Syndrome", an "art of creative coex-
istence born of great peril and the strangest capacity for renewal" (ibid.).
These are the "arts of originality springing out of an age of limbo", which

Harris describes as "a true creative phenomenon of the West Indies" (cited in Jonas 1990, 73).

Harris sees the peoples of the Caribbean sharing a collective culture and believes that the key to its survival is not in the total recall of the African past, but rather a form of social deconstruction, creation, renewal, rebirth and cross-cultural fertilization. He advocates a need to find the light in the heart of "hidden" cultures – not to be found solely in the West or in the Caribbean but in the collision and cross-fertilization *between* the two worlds. Anansi is symbolic of this meeting place, market-place or crossroads in which a creative interaction can take place – a powerful energy of appropriation that points away from "both apartheid and from ghetto fixations" (cited in Jonas 1990, 73). It is in this space, at the crossroads of cultures, that Barry Chevannes also positions Anansi: "The crossroads is a space that is rife with a disorder, where different cultures come and mix, a way to look at it is as a *liminal* space. And this is where these hero figures function best, in that whole sense of disorder. But it is a disorder that changes and brings order . . . that is why in the stories you say 'is Anansi mek it' " (interview with author, November 2005).

Anansi, both African and Caribbean, is representative of a cultural crossroads, as he inhabits multiple cultural, historical and geographical locations. Chevannes states that, as children, he and his friends learned through Anansi tales that "nothing happened unless we are prepared to travel, and nothing will be discovered unless at the *crossroad*" (2001, 5). Representative of both good and evil, as well as journeys, travel, liminal states and multiple possibilities, the crossroads have played an important symbolic role in the folk practices of Jamaicans. On the final night of a nine-night ceremony, the mourning procession travels to the nearest crossroads and performs a ritual, enabling the spirit of the deceased, who is often described in their final hour as "travelling", to journey on whichever path they choose. During this ritual the deceased's home is cleared out and their clothes are disposed of at the crossroads (p. 6).

Joyce Jonas uses Anansi and the great house as two central icons in *Anancy in the Great House: Ways of Reading West Indian Fiction* in order to describe the social and cultural structuring of the Caribbean landscape. The plantation owner's house of the eighteenth and nineteenth centuries, looming over the plantation fields, represents, for Jonas, a colonial worldview of binary oppositions: white/black, exploiter/exploited, "First World"/ "Third World". Anansi, in contrast, is a symbol of the folk and folk-history; he is everything that is rejected by the great house, disregarded as dirt – folk dirt. Jonas uses a host of Anansi-inspired metaphors, similes and puns in her writing, often focusing on the symbolism of the web. Anansi is at its centre, spinning tales and wisdom, as well as representing a deconstructive and re-creative force that finds expression through Caribbean authors. In Jonas's work, Anansi is a celebration of disorder and chaos; he is full of revolutionary energy and lives in the rejected "betwixt" and "between" spaces outside of the institutions and authority of the great house (Jonas 1990, 73).

Jonas sees modern Caribbean writers using "Anansi strategies" to deconstruct the imperialist "text" and transform the landscapes of the formally colonized world, like a rite of passage, into new perceptions and insights. Writers using these strategies in their work break down the authority and binary oppositions of the great house and, using folk icons like Anansi as their muse, weave "folk" techniques into their writing (Jonas 1990, 73). For Jonas, the Caribbean writer is like Anansi, spinning new formations in a postcolonial world. They weave a narrative thread to escape a colonial worldview and climb to new freedoms. Taking the strand of linearity (oppressive history or plot), these writers complicate it by making a patterned web of connections and interrelationships, a woven "text" that transforms history (pp. 2–9). This inclusion of what Jonas terms "Anansi strategies" in the Caribbean writer's text is disruptive of the old order, and challenges the structuring of the colonial physical and spiritual landscape. As Jonas explains, the "Anancy artist is the masquerading carnival figure par excellence, celebrating play in a structured world that threatens momentarily to destroy what is most precious to the human spirit" (p. 5).

Anansi on Stage

The popularity of the pantomime grew rapidly in twentieth-century Jamaica, and Anansi became a star of the stage. The Jamaican National Pantomime started in 1941 when the Little Theatre Movement began its annual Christmas show based on a fusion of traditional English theatre and Jamaican folklore. The shows usually took place between Christmas and the New Year at the downtown Kingston Ward Theatre, until the six-hundred-seat Little Theatre first opened in 1961 on Tom Redcam Avenue in New Kingston. There have been ten major Anansi pantomimes in Jamaican theatres to date: *Blue Beard and Brer Anancy* (1949), *Anancy and the Magic Mirror* (1954), *Anancy and Pandora* (1955), *Anancy and Beeny Bud* (1956), *Anancy and Pandora* (1967), *Anancy and Doumbey* (1968), *Moonshine Anancy* (1969), *Rockstone Anancy* (1970), *Anansi Come Back* (1993) and *Anansi's Web* (1998) (Little Theatre Movement 2004).

In her essay "A Philosophy of Survival: Anancyism in Jamaican Pantomime", Ruth Minott Egglestone, researcher of the Little Theatre Movement, describes Jamaican pantomimes as "multi-layered description[s] of a historically based, complex sociocultural situation which is constantly being articulated and explained in the form of metaphor" (2001, 1). Similar to my interpretation of Anansi, Egglestone portrays him as a resistance figure who plays a central part in Jamaican history and culture. In "'Jamaica Derive Too': The Use of Jamaica Talk in the National Pantomime", Egglestone explains that putting Anansi on stage encourages a "philosophy of resilience" aimed at teaching the individual to "meet hardship with humour, thereby avoiding bitterness" (Egglestone 2003, 1).

In much the same way as among the Asante, where Anansi is a medium through which powerful members of the community such as the chief or even Nyame can be criticized, in a Jamaican Anansi pantomime the plot revolves around Anansi challenging familiar powerful personages such as rich Jamaican business men or women and corrupt politicians. As Egglestone puts it, audiences are shown "Anansi at work ambivalently challenging and serving/ serving-and-challenging the 'Giant' of the day" (2001, 17). As Alex Gradussov states, in these performances "the narrator knows, even if subconsciously, that Anancy is more that just a spider-man who outwits the society: he is the symbol of resistance. He is living manifestation that the outside world, the white world, the commercial world, the oppressive world, has not been able to overpower the folk culture and folk tradition" (cited in Egglestone 2001, 17).

As in Bennett's performances, the use of Creole in Jamaican pantomimes creates a sense of unity, as the jokes are designed to be understood by a Creole-speaking audience, thus complimenting the audience on their perceptiveness and simultaneously reaffirming a bond that excludes non-Creole-speaking people. Bennett explains the defiance inherent in the use of Creole: "We African ancestors-dem pop [meaning confuse/fool] we English fore-fahders dem. Yes! Pop dem an disguise up de English Language fi projec [protect] fi-dem African Language in such a way dat we English forefahders-dem still couldn understan whet we African ancestors-dem wasa talk bout when dem wasa talk dem one annoddor!" (cited in Egglestone 2003, 4).

Anansi's growing popularity in late-twentieth-century Jamaica is based on both his ability to speak the language of the masses and his ability to reflect a contemporary Jamaican experience. This is because, according to Barbara Gloudon, a well-known Jamaican playwright, radio host and author of two Anansi pantomimes, *Moonshine Anancy* (1969) and *Anansi Come Back* (1993), he is an integral part of the national Jamaican consciousness. In her 1983 interview with Paulette Bell, Gloudon explains: "Anancy is part of Jamaica. He is a part of our language. His Anancyisms – his characteristics of always being able to wriggle out of trouble, are taken for granted in Jamaica. These are the characteristics of Anancy that are always in the consciousness of the Jamaican people". In the same interview, she goes on to describe how Anansi's success on stage centres around the portrayal of the trickster as a lovable villain. In pantomime, she states, writers and directors "take the spirit of Anancyism" and incorporate it into their work. She describes the role of Anansi in the pantomime thus:

> [Pantomime is an] obvious theatrical form where good triumphs over evil; there is always a villain who has to be conquered . . . and [who] better than Anancy?
> . . . Because we all know him. He is the village crook, he is the man who is always carrying you down trying to win points and all of that . . . he is so rich; he offers everything – he offers humour, he conquers by laughter. He uses his wits – he's greedy, and so he is a very obvious villain . . . But he has the capacity to say "I'm sorry" when they turn down on him, and says "look, I am very sorry about all of this", and as soon as he reveals himself he begins to wheedle his way back into people's affections.

Gloudon herself wishes to capture the "spirit of Anancyism" in her work and feels drawn to him not only because he is "essentially Caribbean and African", but also because she finds him more complex and ambiguous than European folk figures "where the villain renounces all". Anansi reflects what she calls an "African ethos" as well as being a symbol of humankind: "He is all of us! And therefore you put him in theatre, where it is easy to create his redemption, and this is why children recognise it, adults boo him you know . . . they will throw things at him . . . And even if he says he is not going to do it again – who is going to believe him? Because he is us" (interview with Bell 1983).

For Gloudon, the beauty of using Anansi in the theatre is that he is not spatially bound and confined by the proscenium arch. The proscenium arch is a European invention; a barrier between the audience and the actors that "suggests something that you can't get over" (interview with Bell 1983). Anansi is able to transcend this traditional divide between audience and actors: "Anansi is not bound by it because it is not his invention; if Anansi wants to go and talk to the audience, he will" (ibid.). In Gloudon's *Moonshine Anancy* (1969), Anansi remains hidden at the side of the stage during the beginning of the show. He crouches in the shadows, listening, and the audience fail to notice him. He then "waits until the thing had died down" and makes a big entrance, taking centre stage and saying "now me Anansi, I stand there for a long time and you don't see me!" (ibid.).

Refusing to be overlooked, pantomime Anansi is the hero of poor, struggling Jamaicans living moment-by-moment in grim and unpredictable circumstances. One way to survive or thrive in these conditions is to duck and dive and, most importantly, to use your brains and have a plan. Anansi is, using de Certeau's terms, the champion of oppositional practices in everyday life (de Certeau 1980). As Egglestone explains, "eventually in the pantomime, as in some quarters of Jamaican society, the feeble Spider-man becomes an unlikely symbol of resistance as people learn to employ the creativity of his approach in manoeuvring through challenges of disempowerment" (2001, 4).

In Jamaica today, Anansi appears in theatre productions, pantomimes and storytelling events geared towards historical remembrance and cultural celebration. Several Jamaican storytelling events are held annually and are well attended by both adults and children. Although the relevance of the Anansi tales is being questioned in Jamaica's current political climate, as will be discussed in detail in the following section, there is a conscious movement in Jamaica to ensure the survival of the stories alongside other traditional cultural forms.

Anansi tales started being "performed" in the 1990s on stage by professional storytellers, at a price. These events are still popular today but expensive ticket prices mean they remain unaffordable to most Jamaicans. The events take place in the cultural milieu of the capital, often uptown. They are attended by a cultured middle-class Kingstonian set; people concerned with preserving their traditions and creating new cultural forms which feed from their ancestral roots. As Small explains: "Now that the Anansi tales are done on stage it is *very* different to in a community setting, on a bench in a yard or in a park. Now there are people like me and Amina Blackwood Meeks[8] on a stage, very often with a microphone; all this technology" (interview with author 2005).

This is another stage of Anansi's metamorphosis – Anansi tales are becoming cultural commodities. Anansi is transforming yet again as he is taken from the back yards, streets and villages into the comfortable spaces of the auditorium. Although this allows for the all-important survival of the folktales, they transmute from participatory community activities into buyable and sellable cultural merchandise. Anansi becomes something to be looked at, separated by space, and observed from a distance by a well-heeled audience, rather than an involving medium, ubiquitous and free for all.

Storytellers and artists who use Anansi in their work defend this phase of Anansi's evolution. With numerous social commentators criticizing the folk hero – some calling for the total ban of the telling of Anansi tales – they insist that they can put the controversial character to positive use. They want to depict an Anansi who sees the error of his ways, but, unlike the often sterile Anansi portrayed in colonial collections and school books, he is used to celebrate Afro-Caribbean culture, history and identity. Storytellers such as Eintou Springer and Small are bringing to life "new" Anansis by writing and performing their own Anansi stories and plays. Small's Anansi speaks Creole and is a cunning trickster, but he learns a lesson and has the willingness to alter his behaviour. Springer's Anansi takes a rope across the ocean from the Caribbean to Africa and links his Caribbean brothers and sisters back to their homeland.[9] Small has been making efforts to celebrate Anansi with her local community in Kingston by writing an Anansi puppet play that she performs alongside local children. In the play, Small's Anansi has a fresh message for a changing social context: as a mirror is held up to him he begins to see himself clearly. Anansi cries at the end of this play, entitled *Anansi and the Mirror* (2005): "Me promise dat me will be a good citizen ov AWE DIS COUNTRY, an dat nobody won't haffe wrote no more stories 'bout how Anansi tief, 'bout how Anansi greedy, 'bout how Anansi tell lies. Me will mek a complete change" (p. 10).

In Jamaica today Anansi tales are still told by teachers to schoolchildren, but they are no longer used in school literacy programmes. Representatives at the Jamaican Ministry of Education's Core Curriculum for Arts and Languages unit explain that "Anansi stories do not form a part of the curriculum, but it's up to the individual schools to use Anansi stories if they so wish" (interview with author, December 2005). Schools contacted during the course of my research said that they used Anansi in lessons and school plays. The headmistress of Liberty Academy, in Kingston, whose pupils range from three to eleven years, explained that the school regularly makes use of Anansi in poetry, song and drama. She explained that "Anansi stories are a way of life in Jamaica. Children will always tell them in the playground" (interview with author, December 2005).

Annually, all Jamaican primary and secondary schools enter into the Jamaica Cultural Development Commission (JCDC) competitions; these are nationwide events including competitions in oratory, dance and drama. The oratory category consists of entries for Jamaican dialect prose, dub poetry, storytelling, and Caribbean dialect poems (JCDC 2006). Andrew Brodber, one of the co-ordinators of the event, explained that many participants chose Anansi tales for the storytelling category, some inventing their own, others using set texts and tales (interview with author, December 2005).

As well as appearing in national storytelling competitions, performances on stage, pantomimes, and cultural festivals and celebrations, Anansi is still a central figure in several Jamaican proverbs. Among the favourites are the Anansi inspired "play fool to catch wise" and "cunnin better than strong", as well as "Anancy say 'two chubble betta dan wan'" (two troubles are better than one), and "Anancy say, 'Two hed betta dan wan, eben coco hed'" (two heads are better than one, even coco heads – problems are better solved together) (Morris-Brown 1993, 72). There is also "chubble deh bush, Anancy cyah I'kum a yard" or "Trubble dey in de bush, Nancy come bring a home", which Vivien Morris-Brown, documenter of Jamaican proverbs, translates as "if there is trouble in the bushes, Anancy takes it home". For non-Jamaicans, she explains the proverb as follows: "Anancy, the folk hero of West African

origin, is never satisfied with leaving things in their proper place. He sometimes takes home the spoils of his foraging, many times to the unhappiness
of his family. What does not concern us we should leave well alone"
(1993, 26).

But despite Anansi's continued popularity in contemporary Jamaica, his
status as a national Jamaican folk hero is being challenged. Anansi has numerous critics who claim he has a negative impact on contemporary Jamaican
society. The next section provides an analysis of their arguments and ends
with a refutation of their claims.

Anansi and *Politricks*: The Anansi Syndrome

> Jamaica is in a transition and adjustment phase of development. With rapid
> globalization, the viability and sustainability of Jamaica becomes increasingly
> fragile and the country is challenged . . . to maintain economic and social equi-
> librium. When combined with new global development threats such as terror-
> ism, drug trafficking, money laundering and HIV/AIDS, these factors create the
> need for new development approaches and solutions. (United Nations 2007)

As a folk hero of West African origin, Anansi is steeped in a West African
ethos that celebrates ambiguity and liminality. Diane Austen-Broos argues
that West African religions were based around "notions of good and evil which
were not assigned to separate spheres but were allowed to reside as ambivalent companions in the world", a way of thinking which "was expressed in
African trickster myth" (Austen-Broos 1997, 48). Anansi tales are thought-pro-
voking narratives that deliberately resist clear interpretation, and it is their
ambiguity that encourages the listener to reflect on morals and values.

Through enabling a reflection on one's moral, philosophical and political
outlook and providing scope for a critique of one's sociopolitical situation,
Anansi tales can encourage the use of intelligent means to survive disempowerment. Several Jamaicans have spotted Anansi's potential as a medium
through which to encourage positive action. As we have seen, through focusing on Anansi's intelligence, storytellers Bennett, Small and others have been
using the folk figure to communicate messages aimed at teaching young people to use their brains, not their fists, to overcome challenging situations.

Van Sertima believes that African trickster tales have never been so relevant to the situation in which African Americans find themselves today. He sees many black communities in the Americas as still locked into ideological and economic wars between rebel and institution. He views the trickster as the essence of a revolutionary spirit that has the power to break free from these fixed, programmed ways of seeing the world, a world in which (quoting Matthew Arnold) "ignorant armies clash by night" (2002, 451).

In Jamaica today the Jamaica Labour Party and the People's National Party have been at loggerheads for several decades. Rival politicians circulated firearms to their supporters in impoverished inner-city communities during the 1970s and 1980s. As a result these communities have been locked in a situation of continuous conflict resulting in extreme violence. This violence, often perpetrated by gangs, and further aggravated by a profitable drug trade and the ready availability of guns, has created garrison communities across Kingston and in other major Jamaican towns.

The Jamaican national mantra of "Out of Many, One People", aims to smooth over racial barriers and glaring social inequalities and injustices. However, economic stress and political corruption have resulted in high levels of unemployment and an alarming murder rate – one of the highest per capita in the in world. Human rights campaigners at Amnesty International explain that the economic stress Jamaica faces exacerbates the difficulties of its citizens' full realization of human rights (Amnesty USA 2007). As well as highlighting the problems caused by "political tribalism" and organized gang violence, Amnesty International is trying to raise awareness of the high levels of violence towards homosexuals and women on the island (ibid.).

In this climate of political and social unrest, several Jamaican academics argue that Jamaican communities are in transition and experiencing a radical change of values. For his part, Chevannes explained to me the situation as follows:

> You beginning to see this change of values? And you think "how can we live like that?" We can't, but you see Emily, we are in the midst of accelerated change. That is what we are in the midst of. The value system is changing but it has not settled into a mode in which a new social order is affirmed and we can redefine

our social relationships with one another and how we are going to live together. (Interview with author, November 2005)

Similarly, in an interview, Tanna identified a shift in values in Jamaica but, fearful of the rise in violence and crime, was less positive than Chevannes regarding the "accelerated change". "Guns come in barrels," she stated, "even a thirteen-year-old kid in a garrison community can have a gun. Things *are* changing" (interview with author, November 2005). Although Chevannes predicted the onset of a new (and more harmonious) social order, he admitted that it appeared as if the "whole fabric of society is crumbling" in modern Jamaica (ibid.). Young people's attitudes have undergone radical transformations, he continued, and the "courtesies and sensibilities" expected of young people when he was growing up have been replaced by "coarseness" (ibid.). Chevannes maintains that, since the 1990s, there has been a shift away from traditional principles based on Victorian values of respectability.

These new values are explored in detail by Deborah Thomas in *Modern Blackness: Nationalism, Globalization, and the Politics of Culture in Jamaica* (2004). Thomas takes us back to the independence era of the 1960s in an effort to explain the shift in Jamaican attitudes and values over the following decades. She argues that although the post-independence Jamaican government celebrated certain aspects of Jamaica's African heritage through its cultural policy, it also pursued development strategies aimed at modernizing Jamaica's economy through industrial development and foreign investment, which destabilized the rural lifestyles linked to much celebrated "folk" practice. Paradoxically, it was in the face of these major changes that "Creole nationalist cultural mobilizers" continued to assert the continued relevance of folk practices, which they believed "might provide a base from which to cope with the rapid changes facing Jamaicans after independence and into the contemporary period" (2004, 9).

Thomas argues that traditional Jamaican "values" were linked to "class-coded cultural forms and practices" and a concept of "Jamaicanness" or Jamaican identity "consolidated by political and intellectual elites at the time of independence" (2004, 9). Today these values and identities have been superseded by what Thomas calls "modern blackness" (p. 11). At the close of the twentieth and beginning of the twenty-first century, the influence and power of the "respectable" professional middle-classes on the lives of the poorer classes diminished, and modern blackness became an expression of Jamaicanness not articulated through folk-culture but through a modern, urban mode. It directly challenged the idea that a sense of Jamaican identity should be created through a celebration of folk-culture, African roots and rural traditional respectability. Thomas states that modern blackness is a "notion of blackness that is in the here and now" (p. 11). It is not an articulation of Jamaican identity based on revolutionary or utopian goals, but one which is "loud and proud", influenced by consumerism and black American culture. For Thomas, modern blackness finds its expression in contemporary Jamaican cultural practices, such as dancehall, which reflect the transnational experiences of an urbanized Jamaican youth in a globalized world (p. 13).

Although the popularity of traditional Jamaican cultural forms may be diminishing, it seems that Anansi is still relevant to, and absorbed by, modern young Jamaicans. Pollard explains: "I think people will keep on telling Anansi stories forever. The stories are part of the fabric of our society, and even people who don't tell them, they quote them in the DJ stands. These modern young people – all the time you hear them saying something from an Anansi story, or something from a proverb . . . without even thinking about it they pick up a part of what is Caribbean" (interview with author, October 2005). Despite Anansi's continued cultural relevance, many members of the older generation argue that Anansi has become emblematic of the negative behaviour traits of the younger generation. They see what could be described as the negative aspects of modern blackness – individualism, greed and lack of respect for others – as Anansi characteristics or "Anancyisms". What we see here is Anansi, not being rejected as "folksy", but implemented as a medium through which Jamaicans critique their societal structures and relationships within it.

Anansi has become a symbol of Jamaica's downfall to some, and to others an emblem of hope and change. Storyteller Jean Small, deeply concerned about the levels of gun and domestic violence in Jamaica and the distinct "lack of a respect for life", sees Jamaican society as "spiritless, inhuman, and destructive" (interview with author, November 2005). She interprets Anansi as a redeemer, and believes there is "a need to hold on to Anansi's thread to move upwards; go back in time to the mores of the society of our ancestors, to reach a higher spiritual level" (ibid.). Brother Martin also discussed the destructive drive in the young Jamaicans: "These children now they want to hear about foolishness. They want to hear about fire gunshot. Kill man. You understand. They want to know about the gun, but the gun, it make no sense. They make their war here, but I not like that" (interview with author, December 2005).

The economic and social instability that inflicts Jamaica and its people are a part of a bitter colonial legacy. A sense of hopelessness born of poverty and oppression turns many young Jamaicans towards violence and crime. Over the past few decades, hundreds of thousands of Jamaicans have left the island in search of improved standards of living, some of them leaving behind young children to face poverty and, in certain cases, neglect. These children, brought up without mothers or fathers, are part of the youth of modern Jamaica, and many still suffer from the trauma of being separated from their families and experiencing the breakdown of family life. However, for a country with a longer history of slavery than freedom, Jamaica has successfully overcome terrible shortcomings. According to Chevannes, it is remarkable that Jamaica has been able to establish itself on the map of the world since slavery ended, and that Jamaicans are now "holding their own regionally, nationally and internationally" (interview with author, November 2005). He worries that this achievement is glossed over in the face of Jamaica's problems, and it should not be forgotten (ibid.).

Politicians' contributions to Jamaica's contemporary social problems are explored in detail in Laurie Gunst's journalistic exposé of Jamaican gang violence and political corruption in *Born fi Dead: A Journey Through the Jamaican Posse Underworld* (1995). Gunst spent nearly ten years, from the mid-1980s to the mid-1990s, as an observer-participant researcher, forming relationships with Jamaican gang members in both Jamaica and the United States. Her book offers ground-breaking insight into the world of corrupt Jamaican politics, gun crime and the drug trade over the past few decades. She describes Kingston as a "chessboard of war zones with human pieces", arguing that "as long as Jamaicans can remember, politicians have armed and paid Kingston's most notorious gunmen to enforce their rule in the capital city's thronged slums" (1995, xiii).

Gunst explains that, since the 1970s, many young, poor, inner-city Jamaican men have spent their childhoods in communities in which the ruling "don" (or gangster) is hero-worshipped. Jamaican dons accumulate wealth through the gun and drug trade and self-style themselves as benevolent providers for their communities, giving away presents and organizing parties. Dons are frequently protected by a political leader, whom the community also perceive as a kindly benefactor due to their display of concern to their supporters and capital input into the community. The community will vote for whichever political party – be it the Jamaica Labour Party or the People's National Party – the don and the political leader represent. Some young Jamaicans are willing to die for their loyalties to the don and dream of reaching the don's status (Gunst 1995).

As a result of three decades of political and social turmoil, which Gunst describes so vividly, educator Pauline Bain called for a "ban on Anansi" as a folk hero at a March 2001 conference for the Jamaica Teachers Association. Pauline Bain was quoted in a *Gleaner* article as saying, "If you want to ginnal (cheat) and out-smart people, this is what he represents" ("Ban Anancy" 18 March 2001). Many present agreed that Anansi made an appalling folk hero: he was the ultimate hoaxer, a cunning deceiver, a master of lies and malice, and an inspiration to the gangsters and criminals who have blighted and still blight Jamaican society (ibid.). In the wake of this discussion, the *Jamaica Gleaner* was filled with its readers' fiercely divergent views about Anansi's future. Those in favour of banning Anansi argued that he encouraged "trickery and unscrupulous behaviour among children", an influence believed to instill corrupt values – they termed this the "Anansi syndrome" (4 April 2001). But the proposal to ban Anansi also caused outrage: "If you don't leave Anancy alone I promise the mother of all demonstrations", wrote one *Gleaner* reader (27 March 2001).

Like Bain, Dennis Forsythe, author of *Rastafari: Healing of the Nation*, sees Anansi as representative of the problems in Jamaican society. Although he explains that he understands the necessity of the use of Anansi tactics in times of extreme oppression, he warns: "watch ideas and symbols – they do become people" (1999, 257). Forsythe insists that Jamaican society is saturated in trickery and deceit – a culture of "Anancyism" which has turned Jamaicans into hustlers and "Anancy capitalists" (p. 258). For Forsythe, Anansi can be implemented as a concept or intellectual framework to understand the damaging legacy of Jamaica's colonial past. He blames a Jamaican culture of "Anancy-ism" for breakdown of familial relationships, crime and alcoholism, corrupted bureaucracies, nepotism, racketeering, hustling, conmanship and even the presence of the Central Intelligence Agency in Jamaica – which he calls "the leading Anancy" (ibid.). Anansi, according to Forsythe, is also responsible for the "problem" of "the homosexual upsurgence" (ibid.).

In the late 1970s, Forsythe developed a course in the sociology department at the University of the West Indies' Mona campus in Kingston, Jamaica, which was built around his concept of the culture of Anancyism. The course was eventually dropped and his university contract was terminated. In his writing, Forsythe provides a furious attack on his colleagues who challenged the course; he describes them as "middle-class", "brown", "Marxist" and intellectually committed to "vacuous or abstract intellectualism" as well as "middle-range theorizing" (pp. 252–60). He believes these individuals used Anansi-tactics to destroy his concept as it pointed "too much in the direction of self-criticism and self-responsibility" (p. 251).

Forsythe is a Rastafarian and his militant views are grounded in his faith. He and other Rastafarians envision Jamaica today as "Babylon", which, from Forsythe's perspective, is symbolized by the Anansi figure. In his work, the Babylonian spider is posited against that of the Lion of Judah, emblem of Haile Selassie, the "King of Kings" (1999, 247). Like Forsythe, Horace Campbell asserts that he and other Rastafarians urge Jamaicans to drop the archetypal Anansi character traits of the adaptable hustler and "be straightforward with fellow men and women" (1985, 99). Jamaican folklorist Leonard Barrett also suggests that Anansi has become a problematic part of the "Jamaican personality stereotype" (1976, 33).

During the "Ban Anansi" debate, *Gleaner* readers argued that Anansi was a symbol of the decline in education and the collapse of societal values. Psychiatrist E. Anthony Allen claimed that Anansi was no longer providing humour and lessons of the weak overcoming the powerful, brainpower versus physical destruction, but was "being manipulated to show the power of the individual who seeks their end at whatever cost and regardless of consequence" (*Gleaner*, 31 March 2001). Dr Ralph Thompson wrote that Anansi served a purpose in the plantation era but now only represents fraud and lies: "The sentimental attachment to this character is now spent. What was once a means to an end is no longer appropriate for a black nation facing the new challenges of its destiny. It is time to say goodbye to Anansi in our schools and to be reminded of him only as a quaint curiosity, no longer a suitable role model for our children" (*Gleaner*, 4 April 2001).

Thompson suggested replacing the tales of Anansi with stories such as Pinocchio. Even though Pinocchio is not a Jamaican tale, he saw him as a superior role model by showing the young that you can never get away with lying (*Gleaner*, 4 April 2001). Other *Gleaner* readers argued that Anansi was a part of a legacy that created suspicion in Jamaican society – he mirrored the mistrust among Jamaican people; a distrust of the system and mistrust for one another. They said that an "Anansi syndrome" was a widespread phenomenon practised among rich and poor in Jamaica, although when used by the rich it was disguised by the mask of "respectability".

Readers argued that old Anansi, representing a protest mentality and a survival strategy, was dead. For them the new Anansi represented a selfish individualism created in an atmosphere of fragmented, materialistic modern concerns. The protest mentality that the Anansi of old symbolized was based on a coherent order of values; it assumed that laws that were oppressive and immoral should not be obeyed (*Gleaner*, 31 March 2001). This message, they wrote, was now being twisted to suit the actions of a disassociated youth and to legitimize their devious behaviour towards one another and society at large.

As Gunst illustrates in her text, the most sinister expression of the trickster in modern Jamaica is the growing phenomena of gangsters or *yardies*.[10] In 2003 the former Jamaican prime minister Edward Seaga gave an address in Oxford on the impact of folk-culture on Jamaican identity. When asked his views on the possible negative impact of Anansi on the formation of Jamaican cultural identity, he responded thus: "People need to carve a space for themselves. If they have no education they use their wits and brains for other things. They need to carve a space of their own, something which belongs to them, and using Anansi tactics is the only way they can get it". Those who want to ban Anansi, he claimed, come from the "other" Jamaica: "they have privileges and rights and don't need to carve themselves a little space; they have space enough – although you will find that they too use Anansi tactics to get what they want!" (2003).

Ironically, Seaga himself has been accused of being a member of "the other Jamaica" he criticizes, and he allegedly has deployed quite a number of "Anansi tactics" to get what he wanted. Seaga has sued Gunst for libel, as Gunst makes it very clear that she holds him partly responsible for the political violence of the 1970s and 1980s ("Seaga Gets Multimillion Out-of-Court Libel Award", *Gleaner*, 2 October 2003). I do not align myself with Gunst, but wish to outline her criticism of Seaga to demonstrate the ferocity of the "politricks" debate in Jamaica. Gunst claims that Seaga abused his position as minister of welfare and development (to such an extent that some Jamaicans called him the "Minister of Warfare and Devilment") and recounts, in detail, Seaga's famous and ruthless 1966 bulldozing of the Back o' Wall slum in west Kingston, the event that caused storyteller Brother Martin to lose his home (Gunst 1995, 79). In her description of Seaga in *Born fi Dead*, Gunst uses the very same phrase that he uses in relation to Anansi: "he came home to Jamaica to carve a place for himself" (ibid.). Gunst portrays Seaga as the Anansi politician, stopping at nothing to achieve his aims – an example of the "top-down" political corruption that Bain and others sought to denounce.

In his thesis on Jamaican identity, Kam-au Ron Amen laments the fact that "nowadays Anancy is almost always mentioned in a negative context in Jamaican culture . . . seldom do we invoke Anancy in reference to positive happenings" (2002, iii). Yet, despite the growing perception of Anansi as emblematic of a culture of trickery and individualism, Anansi supporters are numerous and passionately defend his legitimacy as Jamaica's national folk hero. Chevannes believes that the key to understanding people's problems with Anansi lie in his ambiguity: "We just don't know yet how to deal with ambiguity: we don't like to live with it, we fight against it" (interview with author, November 2005).

Ambiguity is difficult to accept and understand in the face of Jamaica's current socio-economic problems. Influenced by Pelton's reading of Anansi, Chevannes explains that people try and eradicate ambiguity in their lives through cultural and religious means: "We gather up all ambiguities and put them into these deities, antiheroes and cross-road figures and built narratives around them to satisfy ourselves that we have gained order by sequestering them in a zone. We then evoke them from time to time, to gain relief and remind ourselves that life is how they find it, full of disorder and trickery" (interview with author, November 2005).

While Chevannes perceives Anansi as representative of the ambiguity, disorder and trickery implicit in life itself, Barbara Gloudon sees him as symbolic of the human condition. For her the tales are symbolic of mankind and the continual cycle of sin and redemption which is central to human life. Her interpretation is heavy with Christian symbolism: "The Anansi tales are symbolic of human nature. I deliberately brought it to a kind of religious analogy; in fact it is saying that man's falling from grace is a constant situation, and man's redemption is a constant situation. He is mankind; that is my reading of him, that he is a *symbol* of mankind" (Gloudon, interview with Bell, 1983). Reverend Daley, from Webster Memorial Church in Kingston, also saw Anansi as symbolic of human nature: "Forgiveness plays a dominant role in the self expression of a society", he stated, and within the Anansi tales he found "always a theme of sin and redemption. Anancy is the errant child who is forgiven" (ibid.).

Gloudon and Reverend Daley may attempt to interpret Anansi in a Christian mode, but Chevannes argues that Anansi does not operate within a Christian framework. He states that one must suspend Christian values, and moral and ethical judgements where Anansi is concerned. Chevannes points out that "many Jamaicans don't think of Anansi as sinful . . . in the same way we don't think of the man that pulls off the clever trick as sinful. You may take advantage of somebody else but you may say the person deserves to be taken advantage of" (interview with author 2005). Sherlock also believed that a focus on Anansi's morality takes one away from a "real" understanding of the stories. The Anansi tales, he explained, are to be used as satirical weapons; through the medium of the tale the storyteller takes revenge on those who have wronged or offended him and raises a laugh at their negative character traits: "Ridicule is a powerful weapon – those that think the Anansi story is immoral and should not be told are missing the point. 'Let us,' says the wronged man, 'enter the world of make believe. Let us pretend. We will not use real names'. In this way the story often becomes a vehicle for satire" (cited in Bennett 1944, 12–13).

Although it may seem to Amen that Anansi is seldom evoked in reference to positive "happenings", it is clear that many Jamaicans, like Chevannes, view

Anansi's impact on contemporary Jamaican society as positive. They argue that it is not Anansi who has a negative influence on the Jamaican youth, but the youths' dwindling interest in Jamaican history and culture, which, paradoxically, an interest in Anansi could help to revive. Isaac Bernard, from the Moore Town community, believes that young Jamaicans are losing touch with their cultural traditions as the way of the gun becomes ever more attractive. He illustrates how the Anansi tales offer alternatives to using force to get what you want:

> Anansi storytelling is dying out because younger people they is coming up now, and some of them full of *pride,* they don't want to learn about this thing, they want to learn about the gun, and the knife, and the bayonet, and all those things. You understand. They don't want to know a little Anansi story, but with Anansi if trouble take you, *you can come out and walk back round.* They don't want to know dem, say that that is *too local,* and they say no. But I am thanking God for we who know. (Interview with author, November 2005)

Like Bernard, Small sees the tales as integral to Jamaican culture and believes the tales inspire community cohesion and understanding:

> All Anansi stories, and there are so many, have a good message which speak to human relations, a harmonious life and understanding on many levels – biological, social, psychological and spiritual. It's really about learning to live in a cohesive society. In African communities a story is told which relates to a problem affecting the whole community. So when the problem is solved in the story, a healing takes place in the community as well. (Interview with author, November 2005)

Bennett also jumped to Anansi's defence when asked whether she thought that the Anansi tales encourage an "Anansi mentality". On the contrary, she explained, the tales illustrate how "we must *not* be tricksters" by pointing out the weaknesses of human nature (Bennett, interview with Bell, n.d.). Everyone can appreciate the clever trick played on one who might deserve it, and Anansi tales illustrate the pitfalls of leaving yourself exposed to trickery. Anansi plays on the weaknesses of others – their pride, overconfidence, greed, naiveté, stupidity – they suffer for their flaws and in this way Anansi shows you how *not* to make yourself vulnerable to tricksters: "Anansi is in human nature. Anansi is showing you human traits, pointing out all the human weaknesses. Showing you how you can be tricked, or how somebody can hurt you if you are greedy, thoughtless or stupid" (interview with Bell, n.d.). Velma Pollard supports Bennett's interpretation of Anansi:

> Anansi deals with the foibles of people and shows you how not to make yourself vulnerable. If you are too proud, he will outwit you, because your Achilles heel is accessible to him. He is not a villain but somebody who can see the opportunity to get to your weakness. It is for *you* to be aware of what he is doing. And there is a lesson there to teach you how to live so that your weaknesses *don't* become your downfall. (Interview with author, October 2005)

Conclusion

As the interpretations of these Anansi commentators illustrate, there are many ways of reading Anansi. He is human nature in all its flaws and glories. He warns against weaknesses, he facilitates the airing of problems within a community, he is a vehicle for satire, parody, play and role-reversal. He is emblematic of the ambiguity, violence and disorder inherent to life itself.

Anansi's critics argue that the tactics of resistance and survival used in the plantation context have a negative impact on Jamaican society today. Their arguments are convincing. With high crime and murder rates, individualism, ruthlessness and greed are not traits one would wish to endorse in contemporary Jamaica. However, those who focus on Anansi's actions in isolation may be missing the point. Anansi can be interpreted differently in a modern context: the tales need not actively encourage the listener to do as Anansi does, but can be implemented to encourage an audience to reflect on Anansi's actions. In this way, they facilitate meditation on moral, social and political values. As Miss Lou advocates, Anansi can act as a warning against the dangers of violence and using brawn over brains. The message is: use your intelligence like Anansi, because if you are stupid, an Anansi will expose your weaknesses. Seen in this context, Anansi offers messages of caution against the weaknesses of self-indulgence, pride and stupidity, as well as advocating thought before action; values which are undoubtedly key to influencing change in Jamaican society today.

Anansi survival tactics played out against fellow Jamaicans in the modern world should not be endorsed, but Anansi can be a facilitator of hope and change. Jamaicans have been forced to look back at their slave past with shame, but Anansi can offer an affirmation of their history and encourage a sense of pride in their heritage. He signifies an unsanitized version of the history of the Jamaican people in all its brutality and triumphs.

Furthermore, Anansi is a champion of the "sufferers" – the Jamaican poor who face extreme violence and oppression in their daily lives. Hero of the dispossessed, Anansi's narratives map out the struggles of African slaves and the continuing struggles of the Jamaican people, celebrating their intelligence, stoicism and bravery, and most importantly, their sense of humour. In the postcolonial world, disadvantaged Jamaicans continue to live in a climate of conflict, fear and unpredictability and in these circumstances Anansi is still highly relevant. The great houses of the rich still loom over the poor in Kingston today: built on the sides of the mountains that surround the city, their mansions look down on the struggling populace below, their geographical positioning starkly reflecting the gross inequality of Jamaica's modern social and economic hierarchy.

Anansi has never been a character who directly endorses cooperation or collective action. He is, nevertheless, an instrument of communication and transformation. In each disparate context, Anansi has been a medium through which the individual can challenge the moral, political and social values of their society. Anansi stories confirm that the world is not constructed in binary oppositions, but is confusing, ambivalent, challenging and contradictory. Full of humour, danger, destruction and creation, the Anansi tales challenge listeners and readers to examine the complexity of their existence and their environment.

In recent decades, as Jamaican comedian and storyteller Ranny Williams points out, Anansi has become a metaphor used to describe the Jamaican experience, serving either to "criticize or to praise" (cited in Egglestone 2001, 7). The Asante had faith in negotiation and the power of words to resolve conflicts, and today Jamaican Anansi is once again being used as a vehicle through which a community debate their sociopolitical landscape. Anansi introduces disorder into the social order and in doing so tests its limits, pushing back its boundaries and showing us the possibilities of new and alternative ways of being and thinking. Brother Martin explains this:

The story teach you wisdom, it teach you knowledge. And it teach you understanding. You supposed to pick out the truth out of what Anansi say. You suppose
to pick out the knowledge and the sense out of it. To put yourself on the right
track. Anansi will say jump in a hole, but you don't do that if you can't see what's
down there. You haffi see the *ginnalship*. You have to work it out in your brain.
You also haffi understand the history. (Interview with author, December 2005)

In my view, Anansi is representative of a human preoccupation with freedom on both a psychological and practical level. Trickster figures embody our
fascination with characters who are free to break the boundaries of the social
world. Trickster tales do not exist solely in an environment of severe oppression, but they can be used as vehicles to escape the "oppression" of the
demands of socialization. One can flee the ties of the human world only in
the imagination, therefore the dream of those living in an "acceptable" social
order, such as the Asante, is that of the individualistic trickster, free from all
moral and social responsibilities. In this context the tales ultimately uphold
the social structure and are mediums through which the world can be
explained and problems aired and solved.

In the context of slavery in the Caribbean, however, West Africans and
their descendants found themselves in a social order they could never accept.
It is in this context of captivity and conflict that Anansi took on renewed roles
and functions. The trickster crossed the threshold into the real world; Anansi
enhanced the desire for freedom from captivity, as well as offering practical
techniques to achieve that freedom which could be implemented in the slaves'
daily lives. As has been demonstrated, Anansi tales reflected and inspired
methods of slave survival and resistance, illustrating the tactics of self-preservation, and strategies of defence and subversion against an oppressive order.
In this context, Anansi tales were defiant "hidden transcripts" aimed at undermining the imperial powers, psychologically, culturally and practically (Scott
1990).

However, while this is the prevailing interpretation of the Anansi tales in
their plantation context, due to the malleability of both oral narratives and
the folk-figure, it would be unworthy of Anansi to attempt a final interpretation applicable to the function of the tales in their many different contexts.
Anansi is a master of modification and metamorphosis; ever-changing and
eternally ambiguous, he is fundamentally a shape-shifter and his resistance

to fixity ensures both his continual survival and appeal. As Salkey writes in his poem dedicated to Anansi, "always, Anancy changes" (1981, 36).

Embodiment of resistance and opposition, universal archetype, tester and extender of boundaries, personification of liminality and crossroads, Anansi exists in a perpetual stream of transformation, and will continue to change to suit the needs of the people across the centuries. That is why, in an Asante tale, when Anansi is captured by Nyame's executioners for his misbehaviour, Ya, Old-Mother-Earth, explains, "Let him go and all shall be well." Anansi, symbol of freedom, fascinates and captivates precisely because he can never be fixed, captured or contained. Hence the saying among the Asante, "You are as wonderful as Anansi."

Sample Interview

Brother Martin
Date: 1 December 2005
Location: 15 Hopedale Avenue, Kingston 6, Jamaica

Description of Interview

Brother Martin, also known as Alexander Parker, is a Rastafarian storyteller. Born in 1925, he was a former resident of the notorious Kingston squatters' slum "Back o' Wall". His home was destroyed three time and he now lives in August Town. He was also interviewed by Laura Tanna in 1976, and his stories appear in her book *Jamaican Folktales and Oral Histories* (1984).

Due to the rise in gang violence in August Town (an area of Kingston), Brother Martin came to visit me in Kingston 6. After eating lunch we sat in the garden outside my bed-sit and started the interview. He talked animatedly and gesticulated dramatically, especially when telling Anansi stories, two of which I have edited from this excerpt due to their length. Towards the end of the interview, Brother Martin started to tire, his eyelids drooping. We finished, and I walked him to his bus. There is a photograph of Brother Martin on page 184.

EMILY ZOBEL MARSHALL: Are you ready Brother Martin? Can I ask you a few questions? I was interested in where you grew up.

BROTHER MARTIN: Where I grew up? Well, I grow up in St Catherine. I grew up in a place name Wakefield in St Catherine. Then I come to Kingston,

Figure 16. Brother Martin, storyteller, Kingston, Jamaica. (Photograph by the author, November 2005.)

St Catherine. All my days as a small youth, me moving around, up and down, you understand? I live in Kingston since 1940. Then I was round about ten or fifteen year old.

EZM: When were you born?

BM: I was born 1925, 15 June. And I come to town, me up and down all about from place to place. Till me start work – Coronation Market, there when I [was a] big bowy, I carry people basket from Coronation Market up to Parade. Three pence, six pence.

Me three years old when me mother die. Me not know the care of me mother personally. Midwife-Granny from public hospital look after me. Understand? I don't know me mother's mother, me don't know me father neither. She take care of me till I come right up, till me come 'bout ten or fifteen year old and me come a town, you understand?

Me a town now, about town, until me a turn bad man, you understand. Me work and thief; me work and thief people. Me stop people come from country in the truck. Take de load off of de truck. Put it on the ground and say "pay me", you understand? Take their money. For five, six person in the truck, me take their money. Me have deal with the truck company. Four people from Manchester, me hustle off a them.

EZM: What kind of goods?

BM: [*In a very high-pitched voice*] Yam, co-co, potato, food, cassava, all kind of food. They come pack it a bag, put it on the bus, me take it off the bus and into hand cart and down market for to sell. Coronation Market. That how me live for many years. Many years that how me live. Then me take up a little house in Back o' Wall. Piece of land. Empty land there. Make up a house. It was Back o' Wall and now it name Tivoli Gardens. Government destroy dem. Seaga take over. So now me in August Town. Me lease a piece of land there. I go when I about fifty.

EZM: So you never lived in the countryside?

BM: No for very long. Let me a tell you. When me youth. When me a big man me a never live a country.

EZM: So do you remember people telling you Anansi stories in town?

BM: No, let me tell you they a not tell Anansi in town. The Anansi story me a know now they from youth days, when me live a country. When me about nine, ten some. At night time we shred the corn, put it off the stick in a barrel for the market. And we pick rotten coffee out of the beans. And in the night time we tell Anansi story and everybody a listen.

EZM: Who would tell the stories?

BM: The adults would tell the stories and the children listen it. And then them tell it to one another after. From me a yout me know dem story.

EZM: Why do you think the children would tell the stories when the adults were not there?

BM: Because they don't want adults to know they know de story. Understand? Because they should have something to do beside telling a story, something to do like sweep yard, go for water. They come to me now, these story, from them times, and me keep them in a my head. Me know all of dem you know. Me know whole heap. You understand.

EZM: How would you describe Anansi?

BM: Well, Anansi is a very very dangerous weapon. Anansi is a man who make trouble, and take himself out of it, and make you gwan in there. Understand? Him ginnal man. Now 'ear, 'ear what Anansi do one time!

Anansi in yard and time is hard, him no have no food give him wife or him pickney dem. Him hear dat Brother John Tuwi go over a Bird Cherry Island cross water good for go look food. Him say, "Me a go over there and get some too." Him see coming through bush Brother John Tuwi. Him say, "Good morning, Brother John Tuwi." Him say, "Good morning, Brother Anansi. It's a long time a don't to see you." Anansi say, "Me food dry out, me hear you go far country for food for de wife and pickney, and we want to go too!" You know why we a call him John Tuwi? Dem a bird named so. "Will you take me?" John Tuwi say, "Yes, but you have to fly go there, and you no have no feather, neither wings." Him say, "*good God*, John Tuwi, *good God*, man! Me see a *whole* heap feather dere, give me a feather, let me make up a wing and fly!"

So John Tuwi say "yes", and when him ago in him yard and give him feather and so Anansi make it up some and put a wing on him and put wing round him and leave him for morning and come back next day. And next morning him get to Bird Cherry Island and him start pick cherry and eat full him belly and full him bag! Every cherry John Tuwi go try pick Anansi say, "Me a first a see dat!" He eat *all* the cherry off the tree and John Tuwi say, "Alright, you have the tree, we go look for more tree." When they come back Brer Anansi eat full him belly and full him bag till him drop asleep. Him eat it *all*, and John Tuwi go take away him feather. And bam! – and him fly away. Gone.

Brother Anansi wake up and him see him alone and feathers gone him say [*crying voice*], "Awwwwww, me see me bag is gone, me feather gone. Me on Cherry Island what a me go do? How a me go back home?" So him get him bag and him a start walk walk walk. He start walk walk walk walk. Until he reach the seaside. Hear him now. Him put a leaf in the water and him a float. He jump on it. And him gwan and gwan and gwan and gwan until get out a BIG sea. And true the sea *rough*, it lick him up pon the leaf! Brer Alligator there now and him watch because parts of the sea you see alligator, and him watch you and grab you and take you down alligator yard at sea bottom. Alligator say, "What sight! Anansi on big sea!" And him a capture him. So him take Anansi down a sea bottom and Anansi hear him have a cousin with a wife with only one eye.

So on Sea bottom he a see shark wife, she have one eye. Him go see shark in him yard and him say, "Good morning, Brer Shark." Brer Shark say, "Good morning, Anansi, what you do down here?" And Anansi say, "Me see your wife have only *one* eye and me can cure her because I am a doctor!" So shark say, "Yes man!" and him give Anansi food fee eat and Anansi sleep in him yard, and the light of morning come and Anansi say, "To cure shark wife eye, she haffi lock in a room by herself. You understand? Otherwise the eye can't cure."

Before he a go in de room him tell shark to give him a knife, give him a frying pan, give him some oil and a pack-a-matches. Him tell shark when he hear sssshhhhh [*pretends to hold a frying pan and makes the sound of meat frying*] he must say "tenga": "Tenga mama you a well, tenga tenga mama you a well!" That mean thank god mama you get better. And shark give him the things and he go in the room and tell shark him a going work on him wife eye. And when they lock up the room him kill shark wife! Cut off her head and cook her out and *nyame* her off!

And when he done that he come out and lock up the door where him been now. Now when Anansi come out now him a lock up the door and tell shark he has to wait three day before he can go into his wife room because the wife haffi get better *perfect* first before she can see him. And in the space of three day she will come out and her eye will get better.

So shark give Anansi boat him and come along out of his yard to take Anansi home, with some fish [*the fish help Anansi to pull the boat*]. And him a row and a row and row and row. But two day gone and Brer Shark can't take it no more, him say, "Me want see me wife man!" And him go home and him open de door and him see no wife at all! Him only see a frying pan, knife. And him go in him yard and say Pooooooo! Poooooo! [*Whale noise?*] Him say, "Bring back Anansi come yaaaa, bring back Anansi come yoooo!"

So Anansi row fast, row fast, and Brer Shark bawling to bring back Anansi. The fish say, "What Brer Shark a say?" Anansi say, "He say row Anansi fast! Row fast!" Now when he reach land now him say to fish, "You can't go back home tonight, you have to wait to the morning. A storm is coming. Come to

yard and sleep up there." And them say, "Alright." They take the boat on land
and decide to follow Brer Anansi to him yard.

But when them go up the road now, they see some boy now – like them
boy who sit pon the corner, you know them boy? Whole heap of boy! So
Anansi turn to the fish and say [*conspiratorial*], "You know what man? You see
dem boy there, they *no* like it when they see fish pass you know!" So he say,
"You know what you haffi do? You have get in me bag there to pass them."
Fish decide to hide in Anansi bag, Anansi *tie* up de bag mouth and carry them
dem straight a yard! Him make up a big fire and boil up a big pot and put de
two fish in. And cook dem and nyame dem off! So from *dat* until *dis* time man
noh say can't eat fish, because man must eat fish! From dat had till dis one,
man a eat fish.

Say a Jack Mandora dat story dere *done*. Me no say no more.

EZM: You know when you say "Jack Mandora", what does that mean?

BM: That mean the story over. Jack Mandora is a man who tell story.

EZM: What do you think Anansi looks like?

BM: Anansi have about ten legs, five a this side and five a that side. Him can
a shake them out and you can see all of them, or hold them in. Anansi is brave
man. And him is man him have *techniques*. He is a man him have *intelligence!*
Anansi is a man who *tief!* You can't find a bigger tief than him.

EZM: Does Anansi play on other people's weakness?

BM: Yes man! . . . Anansi is a *ginnal*. Is a man who will try and apprehend
anything you put in his kingdom!

EZM: Some people say that Anansi is too much of a *ginnal* and his stories
should not be taught to children, but some other people say that Anansi is
important . . .

BM: Yes!!! It have a kind of moral. It will show you that you can defend yourself in every *capasibility* that you can. Because it will help you a get out o' it,
you see?

EZM: Do you know about the history of the stories?

BM: Well them stories come straight from Africa. Because in days gone by
when slave master did a rule slave, African could not speak to African like me
a you go aspeak together. Them a *ketch we, and beat we and tie up* and *rob*

and a *beat* we, so we can't a talk each other. Because if we talk to each other we will form law gainst *dem*!

So Africans get together and them a talk Anansi story, and when them a talk some of the story have *great meaning*. Dem a tell you what fee happen and how to do things, but they talk it a story, so nobody know. You understand? So it happen, right here and true. Whole heap a story, whole heap a meaning. Through them you know what happen to the African.

When them working them talk about the boss and also ina song. While dem work them a tell you which part a meet me tonight. Which part you a go tomorrow, and which part you sister and brother a go to link up and meet you!

Them African story, slave come and set them up among each other. You see the Maroon now, them a one of the *clever* set a people. Because they fight 'gainst the English and the English have to *free* them to get land for themselves.

EZM: Do you think that some church people would disapprove of the Anansi stories?

BM: Yes man! You can't tell some of the people Anansi stories! But every foot step of the way you have good and evil. Good man and de bad man. You have some man in the house of God and they bad people! They try and cheat the poor. In everything you have good and you have evil [*gives examples*].

EZM: Does Anansi show you that in everything you have good and evil?

BM: Yes man, but you have to think it out you know, Anansi no show you that. You have to think it out yourself. You have to watch him. You have to figure the story out.

EZM: What about when people say that Anansi is encouraging gunmen and conmen and tricksters in Jamaica? What would you say to that?

BM: The gunman *noh* be like Anansi. Anansi is a man make you drop in a hole and tie you up. He no *kill* you. You dead by yourself. Gunman now, will see you in the road, take four or five shots and you dead and gone. It's a different thing. You don't call him trickster, you call him *murderer*. Him a *wicked*. Anansi is a different form. You listen to the story and you work it out for yourself. Pick out the sense out of the nonsense.

EZM: You say you can't tell some people Anansi stories. Why?

BM: They no want hear. They say you fool with Anansi! They say when Anansi talk he makes no sense! But a whole *heap* a sense in a it. You pick it out.

More Anansi me a tell a you. [*Tells another Anansi tale.*]

EZM: Is Anansi ever a loser?

BM: Everytime he find some way to get out of it and leave you in a it. He *always* a winner wid him ginnalship. No one stronger that Anansi in a ginnalship.

EZM: How would you describe Tacoma?

BM: Tacoma is a man like Brer Anansi. Also Brer Tiger. Them just have different name. Them people – them a clever people. But out of all of them Anansi is the cleverest one.

EZM: What's your favourite Anansi story?

BM: My favourite is every one of them. I still tell them. In school I tell story you know. To schoolchildren. They call *me* Brother Anansi! Now you can talk story for big profit! For whole heap a money. You can get a big percentage.

EZM: Do the children tell fewer stories now?

BM: Well these children now they want to hear about foolishness. They want to hear about fire gunshot. Kill man. You understand. They want to know about the gun, but the gun, it make no sense. They make their war here. But me not like that.

The story teach you wisdom, it teach you knowledge. And it teach you understanding. You supposed to pick out the truth out of what Anansi say. You suppose to pick out the knowledge out of it and the sense out of it. To put yourself on the right track. Anansi will say jump in a hole, but you don't do that if you can't see what's down there. You haffi see the ginnalship. You have to work it out in your brain. You also haffi understand the history. You see is a funny ting you know. You want to go to Papine [*an area in Kingston*]. But if your hand, your heart, your foot don't come together, you don't go to Papine. You have to know *how* to think and *what* to think.

Notes

Introduction

1. I watched storytellers Amina Blackwood Meeks at the Phillip Sherlock Centre for the Creative Arts, UWI ("Matters Arising", 23 October 2005), a story performance by Enitou Springer at the Marcus Garvey Centre, Kingston (7 December 2005) and storyteller and comedian Paul Keens Douglas at the Jamaica Pegasus Hotel ("Come Mek Wi Laff", 27 November 2005). The interviewee who collected tales was George Campbell from St Thomas.

2. The *Dictionary of Jamaican English* lists the following: Anànse, Anansi, Anancy, Anánsi, Hanáansi, Nansi, Ananzi, Anansay, Annancey, Nancy, Annancy, Nance and Anawasy (Cassidy and Le Page 2002, 10).

3. Anansi is referred to as "Ti malice" in Haiti and "Nansi", "Aunty Nancy" or "Miss Nancy" in southern parts of the United States. In Curaçao they refer to their folktales as "Cuenta de Nansi" and in Suriname as "Anansitore" (Levine 1977, 105; Purchas-Tulloch 1976, 225).

4. "Compair" translates as "godfather", but it is used as a term of endearment similar to "Brer".

5. The trickster, for Jung, is the universal archetype of the unconscious, which is altered as it makes its way into the conscious mind through myth and symbol. It is essentially a "shadow" archetype, harkening back to a time of chaos when man was closer to animal, and it is a sinister and dangerous force. Jung makes some rather dubious and outdated claims regarding the function of the trickster, arguing that "tribal" peoples are closer to this primitive pre-civilized state, which explains the persistence of the trickster archetype in their cultures (1972).

6. See Kouwenberg 2008.

7. Orlando Patterson examined the tribal origins for the Jamaican slaves in his 1967

text *The Sociology of Slavery*. Patterson states that during the earlier half of the period 1655–1700 the largest single group of slaves transported to Jamaica came from among the Akan and Ga-Andangme peoples, a large ethnic group from southeast Ghana. Many of them came via the eastern Caribbean, "and as they were already seasoned, were well placed, both historically and socially, to impose their own patterns of behaviour and speech on the Creole slave society which was then at its nuclear stage" (Patterson 1967, 142). During the period 1675–1700, 20 per cent came from Ghana, but Patterson states that these arrivals would "doubtless have assisted in consolidating the Akan and Ga-Andangme bias which the young Creole slave community would have already had" (p. 142). During 1700–1730, according to Patterson, slaves from Ghana made up the second largest source of slaves. From 1730 to 1775 there was an increase of slaves from Ghana, who made up 40 per cent of the slaves brought to Jamaica, and from 1775 to 1800, 30 per cent came from Ghana (p. 142). It can be concluded, therefore, that due to the large influx of slaves of Akan origin and their position as a dominant tribe in Ghana, Jamaican slave culture was influenced by Akan cultural forms. As is demonstrated in this book, this is evident in the slaves' religious practices, music, dance, folklore and language structures. See Williams 1934; Alleyne 1988; Sherlock 1998.

Chapter 1

1. The Akan calendar is based on what the Akan call "forty days", *adaduanan* (*da* meaning "day", *aduanan* meaning "forty") which is actually made up of forty-two different days (with the forty- third day being the same as the first). The *adaduanan* comprises of both six-day weeks and seven-day weeks. Phillip F.W. Bartle, researcher of Akan culture, states that the European and Akan seven-day week are equivalent and explains that "the *adaduanan* cycle appears to be based on an older six-day week, still in existence in some northern [Ghanaian] communities . . . on which is superimposed a seven-day week which may have been brought south with itinerant traders from the savannah". While "Kwaku" in Twi is translated as "male born of a Wednesday", the "Wednesday" of the Akan seven-day week is termed *Wukuo* and is the "Birthday of Spider" which is connected to, according to Bartle, the "reverse or mortal version of God" (Bartle 1978, 80–84; Twi Dictionary 2007).

2. Comparisons can be drawn between, among others, Barker's "Why Spiders Are Always Found in the Corners of the Ceilings" (p. 69) and Rattray's "How It

Came About That Ananse, the Spider, Went up on the Rafters" (p. 249). Also Barker's "How Beasts and Serpents First Came into the World" (p. 89) and Rattray's "How Spear-Grass Came into the Tribe" (p. 213).

3. Among the Asante the golden stool is believed to have descended from the sky through the power of the priest Okomfo Anokye, Osei Tutu's faithful advisor, who received it as a gift from Nyame to make his people great (Isichei 1977, 65–67).

4. The "Sky-God" is Rattray's English translation of the Twi "Nyame".

5. This is also the case in Jamaica. It is still believed to be dangerous to tell Anansi tales before nightfall in Jamaica today (see chapters 2 and 3).

6. This ending is just one of the many explicit connections between Asante Anansi and Jamaican Anansi. I discuss the Jamaican version of this ending in chapter 3.

7. Williams describes Mmoatia as "little people" and states that among the Asante "these strange creatures are sometimes referred to as being exceedingly swift and used by devils and wizards as messengers" or again as "the speedy messengers of the gods who can go and come like the wind" (1934, 236). Williams cites Rattray, who states: "The most characteristic feature of these Ashanti 'little folk' – the word Mmoatia probably means 'the little animals' – is their feet, which point backwards. They are said to be about a foot in stature, and to be of three distinct varieties: black, red, and white, and they converse by means of whistling. The black fairies are more or less innocuous, but the white and the red Mmoatia are up to all kinds of mischief, such as stealing housewives' palm-wine and the food left over from the previous day" (cited in Williams 1934, 237).

8. For more information on the "liminal" see: Douglas 1966, van Gennep 1960 and Turner 1967.

9. Rattray, Bakhtin and Jung all describe trickster tales as "Rabelaisian". Rattray states the Asante Anansi folktales contain "the most Rabelaisian passages" and Jung draws parallels between the trickster and past "Rabelaisian" ribaldries within the French Catholic Church (Rattray 1930, ix; Jung 1972, 138).

10. Anansi tales focused on the anus or penis include: "How It Came About That the Hinder Part of Kwaku Ananse, the Spider, Became Big, at the Expense of His Head, Which Became Small" and "How Contradiction Came Among the Tribe" (Rattray 1930, 71; 107).

Chapter 2

1. A term derived from the Spanish *Cimarron* meaning "wild", "untamed" or a "hunter of wild cattle" (Cassidy and Le Page 2002, 293).

2. See Cassidy and Le Page 2002 for further information on Twi origins in Jamaican Creole.

3. "Buckra", also spelled "Backra", meaning white master or boss, is derived from the African Ibo word *mbakáre*, meaning "white man who governs" (Cassidy and Le Page 2002, 18).

4. Jeffery-Smith 1899; Beckwith 1924; Bennett 1979; Jekyll 1966.

5. Jekyll explains: "Hafoo: an African word, a kind of yam. 'Kellion: Skellion or scallion, an onion which does not bulb"; "Gungo: Congo, a pea excellent for soups"; "Quatty: A penny" (1966, 19).

6. In Jamaica, the Anansi tales traditionally end with the formulaic statement used by Bennett "Jack Mandora, me no choose none", and there are a variety of interpretations regarding the origins and meaning of this phrase. Livingston describes it as a "kind of spell" (Livingston 1910–50, Ms. 59). Jekyll states that Jack is the person to whom the story is being told: the narrator addresses them and explains they would not like the events and trickery in the tale to befall them. Furthermore, similarly to the Asante beginning discussed in chapter 1 – "we do not really mean, we do not really mean (that what we are going to say is true)" – Jekyll explains that, when told for amusement, the story ends with this formula to explain to listeners that "this story of mine is not aimed at anyone" (Rattray 1930, 55; Jekyll 1966, 10). Bennett, perhaps as a result of her British colonial schooling, learned as a girl that the ending was aimed at disavowing Anansi's wicked ways: "Jack Mandora, the doorman at heaven's door, know that we were not in favour of Annancy's wicked ways. 'Me no choose none' means 'I don't chose to behave in any of these ways' " (cited in Tanna 2000, 31). However, linguist Frederick Cassidy, after considering the possible African or Portuguese roots of this phrase, states that it "turned out to be plain English" and influenced by a British radio broadcast, which was introduced with the verse: "Jackanory, I'll tell you a story, and this is how it's begun, I'll tell you another of Jack and his brother and now my story is done" (ibid.). According to Cassidy, "Jackanory . . . and now my story is done" – the middle part is missed out – became "Jackmandora . . . me no choose none" (ibid.). Again we are faced with the multiple interpretations, which seem to pervade every aspect of the Anansi and the Anansi tales, but, as Tanna points out, not knowing the correct interpretation need not be problematic, "as

long as individuals infuse new meanings into old customs to keep them current" (p. 31).

7. Lewis refers to his cook as "Cookey" in a letter to his friend, dated March 1815 (1999, 259).

8. Alice Werner explains that "tiger" may have been used to describe what was originally a West African leopard or lion; "all over South Africa, leopards are called 'Tigers' by Dutch, English and Germans . . . Tiger is used in the same sense in German Kamerun, and probably elsewhere in West Africa" (cited in Jekyll 1966, xxxviii).

9. An example of Anansi helping Nyame can be found in "How Spear-Grass Came Into the Tribe" in which Anansi offers to assist Nyame and defeat an approaching army (Rattray 1940, 213–21). In "How Kwaku Ananse (the Spider) Got Aso in Marriage", Anansi sleeps with Aso at Nyame's bidding (Rattray 1930, 133–37).

10. Other versions of this tale can be found in Tanna (2000, 63–64) and Sherlock (1989, 105).

11. *Boonoonoonoos* is a term of endearment, meaning very pretty, beautiful, wonderful, glorious; "a term expressing a burst of favourable enthusiasm" (Cassidy and Le Page 2002, 81).

12. Bennett's "Mussirolinkina" is a tale very similar to Lewis's "African Nansi-story" which does not feature Anansi but tells of a headman and obeahman of a "large district in Africa" who loses a considerable amount "at play" to a nobleman. Fearing for his safety the headman's nurse tells the nobleman that he may be harmed when he comes to court to collect his payment and advises him to take the road by the river. On his way he sees the headman's youngest daughter bathing, whom no one can marry unless they can guess her age. He takes her clothes as advised by the nurse and then gives them back to her when she becomes alarmed; in return she helps him guess her age and they marry (Lewis 1999, 191).

13. Jekyll (1907) recorded the musical notations that accompany the songs in his text. Roberts (1924) recorded the music and songs that accompanied the tales collected by Beckwith on phonographic equipment and then transcribed the notations for Beckwith's book. Tanna's text (1984) can be purchased with an audiocassette of the original storytelling performances and songs, as well as a video of the storytellers featured in her book, which was recorded in studio at a later date.

14. Despite the presence of the fiddle in Africa, the fiddle Anansi plays in Jamaican tales is depicted in illustrations accompanying written collections as a European fiddle.

15. The patois *poppesha* originates from "poppy-show" which is derived from "pup-pet-show", meaning "a ridiculous exhibition". This term refers to foolishness, ridiculous talk or actions (Cassidy and Le Page 2002, 359).

16. For references to these Jamaican foods, see, among others, Bennett, "Anancy an de Plantain" (1979, 76); Jekyll, "Dry-Bone" (1961, 48); and "Bird Cherry Island" (Brother Martin, interview with author, December 2005).

17. Brother Martin, interviewed by Tanna in 1976 and by the author in 2005, is a Rastafarian storyteller. Born in 1926, he was a former resident of the notorious Kingston squatters' slum Back o' Wall, which was bulldozed by Seaga's govern-ment. His home was destroyed three times. He now lives in August Town (see interview with Brother Martin in the appendix).

18. "Compè" is derived from the French word *compère*, meaning "godfather", and is the French Creole equivalent of "Brer".

19. "Nayger" is a derogatory term for a "Negro" (Cassidy and Le Page 2002, 317).

20. Comparisons can be drawn between this tale and "Guinea Chick and Dry-Head" (Rocky, interview with author, November 2005).

Chapter 3

1. Lewis writes that slave women on his plantation "preferred to see their own chil-dren dead rather than be obliged to witness their daily punishments" (cited in Sherlock 1998, 195).

2. The ethnic origin of the slaves first imported by the Spanish to Jamaica remains unclear. According to the Trans-Atlantic Slave Trade database, the main source of slaves transported to the Caribbean and Spanish American mainland during the period between the first recorded Spanish voyage in 1526 and British occu-pation in 1655 was Senegal and the Gambia and the offshore Atlantic (9,774 slaves transported) (2009).

3. I interviewed Isaac Bernard while he sat on the porch of his home in Comfort Castle, contemplating the incredible view. His house overlooked hills carpeted in lush vegetation and partly shrouded in wisps of mist. As we arrived, Mr Bernard immediately adopted an Anansi-like persona, feigning naivety and dim-wittedness: "Why you want to come here and speak to a dunce like me? . . . Mr Smith sent you? . . . He said that about me? . . . But I am but a dunce, I cannot read or write." He went on to prove himself to be extremely intelligent and informed.

4. The term "big man" is defined as meaning an "adult man, grown man" (Cassidy and Le Page 2002, 42).

5. For reference to provision grounds in Anansi tales see, among others, Beckwith's recording of "Cunnie-More-Than-Father" (1924, 29) and "The Dumb Wife" (1924, 124). In "Friendship of Bro Anancy and Bro Puss" (Perkins 1910–77), "Puss and Anancy go to a dance one night and became good friends, so they arranged to go to each others provision grounds" (ibid.). At Puss's ground, they enjoy watermelons together, but when they go to Anansi he challenges Puss to see who can throw a knife the furthest. As Puss has no knife and Anansi, true to form, will not share his, Anansi eats melons while Puss watches, declaring "Bro puss, who have knife eat water melon." The story ends, "From that day to this Puss work no ground" (ibid.).

6. Jekyll explains that "yaws" was a disease prevalent among "Negroes" and slaves which caused ulcers on the feet but "does not attack the Whites": "In old slave days every estate had its yaws-house for the accommodation of the sufferers" (1966, 57).

7. "Dry-Head at the Barbers" was recounted to the author by Isaac Bernard and Rocky. It has been referenced in chapter 2.

8. For Scott, trickster tales told by slaves of African descent are a display of veiled cultural resistance to oppression. He claims they are "hidden transcripts"; voices of resistance disguised by the oppressed and then spoken in the public sphere, at times even in the company of the oppressors. Scott uses drama and theatre metaphors to articulate his theory of performativity. He describes how subordinate peoples perform a role of subservience when in the presence of their masters. When they escape the gaze of the dominant, the performance ends. This concept can be applied to the role-playing of Jamaican plantation slaves; slaves performed a particular role "onstage", as Scott puts it, and another "offstage" (1990). Anansi is symbolic of this performance as the content of the tales focuses on the deceptive performances Anansi puts on to undermine the system. Lewis's record of his slaves' performances demonstrates how slaves implemented these performances in their daily lives.

9. Excerpts from Thistlewood's journals, 1748–86, Lincolnshire County Archives, Monson Ms. 31, entries for 18 May and 2 October 1750 (cited in Craton 1982).

Chapter 4

1. Social reformer Josiah Wedgwood I (1730–95) issued a ceramic medallion in 1787 which depicted a kneeling slave and the inscription "Am I not a man and a brother?" It was modelled after the seal of the Committee for the Abolition of the Slave Trade founded by Thomas Clarkson (British Museum 2011).

2. Rattray's tale does not feature Anansi, but, like the tale told to Thistlewood, it
    tells of how a disobedient young girl is kept captive by an old (obeah)woman
    who tells her to dig yams, but not to dig up ones that cry "dig me up", and to
    pound "fu-fu" in her nose. The old lady refuses to share the food with the girl
    until she guesses her real name, and the girl grows weak and thin. As she cries
    by the river one day Crab takes pity on her and tells her the old woman's name,
    which is "Old-woman-Mosono". In her anger, "Old-woman-Mosono" throws a
    calabash at Crab's back and it stays there: "that is why Crab has shell on his
    back" (Rattray 1930, 33–35).

    The tale is also similar to another of Rattray's collection, a story called "How
    Spear-Grass Came into the Tribe" in which Ntikuma sets off to a "certain village"
    and meets "Old-woman-grandmother", a mysterious lady of magical powers who
    sets him tasks, one of which is not to pick the yams in her field that cry "pluck
    me, pluck me", and he is rewarded with food for his obedience (pp. 213–21).
    Anansi fails at these tasks, as he is greedy and then inadvertently kills the "Sky-
    God's" army. In "How Spear-Grass Came into the Tribe", we see Anansi pretend
    to have his monthly period while he eats all the family's yams in a secluded hut
    reserved for women during their period of menstruation. This element of gender
    play – an interesting subversion in itself – has been adapted into Jamaican ver-
    sions of "How Crab Got Its Shell", which amalgamate both of Rattray's tales
    mentioned above (see Sherlock's "How Crab Got a Hard Back").

3. For example, the Kingston Welfare Commission printed a series of pamphlets
    for children named "Caribbean Home Library". See Dorothy Clarke's *The Adven-
    tures of Brer Nancy* (194–).

4. In Rattray's recording of "Why It Is the Elders Say We Should Not Repeat Sleep-
    ing-Mat Confidence", Anansi wins the Sky-God's daughter's hand in marriage
    by rising to a challenge and not scratching while working the Sky-God's land
    (he tells a story and slaps himself where it itches, as if he were gesticulating).
    He explains his trick to his new wife, a "sleeping-mat confidence", and she
    threatens to tell her father (Rattray 1930, 129–33). A Jamaican version recorded
    by Tanna, entitled "Bredda Nansi, de King an Dryhead Anansi" follows the same
    pattern. Anansi scratches while working in the field by asking a local boy:
    "BWOY, de cow dat yu daddy gwine give me have black yah-so? Im say 'no suh'.
    Im say [yells and scratches], 'Im have a white yah-so?' Im say: 'No Suh'. Im say
    [scratches] 'It have a brown yah-so?' Im say 'Yes, suh'." This is repeated four
    times, causing much hilarity among the audience (Tanna 2000, 97–100). Yet
    another version appears in Jekyll's collection entitled "William Tell", in which

the King is replaced by "a man who name William Tell". This man owns many cows and has a tree in his yard called the Huyg. Contact with the tree causes itching, and William Tell offers a cow to anyone who can cut the tree down without scratching him or herself. Anansi cuts the tree down by singing to it. Note here that a European folk character enters the tales, and how he is assumed, because of his heritage, to be prosperous and powerful (Jekyll 1966, 29–30).

5. The word *tebin* is possibly derived from the Creole term *tebba*, from the Ewe *tébee*, meaning "full to the brim" (Cassidy and Le Page 2002, 439).

6. For further details see the *Gargoyles Encyclopedia* 2006.

7. For a fuller discussion of Salkey's Anansi stories, see Marshall 2010.

8. Contemporary Jamaican storyteller and performer.

9. Storytelling event, Marcus Garvey Centre, Kingston (7 December 2005).

10. The term "yardies" is derived from "yard", which refers to the location of one's home or where the home is sited. Although phonetically related to the English term "yard" it is derived from the Kongo *yaandi* (Carter 1996, 125). It is a term still used by Jamaica's Kumina speakers and practitioners whose language, religion, music and dancing is thought to have been introduced by West central African indentured labourers brought to Jamaican after the British abolished the trade in 1807 (Pinn 2009, 207). The term "yardie" is predominantly used to refer to Jamaican criminals or gangsters, but can also be used to describe Jamaicans generally. Jamaica itself can also be referred to as "the Yard" or "Yard" (Williams 2004).

References

Abrahams, R.D. 1982. Storytelling Events: Wake Amusements and the Structure of Nonsense on St Vincent. *Journal of American Folklore* 95, no. 378 (October–December): 389–414.

Alleyne, M.C. 1988. *Roots of Jamaican Culture*. London: Pluto.

Amen, R.K. 2002. Fi Wi Cultural Studies: Film, Culture, Identity. Master's thesis, University of the West Indies, St Augustine, Trinidad and Tobago.

Amnesty USA. 2007. Jamaica Human Rights: Human Rights Concerns. Accessed 6 May 2007. http://www.amnestyusa.org/Jamaica.

A.S.R. 1957. Anancy and Assonu. *Jamaica Historical Society Bulletin* 2, no. 1 (March): 14–16.

Austin-Broos, D. 1997. *Jamaica Genesis: Religion and the Politics of Moral Orders*. Chicago: University of Chicago Press.

Bakhtin, M. 1984. *Rabelais and His World*. Bloomington: Indiana University Press.

Barker, W.H., and C. Sinclair. 1917. *West African Folk Tales*. London: George G. Harrap.

Barker, W.H. 1919. Nyankopon and Ananse in Gold Coast Folklore. *Folklore* 30, no. 2 (June): 158–64.

Barrett, E.L. 1976. *The Sun and the Drum: African Roots in Jamaican Folk Tradition*. Kingston: Sangster's.

Bartle, P.F.W. 1978. Forty Days: The Akan Calendar in Africa. *Journal of the International African Institute* 48, no. 1 (January): 80–84.

Beckwith, M.W. 1924. *Jamaica Anansi Stories*. New York: American Folklore Society.

———. 1969. *Black Roadways*. New York: Negro Universities Press.

Bennett, L. 1944. *Anancy Stories and Poems in Dialect*. Kingston: Gleaner Company.

———. 1950. *Anancy Stories and Dialect Verse*. Kingston: Pioneer Press.

———. 1961. *Laugh with Louise: A Pot-Pourrie of Jamaican Folk-Lore, Stories, Songs and Verses*. Kingston: City Printery.

———. 1966. *Jamaica Labrish*. Kingston: Sangster's.

———. 1979. *Anancy and Miss Lou*. Kingston: Sangster's.

———. n.d. Interview by Paulette Bell. Cassette recording. Kingston, Jamaica. Jamaica Memory Bank.

Bernard, I. 2005. Interview by author. Mini-disk recording. 19 November. Comfort Castle, St Thomas, Jamaica.

Brailsford, D. 2004. *Confessions of Anansi*. Kingston: LMH.

Brathwaite, E.K. 1995. Jazz and the West Indian Novel. In *The Post-Colonial Studies Reader*, edited by B. Ashcroft and G. Griffiths, 327–31. London: Routledge.

British Museum. 2011. Anti-slavery Medallion, by Josiah Wedgwood. Accessed 10 Aug 2011. http://www.britishmuseum.org/explore/highlights/highlight_objects /pe_mla/ a/anti-slavery_medallion,_by_jos.aspx.

Brodber, A. 2005. Interview by author. Telephone recording. 22 November. Kingston, Jamaica.

Burnard, T. 2004. *Mastery, Tyranny and Desire: Thomas Thistlewood and His Slaves in the Anglo-Jamaican World*. Chapel Hill: University of North Carolina Press.

Burton, R. 1997. *Afro-Creole: Power, Opposition and Play in the Caribbean*. Ithaca: Cornell University Press.

Campbell, H. 1985. *Rasta and Resistance: From Marcus Garvey to Walter Rodney*. London: Hansib.

Campbell, M.C. 1988. *The Maroons of Jamaica 1655–1796: A History of Resistance, Collaboration and Betrayal*. Trenton, NJ: Africa World Press.

Carter, H. 1996. Annotated Kumina Lexicon. *African-Caribbean Institute of Jamaica Research Review* 3: 84–129.

Cassidy, F. 1961. *Jamaica Talk*. London: Macmillan.

Cassidy, F.G., and R.B. Le Page, eds. 2002. *Dictionary of Jamaican English*. Kingston: University of the West Indies Press.

Chevannes, B. 2001. *Ambiguity and the Search for Knowledge: An Open-ended Adventure of the Imagination*. Kingston: University of the West Indies.

———. 2005. Interview by author. Mini-disk recording. 23 November. University of the West Indies, Mona, Jamaica.

———. 2006. *Betwixt and Between: Explorations in an African-Caribbean Mindscape*. Kingston: Ian Randle.

Clarke, D. 194–. *The Adventures of Brer Anansi*. Kingston: Jamaica Social Welfare Commission.

Colman Smith, P. 1896. Two Negro Stories from Jamaica. *Journal of American Folklore* 9, no. 35 (October–December): 278.

———. 1899. *Annancy Stories*. New York: D.H. Russell.

Craton, M. 1982. *Testing the Chains: Resistance to Slavery in the British West Indies*. Ithaca: Cornell University Press.

Daley, O. 1983. Interview by Paulette Bell. Cassette recording. 27 June. Webster Memorial Church, Kingston, Jamaica. Jamaica Memory Bank.

Danquah, J.B. 1944. *The Akan Doctrine of God*. London: Lutterworth Press.

DeCamp, D. 1961. Social and Geographic Factors in Jamaican Dialects. In *Creole Language Studies*, edited by R.B. Le Page, 61–84. London: Macmillan.

De Certeau, M. 1980. On the Oppositional Practices of Everyday Life. *Social Text*, no. 3 (Autumn): 3–43.

De Souza, P. 2003. Creolizing Anancy: Signifyin(g) Processes in New World Spider Tales. *Matatu: Journal for African Culture and Society* 27, no. 1: 339–63.

Douglas, M. 1966. *Purity and Danger: An Analysis of the Concepts of Pollution and Taboo*. London: Routledge.

Egglestone, R.M. 2001. A Philosophy of Survival: Anancyism in Jamaican Pantomime. *Society for Caribbean Studies Annual Conference Papers* vol. 2. Accessed 18 March 2003. http://www.caribbeanstudies.org.uk/papers/2001/olv2p5.pdf.

———. 2003. "Jamaica Derive Too": The Use of Jamaica Talk in the National Pantomime. Paper presented at the Society of Caribbean Studies Conference, Bristol University.

Ellis, A.B. 1894. *Yoruba-Speaking Peoples of the Slave Coast of West Africa*. Accessed 2 January 2007. http://www.sacred-texts.com/afr/yor/index.htm.

———. 1966. *The Tchi-Speaking Peoples of the Gold Coast of West Africa*. Oostrerhout: Netherlands Anthropological Publications.

Eltis, D., and D. Richardson. 2003. West Africa and the Transatlantic Slave Trade: New Evidence on Long-Run Trends. In *The Slavery Reader*, edited by G. Heuman and J. Walvin, 42–57. London: Routledge.

Fanon, F. 1986. *Black Masks, White Skins*. London: Pluto.

Folklore of the Negroes of Jamaica. 1904. *Folklore* 15, no. 1 (March): 87–94.

Folklore of the Negroes of Jamaica. 1905. *Folklore* 16, no. 1 (March): 68–77.

Forsyth, D. 1999. *Rastafari: Healing of the Nation*. New York: One Drop Books.

Gargoyles Encyclopedia n.d. Anansi. Accessed 8 May 2007. http://www.reocities.com/demonafan2/gargoyles_myths_legends.htm

Glazier, S.D. 1998. Rites of Passage. In *The Encyclopedia of Religion and Society*, edited by W.H. Swatos. Accessed 10 September 2007. http://hirr.hartsem.edu/ency/index.html.

Gloudon, B. 1983. Interview by Paulette Bell. Cassette recording. 29 June. Kingston, Jamaica. Jamaica Memory Bank.

Gradussov, A. 1971. *Anancy in Love*. Kingston: Jamaica Publishing House.

Grant, J. Institute of Jamaica Folklore Research Project. 1967–69. Ms. 1947, National Library of Jamaica, Kingston.

Gunst, L. 1995. *Born fi Dead: A Journey Through the Jamaican Posse Underworld*. New York: Henry Holt.

Hall, D. 1999. *In Miserable Slavery: Thomas Thistlewood in Jamaica, 1750–86*. Kingston: University of the West Indies Press.

Harris, W. 1981. *Explorations*. Denmark: Dangaroo.

Hart, R. 1998. *From Occupation to Independence: A Short History of the Peoples of the English-speaking Caribbean Region*. London: Pluto.

Hartland, S. 1917. Review: *West African Folk-Tales*, by W.H. Barker, Cecilia Sinclair. *Folklore* 28, no. 3 (September): 333–34.

Herskovits, J.M. 1958. *The New World Negro*. Bloomington: Indiana University Press.

Heuman, G. 1994. *The Killing Time: The Morant Bay Rebellion in Jamaica*. Knoxville: University of Tennessee Press.

Isichei, E. 1977. *A History of West Africa since 1800*. London: Macmillan.

Jamaica Cultural Development Commission (JCDC). 2002. National Festival of the Arts, Performing Arts, Speech. Accessed 3 December 2005. http://www.jcdc.gov.jm.

James, C. 2004. Searching for Anansi: From Orature to Literature in the West Indian Children's Folk Tradition – Jamaican and Trinidadian Trends. Paper presented at IBBY World Congress, Cape Town, South Africa.

Jeffery-Smith, U. 1899. *A Selection of Anancy Stories*. Kingston: Aston W. Gardener.

Jekyll, W. 1966. *Jamaican Song and Story: Annancy Stories, Digging Sings, Dancing Tunes and Ring Tunes*. New York: Dover Publications.

Jonas, J. 1990. *Anansi in the Great House: Ways of Reading West Indian Fiction*. Westport, CT: Greenwood.

Jung, C.G. 1972. *Four Archetypes: Mother Rebirth Spirit Trickster*. London: Routledge.

King, N.Q. 1986. *African Cosmos: An Introduction to Religion in Africa*. Belmont, CA: Wadsworth.

Kopytoff, B.K. 1978. The Early Political Development of Jamaican Maroon Communities. *William and Mary Quarterly*, 3rd ser., 35, no. 2 (April): 287–307.

Kouwenberg, S. 2008. African Languages in Early English Jamaica: The Akan-Dominance Myth. Paper presented at seminar series, University of Puerto Rico, Rio Piedras.

Kyei, T.E. 2001. *Our Days Dwindle: Memories of My Childhood Days in Asante*. Portsmouth, NH: Heinemann.

Levine, L.W. 1977. *Black Culture and Black Consciousness: Afro American Folk Thought, from Slavery to Freedom*. Oxford: Oxford University Press.

Lewis, M.G. 1999. *Matthew Lewis: Journal of a West India Proprietor*. Oxford: Oxford University Press.

———. 2005. *Journal of a Residence among the Negroes in the West Indies*. Gloucestershire, UK: Nonsuch.

Little Theatre Movement. 2004. Timeline. Accessed 30 March 2007. http://ltmpantomime.com/pages/a41_50.html.

Livingston, Sir Noel. Livingston Collection. National Library of Jamaica, Kingston. 1910–50, Ms. 59.

Lockett, J.D. 1999. The Deportation of the Maroons of Trelawny Town to Nova Scotia, then Back to Africa. *Journal of Black Studies* 30, no. 1 (September): 5–14.

MacLean, I.C. 1910. *Children of Jamaica*. London: Oliphant, Anderson and Ferrier.

Makhanlall, D. 1971. *Anancy in Love*. Mahoe Adventure Series. Kingston: Jamaica Publishing House.

———. 1973. *The Best of Brer Anansi*. London: Blackie.

———. 1974. *The Invincible Brer Anansi*. London: Blackie.

———. 1976. *Anansi Strikes Again*. Glasgow: Blackie.

Marshall, E. 2010. "And Always, Anancy Changes": An Exploration of Andrew Salkey's Anancy Stories. In *The Caribbean Short Story: Critical Perspectives*, edited by L. Evans, M. McWatt and E. Smith. Leeds: Peepal Tree Press.

Martin, B. [A. Parker] 2005. Interview by author. Mini-disk recording. 1 December. Hopedale Avenue, Kingston, Jamaica.

Matthews, G. 2006. *Caribbean Slave Revolts and the British Abolitionist Movement*. Baton Rouge: Louisiana State University Press.

Mbiti, J.S. 1969. *African Religions and Philosophy*. London: Heinemann.

McCaskie, T.C. 1995. *State and Society in Pre-Colonial Asante*. Cambridge: Cambridge University Press.

———. 1992. People and Animals: Constru(ct)ing the Asante Experience. *Africa: Journal of the International African Institute* 62, no. 2: 221–47.

McDermott, G. 1972. *Anansi the Spider: A Tale from the Ashanti*. London: Hamish Hamilton.

McLeod, M.D. 1981. *The Asante*. London: British Museum Publications.

Meyerowitz, E. 1949. *The Sacred State of the Akan*. London: Faber and Faber.

Milne-Home, M.P. 1890. *Mama's Black Nurse Stories: West Indian Folklore*. Edinburgh, UK: W. Blackwood.

Morgan, P.D. 1995. Slaves and Livestock in Eighteenth-Century Jamaica: Vineyard Pen, 1750–1751. *William and Mary Quarterly,* 3rd ser. 52, no. 1 (January): 47–76.

Morris-Brown, V. 1993. *The Jamaica Handbook of Proverbs*. Mandeville, Jamaica: Island Heart.

Newman, A.J., and P.M. Sherlock. 1959. *Annancy Stories*. Glasgow: Ginn and Company.

Partinder, G. 1954. *African Traditional Religion*. Hertfordshire, UK: William Benson.

Patterson, O. 1967. *The Sociology of Slavery: An Analysis of the Origins, Development and Structure of Negro Slave Society in Jamaica*. London: Macgibbon and Key.

Pelton, R.D. 1989. *The Trickster in West Africa: A Study of Mythic Irony and Sacred Delight*. Berkeley: University of California Press.

Perkins, L. 1910–77. Lily G. Perkins Collection. National Library of Jamaica, Kingston. Ms. 2019.

Pinn, A. 2009. *African American Religious Cultures*, vol. 1. Westport, CT: Greenwood.

Pollard, V. 2005. Interview by author. Mini-disk recording. 24 October. Kingston, Jamaica.

Purchas-Tulloch, J.A. 1976. Jamaica Anansi: A Survival of the African Oral Tradition. PhD diss., Howard University.

Rampini, C. 1873. *Letters from Jamaica*. Edinburgh, UK: Edmonston and Douglas.

Ramsawack, A. 1973. *Anansi and the Magic Bowly*. Trinidad and Tobago: O.Z. Gonzalez.

Rattray, R.S. 1927. *Religion and Art in the Ashanti*. London: Oxford University Press.

———. 1930. *Akan-Ashanti Folk-Tales*. Oxford: Clarendon Press.

Roberts, H.H. 1926. Possible Survivals of African Song in Jamaica. *Musical Quarterly* 12, no. 3 (July): 340–58.

Robertson, A.F. 1975. Anthropology and Government in Ghana. *African Affairs* 74, no. 294 (January): 51–59.

Rocky. 2005. Interview by author. Mini-disk recording. 19 November. Moore Town, Portland.

Salkey, A. 1973. *Anancy's Score*. London: Bogle-L'Ouverture.

———. 1981. Anancy. In *Caribbean Anthology*, edited by J. Butcher, 5. London: ILEA Learning Materials Service Publishing Centre.

———. 1992. *Anancy, Traveller*. London: Bogle-L'Ouverture.

Schechner, R. 2004. Carnival Theory after Bakhtin. In *Culture in Action: The Trinidad Experience*, edited by M. Riggio, 3–12. New York: Routledge.

Scott, J. 1990. *Domination and the Arts of Resistance: Hidden Transcripts*. New Haven: Yale University Press.

Seaga, E. 2003. The Significance of Folk Culture in the Development of National Identity. Paper presented at Oxford, 21 May.

Sherlock, P.M. 1956. *Anansi the Spider Man: Jamaican Folk Tales*. London: Macmillan.

———. 1959. *The Man in the Web and Other Folktales*. London: Longmans.

———. 1966. *The West Indies*. London: Thames and Hudson.

———. 1989. *West Indian Folk-Tales*. Oxford: Oxford University Press.

———. 1998. *The Story of the Jamaican People*. Kingston: Ian Randle.

Small, J. 2005. Interview by author. Mini-disk recording. 23 November. Sovereign Shopping Centre, Hope Road, Kingston, Jamaica.

———. 2005. *Anansi and the Mirror*. Puppet play, Portmore Missionary Preparatory School Hall, Kingston, 26 December.

———. 2006. Anansi and Spirituality. Letter to the author, 26 January.

Smith, C. 2005. Interview by author. Mini-disk recording. 19 November. Moore Town, Portland, Jamaica.

Stephenson, F. 1998. Remembering Remus. *Research in Review: Remembering Remus Issue*. Accessed 1 May 2007. http://www.rinr.fsu.edu/springsummer98/cover.html.

Stewart, M. 1982. Jamaican Anansi Stories and West African Oral Literature: A Comparative Introduction. *African-Caribbean Institute of Jamaica: Newsletter*, no. 8 (December): 3–36.

Sutherland, W. 2005. Interview by author. Mini-disk recording. 11 October. Hayfield, St Thomas, Jamaica.

Tanna, L. 1983. Anansi: Jamaica's Trickster Hero. *Jamaica Journal* 16, no. 2: 22–34.

———. 2000. *Jamaican Folktales and Oral Histories*. Kingston: Institute of Jamaica Publications.

———. 2005. Interview by author. Mini-disk recording. 28 November. Kingston, Jamaica.

Terry, J., ed. 1999. Introduction. *Matthew Lewis: Journal of a West India Proprietor*. Oxford: Oxford University Press.

Thomas, D. 2004. *Modern Blackness: Nationalism, Globalization, and the Politics of Culture in Jamaica*. Durham, NC: Duke University Press.

Thompson, E.P. 1965. The Peculiarities of the English. In *The Socialist Register*, edited by R. Milliband and J. Saville, 311–62. London: Merlin Press.

Tiffin, H. 1984. The Metaphor of Anancy in Caribbean Literature. In *Myth and Metaphor*, edited by R. Sellick, 3–21. Adelaide, Australia: Centre for Research in the New Literatures in English.

Trans-Atlantic Slave Trade Database: Voyages. 2009. Emory University. Accessed 1 July 2010. http://www.slavevoyages.org.

Trowbridge, A.W. 1869. Customs and Folk-Stories of Jamaica. *Journal of American Folklore* 9, no. 35 (October–December): 279–87.

Turner, V. 1967. *The Forest of Symbols*. Ithaca: Cornell University Press.

Twi Dictionary. 2007. Fie.nipa cooperative. Accessed 1 July 2007. http://dictionary.kasa horow.com/node/5178.

United Nations. United Nations Development Program: Jamaica. *UNDP: Country Programme Document for Jamaica, 2007–11*. http://www.jm.undp.org.

Van Dyck, C. 1967. An Analytic Study of the Folktales of Selected People of West Africa. PhD diss., Oxford University.

Van Gennep, A. 1960. *The Rites of Passage*. Chicago: University of Chicago Press.

Van Sertima, I. 2002. Trickster: The Revolutionary Hero. In *Egypt: Child of Africa, Journal of African Civilizations*, edited by I. Van Sertima, 444–51. London: Transaction.

Vecsey, C. 1993. The Exception who Proves the Rules: Ananse the Akan Trickster. In *Mythical Trickster Figures: Contours, Contexts, and Criticisms,* edited by W.J. Hynes and W.G. Doty, 106–21. Tuscaloosa: University of Alabama Press.

Vice, S. 1997. *Introducing Bakhtin*. Manchester: Manchester University Press.

Walvin, J. 1999. *The Slave Trade*. Gloucestershire: Sutton.

———. 2000. *Making the Black Atlantic: Britain and the African Diaspora*. Leicester: University of Leicester Press.

Wilks, L. 2005. Interview by author. Mini-disk recording. 5 November. Mill Bank, Portland, Jamaica.

Williams, J. 2004. *Back a Yard 6*. Kingston: Yard Publications.

Williams, J.J. 1930–31. Rev. Joseph Williams Collection: Anancy Stories of Jamaica, c. 5,000 items, Mss. 1–4999, National Library of Jamaica, Kingston.

———. 1934. *Psychic Phenomena of Jamaica*. New York: Dial.

———. 1979. *Psychic Phenomena of Jamaica*. Westport, CT: Greenwood.

Wilson, U. 1947. *Anancy Stories Retold*. Kingston: Jamaica Times.

Yanka, K. 1983. The Akan Trickster Cycle: Myth or Folktale? Graduate student term paper, African Studies Program, Indiana University, Bloomington, Indiana.

Index

Note: Figures are denoted by *f*. Titles of Anansi stories are listed under folktales.

www.ingramcontent.com/pod-product-compliance
Lightning Source LLC
Chambersburg PA
CBHW030649270326
41929CB00007B/272